Becoming a Legal Writer

Pg. 373

Effective Memo.

Becoming a Legal Writer

A Workbook with Explanations
to Develop Objective Legal Analysis
and Writing Skills

Robin Boyle-Laisure
PROFESSOR OF LEGAL WRITING
ST. JOHN'S UNIVERSITY SCHOOL OF LAW

Christine Coughlin
PROFESSOR OF LEGAL ANALYSIS, WRITING, AND RESEARCH
WAKE FOREST UNIVERSITY SCHOOL OF LAW

Sandy Patrick
PROFESSOR OF LAWYERING
LEWIS & CLARK LAW SCHOOL

CAROLINA ACADEMIC PRESS
Durham, North Carolina

ISBN   978-1-5310-0448-4
e-ISBN 978-1-5310-0447-7
LCCN   2019941883

Carolina Academic Press
700 Kent Street
Durham, North Carolina 27701
Telephone (919) 489-7486
Fax (919) 493-5668
www.cap-press.com

Printed in the United States of America

To my late grandparents (Jeanette, Hugh, Margaret, and Anthony) who, despite limited educational opportunities, impressed upon me the importance of education; my mother (Verna) who, paving a career in education, showed me how much one can love school and students; my father (Wallace) who passionately taught high school math, modeling the technique of teaching skills to acquire mastery of material, and later pursued a law degree at St. John's (where I have spent 25 years of my career); my stepmother (Deborah) who ascended to great heights in a university; my husband (Paul Skip Laisure) who uses his legal skills every day to make a difference in this world; and to my children (Andrea and Corey), and nieces and nephews, who embody the unlimited potential in today's youthful generation.

—ROBIN BOYLE-LAISURE

To my brother, Tom, and sister, Susan, their partners, Elizabeth and Olivier, and their children Morgan, Gabi, and Henry. Also, to my brothers-in-law, Tom and Dan, and their partners, Sarah and Karie. Family is everything.

—CHRISTINE COUGHLIN

To the memory of my Dad and my Grandmother. Thank you both for showing me what grit, determination, and a strong work ethic look like. Thank you most of all for shining your light on me.

—SANDY PATRICK

Contents

Acknowledgments

Some of the exercises in this book had their genesis decades ago, taking shape into the semblance of a workbook in Professor Robin Boyle's office. Then the successful legal writing book appeared on the market—*A Lawyer Writes* by Christine Nero Coughlin, Joan Malmud Rocklin, and Sandy Patrick (3d ed. Carolina Academic Press). The workbook draft seemed like a natural fit as a companion to the published textbook, and Professor Boyle, together with the amazing synergy of Professors Chris Coughlin and Sandy Patrick, endeavored to continue writing and polishing this workbook. Professor Boyle gives much credit for the quality of this workbook to her co-authors for working with her as a team, creating fresh material, and editing thoroughly; the book is a significantly better product as a result of their expertise and the assistance of staff support at their respective schools.

Joan Rocklin has graciously permitted us to model chapter topics, phrasing, and material from *A Lawyer Writes*. She also contributed some fresh copy, and more importantly, her insightful and precise advice. Thank you for getting us started on the path.

Exercises develop skill sets, and skills can be incorporated into many academic settings. Although this workbook can be a companion to *A Lawyer Writes*, we drafted it in such a way that it can be used alongside any legal writing text. We also wrote it for purposes of academic support and for pipeline programs.

Thank you to the greater legal writing community for inspiring us with your exercises and to our colleagues inside and outside of our schools who graciously shared their materials. We took liberties in adapting your material to fit within our chapters, but we endeavored to acknowledge your work where the exercise appears. Special thanks goes to: Jennifer Cooper, (late) Rita Dunn, Paul Figley, Joe Fore, Steven I. Friedland, Bryan A. Garner, Russell Gold, Laura Graham, Sue Grebeldinger, Kate Irwin-Smiler, Lucy Jewel, Liz Johnson, John Korzen, and Hadley Van Vactor. Any errors or omissions of attribution are purely unintentional. With every project, we realize the immense contribution that legal writing colleagues across the country have made—you have not only sparked ideas, but you have also shaped who we are as teachers. Thank you.

We acknowledge the inspiration we received from entities, such as the helpful Idea Bank of the Legal Writing Institute and from National Public Radio. We did our best to credit contributing authors to the Idea Bank. NPR's insightful reporting of news stories inspired at least two of the fact patterns in the book.

We also thank our Teaching Assistants for guiding our law students through the exercises in class, proofreading rough drafts, and giving us feedback. Thanks goes to Research and Teaching Assistants at St. John's University School of Law who contributed over the past several years: Divya Acharya, Charles Akinboyewa, Brian Auricchio, Max Bartell, Grant Bercari, Laura Berry, Michael Bloom, Jamie Caponera, Jennifer Carnovale, Kaveh Dabashi, Andrew Esposito, Gregory Klubok, and Veronica Reyes. At Lewis & Clark School of Law, we thank Cassandra Dawn, Carolyn Griffin, Stephanie Keys, and Kristen Kinneary. Thank you also to Cyd Maurer and Nicole Burke for their help and support. At Wake Forest School of Law, we thank Nikki Arcodia, Nick Bedo, Tim Day, Corri Hopkins, Henry Hilston, Kaylen Lofin, Melissa McKinney, Adam Messenlehner, and Josh Revilla.

Thank you to our respective law schools for their institutional support. Professor Boyle appreciates the support from St. John's University School of Law for her summer scholarship stipend to engage in the writing of the book, and from former and current law school deans—(late) Mary Daly, Michael Simons; dean for faculty scholarship, Anita Krishnakumar; and the dean-who-always-has-your-back—Andrew Simons, Vice Dean Emeritus. Thanks also to her legal writing colleagues and the secretarial assistance from Janet Ruiz-Kroll over the years. Professor Patrick thanks Lewis & Clark School of Law, especially Dean Jennifer Johnson and Associate Dean of Faculty John Parry for the summer research grant that funded this writing opportunity. Professor Patrick also thanks her incredibly supportive colleagues at Lewis & Clark: Steve Johansen, Judith Miller, Hadley Van Vactor, Bill Chin, Aliza Kaplan, Toni Berres-Paul, and Lora Keenan. Professor Coughlin thanks Wake Forest School of Law for its support, particularly Dean Suzanne Reynolds and Associate Executive Dean for Academic Affairs Jonathan Cardi. Professor Coughlin also thanks her other Wake Forest legal writing colleagues who provided invaluable feedback on drafts and who are so generous in sharing their teaching ideas and materials: Tiffany Atkins, Tracey Coan, Luellen Curry, Heather Gram, Sally Irvin, Chris Knott, Hal Lloyd, Mary Susan Lucas, Ruth Morton, Abby Perdue, Vanessa Zboreak. In addition, Professor Coughlin would like to thank her Administrative Assistant, Ms. Cynthia Ring, for her extraordinary help and patience.

Thank you to family and friends. Special thanks to Anna Blake Patrick for the graphic illustration she provided. Professor Boyle's husband, Paul Skip Laisure, gave us insightful advice on criminal law and other topics. Professor Boyle also thanks her family, close friends, and book club for their encouragement. Professor Patrick thanks her family for letting her use nights and weekends to focus on work. Professor Coughlin thanks her family, extended family, and circle of friends. She knows how lucky she is to have their constant support and inspiration.

And finally, special thanks to our publisher, Carolina Academic Press. CAP is a pleasure to have as our publisher. We could not ask for a more competent, caring, and gracious group of people to help us along this journey.

Introduction

Welcome to *Becoming a Legal Writer: A Workbook with Explanations to Develop Objective Legal Analysis and Writing Skills.* This workbook will help you develop two essential lawyering skills: objective analysis and writing.

All lawyers are writers. As an attorney, you will undoubtedly devote a substantial portion of your time to drafting office memoranda, letters, pleadings, motions, briefs, contracts, and wills, as well as client letters, affidavits, and so forth. In a litigation practice, legal writing falls into two main categories: objective analysis and persuasive analysis.

All legal writing begins with an analysis of the law. Analyzing the law includes synthesizing the law from a variety of sources to determine the standards that currently apply. The analysis continues as you assess how that law will apply to a client's problem.

After analyzing the law, you will need to communicate your analysis to someone else—a client, a colleague, or a court. Your analysis may be communicated in a memo, a letter, an email, or a brief to a court.

This workbook will help you develop the skills you need to analyze the law and communicate that analysis. This workbook will help you develop those skills by providing you with practice—lots of practice.

However, before jumping into that practice, some background is in order. This introduction first describes, in Part I, the different kinds of writing that lawyers do. Then, Part II explains what it takes to become an excellent legal writer—namely, lots of practice, making mistakes, receiving feedback, and learning from the mistakes and feedback. Because learning can proceed more smoothly if you understand how you learn best, Part III explains different learning styles and how you can assess your own learning style. At the end of this chapter, Part IV provides advice about how to use this workbook.

I. Lawyers Write

Simply stated, legal writing encompasses a broad spectrum of legal analysis, objective legal writing, and persuasive legal writing. Lawyers engage in objective legal writing by providing advice to clients about the likely outcome of a legal dispute. Objective legal writing is also called predictive writing because the goal of an objective analysis is to predict how a court would most likely rule if presented with the client's case. Lawyers also engage in persuasive legal writing. When writing persuasively, lawyers advocate on behalf of their client in a court of law.

The fundamental skills of legal analysis and writing remain the same whether writing to predict an outcome or to persuade a court of the appropriate outcome. In both cases, you must first understand the law. Then, your explanation of the law must be organized, accurate, and clear; it should be free from grammatical errors; and it must be cited appropriately. This workbook is intended to introduce you to all of these qualities of legal writing. But the learning does not end within a few months, nor at graduation. For the remaining years of your legal career, you will need to keep within your reach a dictionary and books on grammar, citation, and style.

II. Developing as a Legal Writer

An essential component of becoming a strong legal writer is to practice that skill and to receive feedback about your writing. The more you write and receive feedback, the more your writing will improve.

Do not feel defeated with critique. All lawyers—including your professors—received plenty of critique, and they will impart critique upon your work. Critique is part of the learning process of legal analysis and writing. To succeed in law school, read your professors' comments on legal writing assignments carefully and take advantage of them. Learn from them and improve your skills. If you are lucky, your work will be continually critiqued—not just in law school but also as you practice. The savvy lawyer learns from the feedback. One day, after your writing and analysis has become sharp, accurate, and organized, the roles will change, and you will be in a position to help other new lawyers who will be just starting off as you are now.

Along the way, you should develop self-confidence in your writing—an aspect of writing that is difficult to teach but that you should nonetheless hope to acquire. Confidence will develop as you learn to make strategic writing decisions. As a first-year law student, you may be surprised how many factors play into a draft and how many decisions you will need to make—such as, "Is the law stated accurately? Have I drawn a conclusion? Have I applied the law to the facts with sufficient clarity? Do I have thesis sentences? Should this broader statement be placed in spot 'x' or 'y'?" One of your goals should be to develop confidence to make macro- and micro-decisions about how you communicate your analysis.

Finally, keep reading. Read for pleasure, and read books that are well written. In doing so, you'll develop a fondness of words as well as an intuitive sense of good writing.

III. Learning Styles

Up until 25 years ago, the prevailing view was that all law students learned by listening, and thus, a typical law school classroom had 100% auditory learners. This faulty premise helped to support the predominance of Socratic-method questioning in a traditional amphitheater-styled classroom. That view was shattered with the first empirical study done in a law school, which demonstrated that "law students were diverse in their learning styles."[1] The Dunn and Dunn Learning Style Model was used in that study, but there are other models as well. The Dunn and Dunn Model categorizes twenty-six different elements that affect how one best learns and studies. To understand "learning styles," it is necessary to examine how individuals process and incorporate new and difficult information into their study habits.

To better understand how you learn, we recommend that you take a learning-style assessment by accessing the following website: www.learningstyles.net. Select the adult learning-style tool called "Building Excellence." It will cost a nominal fee. During your experience in law school, it would be helpful for you to pay attention to how you best learn. Although recently skepticism has emerged about the significance learning styles should be given, understanding the strategies through which you best learn and retain information remains a vital part of learning. The science is clear about one thing: repeated practice and engagement with new material leads to more durable, long-term learning.[2] This workbook is intended to give you opportunities for that practice and engagement.

Exploring how you learn and using instructional materials in creative ways would be helpful in gaining the skills of legal writing proficiency. Here are some preliminary questions you may want to ask yourself, based upon five learning-style categories:

Physiological Factors:
- Do you learn by listening (auditory)?
- Do you learn by what you see in text (visual) or in a graph/picture mode (visual picture)?
- Do you prefer to work with your hands, as in turning flash cards (tactual)?
- Do you prefer to learn by doing (kinesthetic)?

Psychological Factors:
- Do you prefer to learn step by step (analytic learners) or through the "big picture" (global learners)?
- Do you find yourself blurting out answers (impulsive) or needing time to think through an answer (reflective learner)?

Emotional Factors:
- Are you motivated by a desire to succeed that is fueled by your own ambitions or from an external source?
- Are you driven to finish a task or can you leave something unfinished (persistence)?
- Do you follow rules or avoid conformity (responsibility and conformity)?
- Do you feel a need for structure imposed from the outside or do you supply your own way of doing things?

Environmental Factors:
- Do you require silence when studying new and difficult information, or do you prefer a bit of a hum of noise or music?
- Do you need bright light when studying or dim lighting?
- Does the temperature of the room affect your ability to concentrate?

---

1. Robin A. Boyle & Rita Dunn, *Teaching Law Students Through Individual Learning Styles*, 62 Alb. L. Rev. 213, 216 (1998).

2. Jennifer Cooper, *Smarter Law Learning: Using Cognitive Science to Maximize Law Learning*, 44 Cap. U. L. Rev. 551, 560–61 (2016).

- When reading something challenging, can you absorb the material while you are seated in a soft beanbag-type chair, or do you need a traditional chair with back support?

Sociological Factors:
- Do you learn best while working alone, with one other in a pair, or in small groups?
- Do you prefer to have an expert in the field overseeing your work?
- Do you prefer to learn in a variety of ways, or do you prefer to do the same work in consistent patterns?

As you reflect on your answers to these questions, think about how to create a strong learning experience that incorporates your preferences. Try to experiment on your own by transforming your reading materials into products that you can better absorb. For instance, auditory learners learn by listening; however, they will remember only 75% of what they hear in a 40- to 50-minute lecture. Thus, even for students who show a strong preference for auditory learning, they still should be relying upon secondary and tertiary strengths to solidify their note-taking in class. For others, they may be learning by listening but only if they are interested in the topic. And for some, learning by listening may not be effective after a short period of time in the lecture.

Visual learners may have a strong preference for visual pictures, meaning they learn by putting concepts into graphs and pictures, rather than course outlines that are heavy with text and are linear in format. Such learners create charts, graphs, and diagrams. Later in this book, we provide examples of charts and diagrams for mapping cases. Word processing systems can help create visual images that are suitable for this learning style.

Tactual learners use their fine motor skills, fingers, and hands while concentrating. If your assessment shows that you have a strong preference for this type of learning, then the sense of touch is important and working with materials that you can manipulate will help you learn. You can create index cards and flip them over with questions on one side and answers on the other. The creation of materials with your hands will help solidify concepts, and you can experiment with maps, charts, graphs, and timelines.

Kinesthetic learners need to role-play because they experience by doing. Interactive exercises are helpful. In legal writing, the classroom exercises often simulate client counseling or, eventually, courtroom arguments. Kinesthetic learners will benefit from peer teaching, which is a popular exercise in legal writing.

You may find that you have a strong tendency toward one learning style or you may utilize aspects of different learning styles. Ultimately, as you work through this workbook and your first semester of law school, take inventory of your own learning-style preferences and the strategies through which you learn best, and tailor your study habits to maximize your preferences.

IV. Using This Book

Use this workbook as a supplement to an assigned legal writing text. We have designed the workbook so that you may write inside the book. The goals of this workbook are to reinforce the core principles of good legal analysis and writing and to give you a chance to practice what you are learning.

Cases and other authorities have been adapted throughout the book to work in concise exercise format.

Becoming a Legal Writer

Chapter 1
Assessing a Client's Case

Imagine you graduate from law school and open up your own law practice. A stranger knocks on your door. She is a prospective client and wants you to take her case. Do you do it? Before answering that question, you will need to investigate her case and analyze whether her claims are likely to succeed. That is, if this client files a complaint in court, what is the likelihood that a judge or jury would find in her favor? If she seeks to negotiate a settlement, what is the likelihood that she could reach a satisfactory settlement?

For many reasons, a lawyer's first step after meeting a client is to assess the client's case. One reason to pause and assess is that, for many lawyers, their practice is a business. As a business person, the lawyer must determine whether a client's case is financially worthwhile (and ethically appropriate) to take on. Thus, in private practice, before deciding whether to take the client's case, you would want to first investigate the client's claim and then objectively assess the strengths and weaknesses of the client's claim.

Lawyers who are not in private practice must also stop to assess a case before proceeding. Imagine you are an attorney at a nonprofit organization that investigates environmental hazards. Before committing your organization to litigation, you would want to assess the proposed claims to ensure that you are allocating your firm's resources in the most appropriate way. Thus, for all lawyers, practical self-interest requires an initial assessment.

More importantly, lawyers have an ethical duty to assess the strengths and weaknesses of a client's case before proceeding. The Model Rules of Professional Conduct require lawyers to exercise independent professional judgment and provide a client with candid advice.[1] And lawyers cannot assert a legal claim unless there is a viable legal and factual basis for doing so.[2]

---

1. Model Rules of Prof'l Conduct r. 2.1 (Am. Bar Ass'n 2018). Each state adopts its own version of the Rules of Professional Conduct; therefore, the rules vary from state to state.

2. Model Rules of Prof'l Conduct r. 3.1 (Am. Bar Ass'n 2018) (prohibiting lawyers from advancing frivolous claims or defenses).

For all of these reasons, an attorney must investigate a claim and objectively assess its strengths and weaknesses before proceeding. This chapter introduces you to those steps in a lawyer's practice: How does an attorney investigate a client's claim? And what does an objective analysis of a client's claim look like?

Those two steps—investigating a client's claim and producing a polished, objective analysis—represent the first and last steps of a process that allows an attorney to objectively assess a client's case. The purpose of this chapter is to give you experience with that first step—investigating a client's claim—and a look at the last step—producing a polished written analysis—so that you will have a sense of the road ahead. Table 1.A provides a more detailed overview of the steps in the process that allow an attorney to produce a polished objective assessment of a client's claims.

Table 1.A: The Process of Analyzing and Evaluating Your Client's Legal Question

Stage of the Process		Steps
Investigate a client's case	1. Investigate the facts	• Understand your client's factual situation by asking questions about who, what, where, when, and why. • Determine the client's concerns and goals. • Consider legal claims that the facts may support.
	2. Research the law	• Find the sources of law that will apply to your client's case. • Critically read the relevant authorities. • Determine legal claims that are supported by the facts.
Prepare to write	3. Organize your authorities	• Organize to understand the relationship among the relevant authorities by using a case chart or other method. • Outline the legal principles at issue and the legal authorities that will guide your analysis of the client's legal question.
Produce a polished objective analysis	4. Draft your work product	• Determine whether you need to draft a memorandum of law, an email, or a client letter. • Draft.
	5. Edit and polish your work product	• Review the relevant authorities to ensure your analysis is consistent. • Edit the substance of the draft to ensure your argument is complete and logically ordered. • Polish to weed out words that might confuse and to eliminate errors in grammar, punctuation, legal style, and citation. • Reread one last time carefully before submitting to your supervising attorney.

I. Investigating a Client's Case

After addressing any ethical issues that may prevent you from taking the case, the first step in assessing a client's case is to gather information. The information to be gathered is usually of two kinds: facts and law. The two are interdependent. The facts of a client's case determine the law that will be relevant. Meanwhile, the law determines which facts will be relevant. Thus, as you know more about the facts, you can expand your legal research to look for other legal theories, or you can toss out legal theories that are inapplicable to the facts of the case. Similarly, as you know more about the law that might be relevant, you can expand your factual investigation to determine whether the facts will support a particular claim, or you can dive deeper into the facts to search for additional support for a legal claim.

At the beginning of your legal career, your knowledge about the law will have less depth and, therefore, you will likely find yourself seesawing between fact investigation and legal investigation. As your knowledge of the law deepens and expands, you will have greater ability to gather the relevant facts more immediately. With time and experience, your legal research will likely be more focused on particular or novel aspects of your client's case rather than on learning entirely new areas of law.

II. Drafting an Objective Analysis

As you are researching the facts and law and organizing your authorities, you will begin to assess the strength of your client's case. Whether you are working in a solo office or as a junior attorney in a larger legal practice, you will undoubtedly need to communicate your analysis to your client or a senior attorney. This communication summarizing your analysis can be done in many ways. You may, for example, communicate your analysis orally. Often, though, attorneys will communicate and memorialize their analysis in either an "interoffice memorandum" ("memo" for short) or an email.

III. Exercises

Two fact patterns below will give you the opportunity to meet clients, think about the information that you need to gather, and decide how you would gather that information. As you read, think about not only the information that the potential client can give you, but what other information you might be able to collect from other sources.

Exercise 1.1: Investigating Ethan Tseng's Potential Claim for IIED

Mr. Ethan Tseng, a nineteen-year-old college student, is a prospective client of your firm. You and another attorney in your office, Carla Perez, meet with Mr. Tseng for an initial interview. He tells you that his college professor, Dr. Susan Fume, has been posting "terrible, absolutely terrible" things on social media about her experiences teaching at Park College in North Carolina, and he is one of the students in her class. The things she has said have made him "sick." He wants to know whether he can sue her under North Carolina law and if you will take the case.

Questions:

1. **What initial questions should you and Carla ask Mr. Tseng about the facts of the case?**

_____

_____

_____

_____

_____

After conducting some research, you learn that the most appropriate claim would be a tort action for intentional infliction of emotional distress. In North Carolina, a claim for intentional infliction of emotional distress requires a plaintiff to prove that the defendant's conduct: (1) was extreme and outrageous, (2) was intended to cause severe emotional distress, and (3) did cause severe emotional distress. *See Woodruff v. Miller*, 307 S.E.2d 176, 178 (N.C. Ct. App. 1983). A plaintiff can prove intent by showing the defendant's "reckless indifference to the likelihood that he will cause emotional distress." *Bryant v. Thalhimer Bros.*, 437 S.E.2d 519, 522–23 (N.C. Ct. App. 1993). A person acts "recklessly" if that person acts "in deliberate disregard of the high degree of probability that the emotional distress will follow." *Dickens v. Puryear*, 276 S.E.2d 325, 333 (N.C. 1981).

Now that you understand the elements of the cause of action, your supervisor suggests that you focus on element (1) for now: Was the conduct extreme and outrageous?

Questions (continued):

2. What questions do you now ask of Mr. Tseng as you narrow your facts under element (1)?

_____

_____

_____

_____

_____

_____

3. If Mr. Tseng brings a claim against Dr. Fume, who would be the plaintiff, and who would be the defendant?

Plaintiff _____

Defendant _____

Now, you conduct a little more research and find the following case:

Briggs v. Rosenthal
327 S.E.2d 308 (N.C. Ct. App. 1985).

Plaintiffs' complaint is premised on the theory of intentional infliction of emotional distress. In summary, the complaint alleges that their only son, Warren Briggs, Jr., died in an automobile accident on 30 June 1982. In October 1982 defendant Rosenthal wrote an article about Warren, which was published by defendant Sun Publishing Company in a magazine-periodical called *The Sun*. According to the complaint, the article described several unpleasant characteristics of Warren in a manner calculated to cause outrage, it was published recklessly and irresponsibly, and defendants knew or should have known that the article would cause great pain to plaintiffs.

In the article, "Saying Goodbye to Warren," defendant Rosenthal described his friend Warren as being a heavy drinker, but also honest, full of life, tender, happy, free and optimistic:

> No categories really work for Warren. Because I can't place him, I am driven to write this piece which might enable me to touch on his complexity . . . .
>
> For instance, strangers usually disliked him when he was drinking, which was a lot of the time, because he wasn't serene: he rolled around town with a raucous energy, his eyes on fire, his tongue constantly testing out accents from weird countries. His life would pour out of his stunning sea-green eyes and out of his red, red face. He would sputter, hold his head in his hands, and whirl around in circles.
>
> Yet I don't want to take anything away from my friend as I try to understand him, now that his death makes that an obligation. He was confused, but so are we. He traded in a lot of possibilities for good times but almost everyone else trades in the good times for possibilities, which to Warren were unimaginable. And the things he kept were wonderful—his spirit, his insistence that boredom was the enemy, his refusal to be false or dishonest . . . .

After reading the article, "Saying Goodbye to Warren," this court concludes that the plaintiffs cannot state a claim for intentional infliction of emotional distress. To prove intentional infliction of emotional distress, plaintiffs must prove: (i) extreme and outrageous conduct, (ii) that is intended to cause severe emotional distress to another, and (iii) does cause severe emotional distress. *Dickens v. Puryear*, 276 S.E.2d 325, 333 (N.C. 1981).

As to what is sufficiently outrageous to give rise to liability, the comments in the Restatement are instructive. Liability has been found only where the conduct has been so outrageous in character, and so extreme in degree, as to go beyond all possible bounds of decency, and to be regarded as atrocious, and utterly intolerable in a civilized community.

Here, plaintiffs cannot prove that publication of the article was extreme and outrageous conduct. To prove extreme and outrageous conduct, the actions must extend beyond mere insults, indignities, threats, annoyances, petty oppressions, or other trivialities. There must still be freedom to express an unflattering opinion. *See* Restatement § 46, Comment d.

Although perhaps not flattering, the article was honest, sincere, and sensitive. Although we recognize that to plaintiffs, grieving parents bereft of their son, the article was offensive, we find that the article does not reach the level of extreme and outrageous conduct necessary to sustain a cause of action.

Upon further questioning of Mr. Tseng, you learn that he claims to have seen the following two Facebook posts, which were posted by Dr. Fume:

> **September 5**. I just reviewed the first set of papers from my English Comp students. They are totally incapable of putting together a grammatically correct sentence! What is the world coming to?
>
> **September 21**. Another set of papers from my dopey English Comp students. Here is an example of ludicrous writing: "My life has been a challenge, a swamp. Like the trials and tribulations of a porn star or a heroin addict, I to [sic] have my demons."

Mr. Tseng claims to have written that quoted sentence in one of his papers for Dr. Fume's class and now feels "outed."

Dr. Fume's facebook page includes 100 of her personal friends and family, plus approximately forty former students and five current students from Mr. Tseng's composition class. The current composition class has thirty students.

Questions (continued):

4. Having read *Briggs v. Rosenthal*, what are your initial thoughts about the likelihood that Mr. Tseng should pursue his claim?

_____

_____

_____

_____

_____

_____

_____

_____

5. Are there additional questions you would like to ask Mr. Tseng or additional information you would like to pursue to understand his litigation goals?

_____

_____

_____

_____

_____

_____

_____

_____

Carla now asks you to examine whether Mr. Tseng will be able to prove that his college professor's conduct was extreme and outrageous. Below, you will see two analyses, both of which objectively analyze whether Mr. Tseng could successfully prove a claim for intentional infliction of emotional distress. The first analysis is delivered in an email. The second analysis is delivered in a memo.

The first purpose of this exercise is for you to see what an objective analysis looks like—whether in a memorandum or in an email. The second purpose is for you to begin thinking about the circumstances under which you would want to use one format or the other.

Model 1—An Email Analysis

From: Associate
Sent: Thursday, August 10
To: Carla Perez [cperez@zalassociates.com]
Subject: Tseng's IIED claim
Attachments: Woodruff.docx
                 Briggs.docx

Carla:

You asked that I research whether Ethan Tseng can prove a claim based upon Intentional Infliction of Emotional Distress against Dr. Susan Fume, a college professor. Specifically, you asked that my analysis focus on the element of extreme and outrageous conduct. Although Dr. Fume's conduct lacked professionalism and tact, her conduct did not rise to the level of extreme and outrageous.

A defendant's conduct is extreme and outrageous when the defendant persistently and publicly distributes derogatory, misleading information. *See Woodruff v. Miller*, 307 S.E.2d 176, 178 (N.C. Ct. App. 1983); *West v. King's Dept. Store, Inc.*, 365 S.E.2d 621, 625 (N.C. 1988). However, liability cannot be found when the conduct or written word falls into a category of merely "insults, indignities, threats, annoyances, petty oppressions, or other trivialities." *Briggs v. Rosenthal*, 327 S.E.2d 308 (N.C. Ct. App. 1985).

According to Mr. Tseng, Dr. Fume posted derogatory messages on her Facebook page that were humiliating to her current college students. Although these comments were negative, they did not rise to the high standard of extreme and outrageous conduct. In the *Briggs* case, the court held that a newspaper columnist who wrote an unflattering obituary was not liable for the tort of intentional infliction of mental distress. *Id.* at 312. Affirming the lower court's decision to dismiss the complaint, the court found that sentiments were not "flattering," but the article was "honest, sincere and sensitive." *Id.* Similarly here, although the comments were unflattering, it appears that the professor was expressing an opinion.

In addition, Mr. Tseng's claim that he was "outed," and thus singled-out, is not supported by the facts and the case law. There is no indication that a person reading Dr. Fume's page would connect the quoted material to this particular student. Accordingly, Mr. Tseng probably does not have sufficient facts to file a complaint based upon the tort of Intentional Infliction of Emotional Distress because a required element is missing—conduct that was extreme and outrageous.

Please let me know if you have any questions.

Best regards,

Associate
Zal Associates, LLP
800 SW Fifth Avenue, Suite 200 | Portland, OR 97204
Direct: 555-222-5556 | Fax: 555-222-5550
associate@zalassociates.com | www.zalassociates.com

Sidebar annotations:

The email begins with an introduction that identifies the issue to be addressed and the resolution to the legal question.

The conclusion is stated at the outset of the analysis.

The email then explains the most important rules that will dictate the outcome in this case.

Using analogical reasoning, the lawyer analogizes and distinguishes the facts from prior cases with the facts of the client's case.

Model 2—A Memorandum of Law

MEMORANDUM

To: Carla Perez
From: Associate
Date: August 10
Re: Ethan Tseng's potential claims for Intentional Infliction of Emotional Distress

Question Presented

Under North Carolina common law, which provides for a claim of Intentional Infliction of Emotional Distress, and more specifically includes an element of extreme and outrageous conduct, can a college student recover when his college professor posts on social media disparaging statements about her students' class work and includes a quotation from the student's paper?

Brief Answer

Probably not. Conduct is extreme and outrageous when the defendant persistently and publicly distributes derogatory, misleading information. The law does not provide a remedy for matters of opinion. Here, the information was unflattering, but posting the information did not rise to the level of extreme or outrageous conduct.

Statement of Facts

Our client, Ethan Tseng, is 19 years old and a student at Park College, a private school in North Carolina. He was in an English Composition class taught by Dr. Susan Fume, who has a doctorate in English Composition. She has posted negative comments about her students' writing on social media, specifically on her Facebook page.

He describes her postings as stating "terrible, absolutely terrible" things about her experiences teaching at Park College. Her statements have made him "sick." The following are two of the Facebook posts Mr. Tseng saw:

> **September 5**. I just reviewed the first set of papers from my English Comp students. They are totally incapable of putting together a grammatically correct sentence! What is the world coming to?

> **September 21**. Another set of papers from my dopey English Comp students. Here is an example of ludicrous writing: "My life has been a challenge, a swamp. Like the trials and tribulations of a porn star or a heroin addict, I to [sic] have my demons."

Mr. Tseng claims to have written that quoted sentence in one of his papers for Dr. Fume's class and now feels "outed."

The Facebook page of Dr. Fume's friends includes 100 of her personal friends and family, plus approximately forty former students and five current students from Mr. Tseng's composition class. The current composition class has thirty students.

Mr. Tseng comes to the firm as a prospective client asking if he could bring a tort claim of intentional infliction of emotional distress against his professor.

---

*Most legal memoranda begin with a **Question Presented** and a **Brief Answer**. Together, they act as an executive summary of the analysis below. Note that the Question Presented and Brief Answer use generic nouns rather than proper names.*

*The **Statement of Facts** describes the specific facts that impact the legal analysis.*

Discussion

Although Dr. Fume's conduct lacked professionalism and tact, her conduct did not rise to the level of extreme and outrageous required for an intentional infliction of emotional distress claim. In North Carolina, a claim for intentional infliction of emotional distress requires a plaintiff to prove that the defendant's conduct (1) was extreme and outrageous, (2) was intended to cause severe emotional distress, and (3) did cause severe emotional distress. *See Woodruff v. Miller*, 307 S.E.2d 176, 178 (N.C. 1983). Whether the defendant's conduct reaches the level of extreme and outrageous conduct is one element of the tort and is usually a question of fact for a jury to decide. *Briggs v. Rosenthal*, 327 S.E.2d 308, 311 (N.C. Ct. App. 1985). However, when it is clear to a court that the alleged facts do not approach that high standard, courts can decide as a matter of law that the element is not met. *Id.*

The Restatement (Second) of Torts addressed this first element. "[O]utrage is essential to the tort; and the mere fact that an actor knows that the other will regard the conduct as insulting, or will have his feelings hurt is not enough." Restatement (Second) of Torts § 46, Cmt. f (1965). Liability has been found only where the conduct has been so outrageous in character, and so extreme in degree, as to go beyond all possible bounds of decency, and to be regarded as atrocious, and utterly intolerable in a civilized community. *Briggs*, 327 S.E.2d at 308, 311.

Generally courts are reluctant to find that the allegations meet the high standard of extreme and outrageous conduct. Liability cannot be found when the conduct or written word falls into a category of merely "insults, indignities, threats, annoyances, petty oppressions, or other trivialities." *Id.* at 311. For instance, unflattering information published to provide an "honest, sincere, and sensitive" portrait of a person is not extreme and outrageous conduct. *Id.* at 312. In *Briggs*, the plaintiffs were parents whose son had recently died. They sued the defendants, a journalist and a newspaper publisher, after the newspaper published an article about their recently deceased son. *Id.* at 309. The article described the son's drinking and antisocial behavior but it also described the son as an "immensely substantial person, as fine, as dignified . . . as important as any solid citizen I ever met." *Id.* The *Briggs* court found that the article, although offensive to the parents, was "honest, sincere, and sensitive." *Id.* at 312. The court then upheld the lower court's decision to dismiss the case. *Id.* Similarly, in a case where a newspaper published an article stating that a decedent had a long history of drug use, the court found this statement neither extreme nor outrageous. *Casamasina v. Worcester Telegram & Gazette, Inc.*, 307 N.E.2d 865, 867 (Mass. App. Ct. 1974).

However, when a defendant persistently distributes derogatory information for no purpose other than spite, the evidence is sufficient to establish extreme and outrageous conduct. *Woodruff*, 307 S.E.2d at 178. In *Woodruff*, the plaintiff was the superintendent of the local school system. *Id.* at 177. Thirty years ago, he had participated in a college prank and been arrested. *Id.* The defendant, after losing two recent lawsuits to the superintendent, posted copies of the superintendent's former arrest record on the "Wanted" board at the local post office and on bulletin boards at the local high school. *Id.* The defendant also showed the "Wanted" poster to at least one prominent citizen in the community. *Id.* A jury found that the defendant had intentionally inflicted emotional distress on the superintendent. *Id.* In upholding the jury decision, the *Woodruff* court explained that distributing derogatory information as part of a "calculated, persistent plan to disturb, humiliate, harass

---

The **Discussion section** explains the legal analysis.

The introductory roadmap explains the governing rule. Notice that this initial rule paragraph uses the broad rule to provide the big picture, and then continues to narrow the rule with a synthesized rule statement that focuses on the precise issue the writer is analyzing.

To **explain the law**, the writer starts with the applicable rule, in this case the Restatement.

Here, the Restatement is further explained by the **sub-rule** in *Briggs*, followed by a case illustration from *Briggs*, which sets out the facts, holding, and reasoning to provide the reader an understanding of how the rules have functioned in past cases.

and ruin the plaintiff for no other purpose but defendant's own spiteful satisfaction" was extreme and outrageous conduct. *Id.* at 178.

> The heart of the analysis is **the application of law** to facts. This analysis uses analogical reasoning to compare the specific facts and reasoning from the prior cases with the facts and reasoning of the client's case.

Dr. Susan Fume's postings on Facebook do not rise to the level of extreme and outrageous conduct. Her statements are similar to the unflattering matters of opinion expressed in the *Briggs* and *Casamasina* cases. Dr. Fume's statements were introduced by explaining she had read a set of student papers, and what followed were her general impressions. Although the statements could be seen as "indignities or insults," these statements are no more offensive than the obituary descriptions that appeared to lack malicious intent but stated unflattering opinions. Dr. Fume's posted comments are not so extreme in degree as to exceed the bounds of human decency.

> Here, the writer shows another facet of how the element is not met by explaining how the facts of the current case can be distinguished from the facts of a prior case in which the conduct rose to the standard required by the element.

In contrast, the *Woodruff* defendant's conduct differs from the facts of this case. In that case, the defendant had targeted the plaintiff in a campaign designed to hurt the single individual. Although Mr. Tseng feels "sick" about his paper being quoted, Dr. Fume's postings did not identify him, and quoting him in one posting is not the equivalent of the conduct in *Woodruff* in which multiple postings disparaged an identified individual. Mr. Tseng has not alleged any other facts that explain how students in the class would be able to identify him.

Conclusion

> The **Conclusion** restates the writer's prediction of the likely outcome of the issue.

A complaint filed on behalf of Mr. Tseng would not likely withstand a motion to dismiss for failure to state a claim. A court would likely conclude that as a matter of law, he has not stated facts constituting extreme and outrageous conduct on the part of his college professor.

6. What are some differences you notice between the analysis in the email and the analysis in the memorandum? Fill in the blanks.

	Email	Memorandum
Length		
Question Presented and Brief Answer		
Statement of Facts		

Introduction		
Explanation of law		
Application of law to facts		

7. Why might an attorney prefer to receive legal analysis via email?

_____

_____

_____

_____

_____

_____

_____

8. Why might an attorney prefer to receive legal analysis via a formal memorandum?

_____

_____

_____

_____

_____

_____

_____

Exercise 1.2: Investigating Anthony Lillo's Claim for Personal Injury

Anthony Lillo wants you to take his case. Mr. Lillo tells you that he tripped on a neighbor's sidewalk near his residence in the suburbs, and he broke his ankle. He feels he should be compensated for his injury.

1. What initial questions would you ask to begin your investigation of Mr. Lillo's case?

_____

_____

_____

_____

_____

_____

By asking those questions, you learn that Mr. Lillo fell on the sidewalk outside of Danielle Holmes's house. He gave you the address where the accident took place, which he claimed was in the suburbs. You enter the address into Google Maps and you find that the accident actually occurred within New York City. (The neighborhood is leafy, so Mr. Lillo thinks of it as suburban.) You do some legal research and find this city ordinance:

City Code:

Section 7-210, Administrative Code, City of New York

Notwithstanding any other provision of law, the city shall not be liable for any injury to property or personal injury, including death, proximately caused by the failure to maintain sidewalks (other than sidewalks abutting one-, two-, or three-family residential real property that is (i) in whole or in part owner occupied, and (ii) used exclusively for residential purposes) in reasonably safe condition.

The ordinance is a little confusing, so break it down into its component parts.

2. Rewrite the ordinance in your own words.

_____

_____

_____

_____

_____

_____

3. Now that you understand the ordinance better, what additional questions would you ask? Why?

_____

_____

_____

_____

_____

_____

After speaking with Mr. Lillo again, you learn the following:

- Ms. Holmes lives in a one-family home that Mr. Lillo believes she owns. Mr. Lillo said that the previous owners were trying to sell it, but that if they couldn't sell it they were going to rent it out. He has seen Ms. Holmes making improvements, like putting in a new fence and painting the house, so he believes she owns it.

- Mr. Lillo fell near the driveway, where there is a crack in the sidewalk.

- Mr. Lillo frequently sees trucks—plain white trucks—parked in the driveway.

4. Check the boxes indicating the searches you would conduct to start researching this issue. If more than one apply, identify the order of the searches in your research.

❏ Conduct a property record check to see who owns the house.

❏ Conduct a Google search to determine if there is any commercial activity at the house.

❏ Search the Secretary of State's database to determine whether Ms. Holmes has registered a business or whether any business is being conducted at that address.

❏ Search court databases to see if any other litigation has been instigated against the owner of the house.

❏ Search NY State case databases to find cases that explain how this ordinance has been applied.

❏ Search federal case databases to find cases that explain how this ordinance has been applied.

❏ Search databases for neighboring states, such as NJ.

Now, you conduct a little more research, and you find the following case: *Schwartz v. Pezzolanti*, 24 Misc. 3d 1231(a), 899 N.Y.S.2d 63 (Kings Cty. Sup. Ct. 2009):

> Plaintiff Schwartz seeks to recover against Defendants Mr. and Mrs. Pezzolanti for injuries when plaintiff fell on a portion of cracked sidewalk in front of the defendants' property.
>
> The legal rule is "that the owner of land abutting a public sidewalk owes no duty to the public to keep the sidewalk in a safe condition unless the landowner creates a defective condition in the sidewalk or uses it for a special purpose." *Otero v. City of New York*, 213 A.D.2d 339, 339–40, 624 N.Y.S.2d 157, 158 (1st Dep't 1995). However, "[w]here a landowner's driveway crosses a sidewalk, the landowner is the beneficiary of a 'special use' of the sidewalk and is obligated to keep said sidewalk in a reasonably safe condition." *Adorno v. Carty*, 23 A.D.3d 590, 591, 804 N.Y.S.2d 798, 799 (2d Dep't 2005). Here plaintiff contends that he fell on a cracked sidewalk at or adjacent to the driveway in front of Pezzolanti's home.
>
> Defendant has moved for summary judgment dismissing the complaint. Plaintiff offers photographic evidence showing two vehicles parked in the driveway as well as deposition testimony stating the same. The driveway is adjacent to the area where plaintiff tripped and fell.
>
> The Court finds that there are triable issues of fact as to whether the cracked area where plaintiff fell was caused by Pezzolanti's use of the driveway because plaintiff fell very close to the part of the driveway that was damaged. Even if he did not fall directly on the driveway, if the weight of traffic on the driveway could have been a concurrent cause of the defect in the sidewalk, the motion for summary judgment dismissing the complaint should be denied.

5. Having read *Schwartz v. Pezzolanti,* what are your initial thoughts about whether a court would likely dismiss Mr. Lillo's case? Are there additional questions you would like to ask Mr. Lillo or additional information you would like to pursue?

_____

_____

_____

_____

_____

_____

Below you will see two emails addressed to a supervising attorney. Both analyze whether Mr. Lillo could succeed in a claim against Ms. Holmes. Read and compare the following email analyses.

An Email Analysis: Version 1

From: Donovan Bonner
To: Hannah Harding
Date: February 1
Subject: Lillo's claim based on injuries from faulty sidewalk

Dear Hannah:

I found the relevant ordinance governing the question you asked me to research. That statute is New York City's administrative code section 7-210. For your convenience, I have attached a copy of that section to this email. The ordinance was a bit difficult to find because New York's administrative code is not included in the major legal databases. The administrative code was, however, referenced in a number of cases. After seeing the reference there, I looked for the code on New York City's website. I was able to download the relevant section there.

My research also revealed several relevant cases. After carefully analyzing and reviewing the cases, I believe the most factually analogous case to Mr. Lillo's case is *Schwartz v. Pezzolanti*. I believe that after you read the case, you will find the similarities striking. For your convenience, I have attached that case as well.

After you review both the ordinance and *Schwartz v. Pezzolanti*, I believe you will likely conclude that Mr. Lillo can, without question, succeed in an action against Ms. Holmes.

Please let me know if you need further assistance in this matter.

Donovan

An Email Analysis: Version 2

From: Donovan Bonner
To: Hannah Harding
Date: February 1
Subject: Lillo's claim based on defective sidewalk

Dear Ms. Harding:

You asked that I research whether Mr. Lillo could bring a claim against Ms. Holmes after he tripped on the sidewalk in front of Ms. Holmes's home. Based upon the facts as we understand them, Mr. Lillo could probably succeed in an action against Ms. Holmes, but only if he can prove that her use of her driveway falls within the "special use" exception to the City's Sidewalk Law.

New York City's sidewalk law makes the City, not the homeowner, liable for injuries occurring on sidewalks serving residential homes. New York, N.Y., Admin. Code § 7-210 (Westlaw 2018). However, there is a common law exception. Under that exception, a homeowner of a one-family residence is liable to a plaintiff injured on the sidewalk if the defendant's use of his or her driveway caused the defect. *See Schwartz v. Pezzolanti*, 24 Misc. 3d 1231(A), 899 N.Y.S.2d 63 (Kings Cty. Sup. Ct. 2009).

Whether Ms. Holmes used her driveway in a way that caused the defect, and whether Mr. Lillo tripped on the portion of the sidewalk affected by the driveway, are questions of fact. Those questions of fact would ultimately be decided by a jury trial. Before a trial, we would need to conduct further discovery to determine whether we could likely prove that he tripped because of the way in which Ms. Holmes was using her driveway.

Please let me know if you want me to research possible claims against the City, or if you have any further questions about the research above.

Best regards,

Donovan

6. Which email is more effective? Why?

_____

_____

_____

_____

_____

_____

7. Which email better informs the supervising attorney about the legal rule and its application to the facts of Mr. Lillo's case? Why?

_____

_____

_____

_____

_____

_____

8. Would a supervising attorney need the details about how the associate found the ordinance, as provided in Version 1?

_____

_____

_____

_____

_____

_____

Chapter 2
Sources and Systems of the Law

To successfully analyze a client's legal problem, you will need to find the potentially relevant law and then determine the law that will be applicable. To do that, you must understand the sources of law in the United States, and you must be able to assess the weight of each legal authority—that is, the likelihood that a court would rely on a particular authority in reaching a conclusion. This chapter will introduce you to the most common sources of law in the United States and help you develop the skills necessary to select the authorities that will be most relevant to a court's analysis.

I. Sources of the Law

In the United States, each branch of government—the legislative, judicial, and executive—has the capacity to produce law. Figure 2.A illustrates the most common kind of law each branch produces.[1] Any law emanating from a branch of government is a **primary authority**. By contrast, a **secondary authority** (such as a treatise, hornbook or law review article) describes the law. That is to say, primary authority in a jurisdiction is the law, while secondary authority will help researchers understand and locate the law.

---

1. As you continue through law school, you will learn more about additional kinds of primary authority—such as Executive Orders—but the primary point here is to understand that each branch of our government produces law.

Figure 2.A: Sources of Primary Law

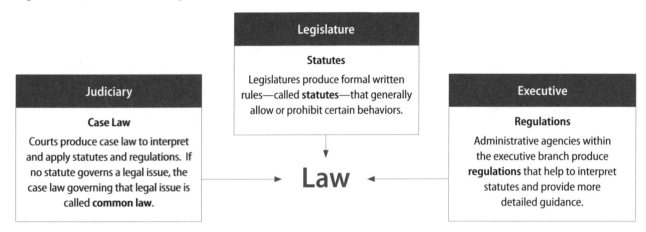

II. Systems within the Law

When confronted with a legal question, a court must decide which law to rely on to reach a decision. As a lawyer, you must therefore understand the "weight" that a court will attach to different kinds of authority. Four principles help determine the weight afforded to different kinds: jurisdiction, legislative authority, court hierarchies, and stare decisis. Figure 2.B explains the role of each of those principles.

Figure 2.B: Four Principles for Determining the Weight of Authority

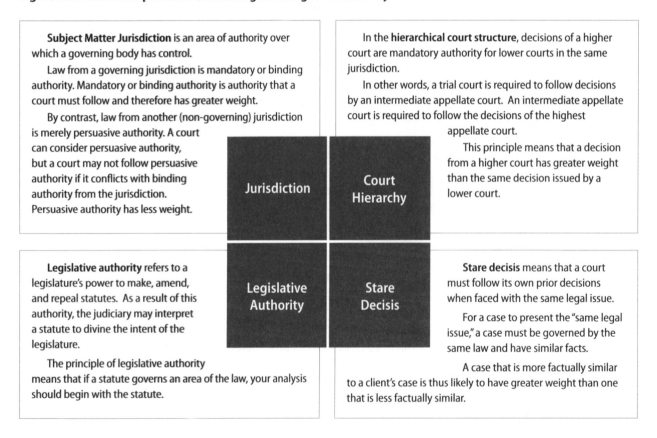

III. Questions to Ask Before You Research

The above principles will guide your research and analysis. Now, you need to apply those principles to your client's legal questions. To begin, you must ask these questions: "Which jurisdictions will govern my client's legal questions?" and "What is the court structure within those jurisdictions?" The answer to those questions will help you select and weigh relevant authorities.

A. Which Jurisdiction Governs My Client's Legal Questions?

You should begin your research by asking which jurisdiction will govern the client's legal questions because the primary law in the governing jurisdiction is binding, mandatory authority. It is the authority you will want your analysis to rely on.

Although many different kinds of jurisdiction exist, for lawyers, one of the most important jurisdictional divisions is between state governments and the federal government.

Article III of the U.S. Constitution provides for Congress to determine the structure of the federal courts within constitutional limits. That is, the federal government has authority to govern (and, thus, to exercise jurisdiction) in limited situations, primarily:

1. If the case involves a federal question or issue of federal law; or
2. If the parties involved in the case are from separate states and the amount in controversy exceeds $75,000.

All other governing authority remains with the states, which is (typically) made up of courts of general jurisdiction, meaning courts that can hear any kinds of cases. Each state has authority to promulgate and enforce laws only within its own borders.

B. What Is the Structure of the Courts in the Governing Jurisdiction?

To assess case law, you will also have to know the structure of the governing jurisdiction's court system. Most—but not every—court system has three levels: trial courts; intermediate courts of appeal (to which a claimant often has an appeal as of right); and the highest appellate court (which may have some discretion to grant appeals), sometimes called "the court of last resort."

1. Federal court system

In the federal system, trial courts are called **district courts**. Federal cases begin in a district court. The United States is divided into ninety-four districts. States that are more populous are divided into more districts. New York, for example, has four federal districts: the Northern District of New York, the Southern District of New York, the Eastern District of New York, and the Western District of New York. By contrast, Oregon has only one federal district—the District of Oregon.

A party dissatisfied with a district court decision has the right to appeal to an intermediate court of appeal. In the federal system, these courts are called **Circuit Courts of Appeal.** The United States is divided into thirteen circuits, as illustrated in Figure 2.C.

Figure 2.C: The Thirteen Federal Circuits

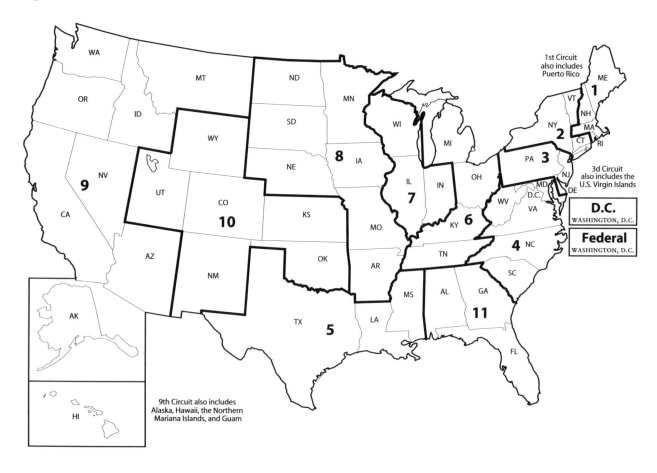

Finally, a party dissatisfied with a circuit court decision may petition the U.S. Supreme Court and ask that the Supreme Court take up the case. While there are some appeals as of right, in most cases, the Supreme Court can choose whether or not to hear a case.

2. State court systems

While the majority of state courts follow the three-tier structure, they do vary somewhat. Some states, such as Delaware, Maine, Montana, New Hampshire, Rhode Island, South Dakota, Vermont, West Virginia, and Wyoming do not have a typical intermediate court of appeal. States also vary in the names they give their courts. For example, in New York, the highest court is called the New York Court of Appeals, and trial courts are called Supreme Courts.

Especially before you begin researching in any unfamiliar jurisdiction, you should research the structure of the jurisdiction's court system. Most court systems have a public website that describes the structure of the courts in that jurisdiction. You can also look at Table 1 in the *Bluebook* citation manual or Appendix 1 in the *ALWD Guide to Legal Citation*. Each table lists state courts in their hierarchical order, with the highest appellate court listed first. In addition, those tables will tell you the names of the reporters in which the judicial opinions are published. (A "reporter" is the name for a book that publishes judicial opinions.)

3. The relationship between federal and state court systems

The federal court system is not hierarchically above the state court systems. Rather, the two court systems exist side by side. State courts have ultimate authority to interpret state law, and federal courts have the ultimate authority to interpret federal law. That means, for example, that the Colorado Supreme Court (not the U.S. Supreme Court) has the ultimate authority to determine Colorado law.

Generally speaking, federal courts review a state court decision only when the state court decision arguably conflicts with federal law—either a federal statute or the U.S. Constitution. In that case, the U.S. Supreme Court would review the decision of the state's highest court.

In matters of state law, the state's highest court has the final say on how state law should be understood. If that decision does not implicate a federal statute or the U.S. Constitution, the decision cannot be reviewed by a federal court. Figure 2.D illustrates the relationship between the two judicial systems.

Figure 2.D: Side-by-side Comparisons of State and Federal Court Systems

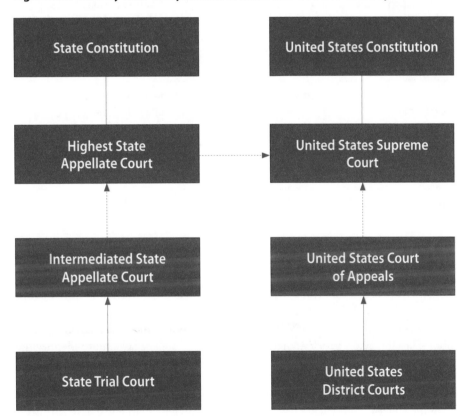

The chart[2] on the next page explains in more detail the path a case may take in either the state or federal court system.

---

2. Adapted from *U.S. Courts, Comparing the State and Federal Court Systems*, http://www.uscourts.gov/about -federal-courts/court-role-and-structure/comparing-federal-state-courts (last visited March 3, 2019).

Figure 2.E: The Path a Case May Take in State or Federal Courts

The State Court System	The Federal Court System
The constitution and laws of each state establish the state courts. A "court of last resort" (often known as a Supreme Court) is usually the highest state court. Some states also have an intermediate Court of Appeals. Below these appeals courts are the state trial courts. Some are referred to as Circuit or District Courts.	Article III of the U.S. Constitution vests the judicial power of the United States in the federal court system. Article III, Section 1 specifically creates the U.S. Supreme Court and gives Congress the authority to create the lower federal courts. (There are also some Article I courts that have been established through Congress.)
States also have some courts that handle specialized legal matters, e.g., business courts, probate court (wills and estates), juvenile court, family court. In forty-one states, parties dissatisfied with the decision of the trial court may take their case to the intermediate Court of Appeals. In the nine states without intermediate appellate courts, appeals go directly to the state's court of last resort.	Congress has used this power to establish the thirteen U.S. Courts of Appeals, the ninety-four U.S. District Courts, the U.S. Court of Claims, and the U.S. Court of International Trade. Parties dissatisfied with a decision of a U.S. District Court, the U.S. Court of Claims, or the U.S. Court of International Trade may appeal to a U.S. Circuit Court of Appeals.
Parties have the option to ask the highest state court to hear the case.	A party may ask the U.S. Supreme Court to review a decision of the U.S. Court of Appeals, but the Supreme Court usually is under no obligation to do so. The U.S. Supreme Court is the final arbiter of federal constitutional questions.
Only certain cases are eligible for review by the U.S. Supreme Court.	

IV. Weighing the Authorities You Gather

As you gather the legal authorities that relate to your client's question, keep the above principles in mind so that you can assess the weight of each authority. (Hint: when researching, it is a good idea to first consult a **secondary authority** like a treatise, encyclopedia, hornbook or law review article to help understand the area of law and to identify the **primary authorities**.)

- Focus on **primary authorities** from the governing **jurisdiction** first.
- If a statute governs your client's legal question, that statement of **legislative authority** is the starting point of your analysis.
- The **court hierarchy** in the governing jurisdiction dictates that opinions issued from a higher court have more authority than opinions from a lower court.
- The principle of **stare decisis** means that factually similar cases have more weight than less factually similar cases when those cases are addressing the same legal issue.

Sometimes, these principles will pull in opposite directions. For example, a trial court may have issued a decision that addresses nearly identical facts to the facts in your client's case. Although, ordinarily, trial court decisions have less weight than decisions from a higher court, the similarity in the facts may significantly increase the weight accorded to that trial court decision. The exercises below will provide you with experience assessing the weight of different authorities.

V. Exercises

The exercises on the following pages will help you improve your legal vocabulary and identify information about the federal and state jurisdictions. The exercises will also provide experience assessing the weight of different authorities and help in gauging various factual and legal considerations necessary to file a lawsuit.

Exercise 2.1: Improving Your Legal Vocabulary

Match the legal term on the left with the correct definition on the right.[3]

1. Statutes

2. Case law

3. Common law

4. Precedent

5. Stare decisis

6. Court hierarchy

7. Subject matter jurisdiction

8. Primary authority

9. Secondary authority

10. Binding authority

11. Persuasive authority

A. A judicial decision that dictates how a court should resolve a similar question of law involving similar facts

B. A kind of authority—statutory, judicial, or regulatory—that a court is required to follow

C. Court-created law in the absence of state or federal legislation

D. This kind of authority is the law

E. The law that is created by judicial decisions

F. A principle that requires courts to follow precedent when deciding similar cases

G. Law that is not binding on a court and other commentary about the law

H. Different levels of a court within a jurisdiction

I. Written descriptions of or commentary about the law, including law reviews, legal treatises, hornbooks, and encyclopedias

J. An area of authority

K. The written enactment of a legislature

---

3. Adapted from teaching materials created by Professor John Korzen, Wake Forest University School of Law.

Exercise 2.2: Legal Vocabulary at the Crossroads [4]

Down

2. A branch of government that produces administrative law.

3. A court can interpret but not change the language of this kind of law.

4. This kind of authority helps lawyers understand the law, but it is not itself the law.

5. Examples include statutes, case law, and regulations.

6. The branch of government that enacts statutes.

10. In the federal judicial system, this word is used to designate intermediate appellate courts.

11. Judicial opinions are also called this.

Across

1. This principle helps to create consistency in court decisions.

5. A judicial decision that is legally and factually similar to a current case.

7. A court is required to follow this kind of authority.

8. This branch of government creates 5-across and 11-down.

9. This kind of authority is not binding on a court.

12. Judicially created law when no statute governs that area of law.

13. An area of authority.

14. In the federal judicial system, this word is used to designate trial courts.

4. Adapted from materials created by Professor John Korzen, Wake Forest University School of Law. Thank you to Joan Rocklin for contributions in this chapter.

Exercise 2.3: Identifying Your Federal Jurisdiction

Use the Internet or other resources as needed to find the answers to the questions below.

1. What federal circuit are you in right now?

_____

2. Which states are included within that federal circuit?

_____

_____

_____

3. List the federal districts that are included within your state.

_____

_____

_____

_____

Exercise 2.4: Identifying Your State Jurisdiction

Use the Internet or other resources as needed to find the answers to the questions below.

1. What is the name of your state's highest appellate court?

_____

2. Does your state have an intermediate appellate court, and if so, what is the name of your state's intermediate appellate court?

_____

3. What is the name (or what are the names) of the trial courts in your state? If your state has more than one kind of trial court, what kinds of cases does each trial court hear?

_____

_____

_____

_____

Exercise 2.5: Assessing Weight of Authority

Your client, who works at a food processing plant in Michigan, has been fired from her job. She believes she was fired because she was about to report that her employer was violating state law. You are researching whether Michigan law should protect her from being fired. You find the authorities listed below.

Rank the authorities below according to their weight of authority, with 1 being the most weighty authority and 6 being the least weighty authority. Assume all cases are factually similar to your client's case.

In addition to ranking the authorities, designate each authority as a (1) primary or secondary authority and as a (2) mandatory or persuasive authority on a trial court hearing the case. Remember that to understand the weight of authority of judicial opinions, you must first determine the court hierarchy within the relevant jurisdiction. (Hint: You can do this by looking in the *Bluebook*, the *ALWD Guide*, or by doing an online search.)

An **encyclopedia** entry that describes whistleblower protection laws.	Primary or secondary Mandatory or persuasive
An **opinion issued by the Michigan Supreme Court** that addresses whether, under state law, a bus driver should be protected from discharge because she was about to report her employer's violation of law.	Primary or secondary Mandatory or persuasive
An **opinion issued by the United States Court of Appeals for the Ninth Circuit**, which addresses whether, under Michigan state law, an employee is protected by Michigan's Whistleblowers' Protection Act.	Primary or secondary Mandatory or persuasive
Michigan's Whistleblowers' Protection Act, a statute first enacted in 1972 by the Michigan legislature.	Primary or secondary Mandatory or persuasive
A **law review article** written by an eminent scholar that addresses the circumstances under which a court should find that an employee was about to report a violation of law.	Primary or secondary Mandatory or persuasive
An **opinion issued by the Michigan Court of Appeals** addressing whether an administrator in a nursing home was protected from discharge after writing an email to a co-worker stating she was going to report the facility to the state licensure board.	Primary or secondary Mandatory or persuasive

Exercise 2.6: Factual and Legal Considerations Before Filing a Lawsuit

Jordan Jones[5] has come to your office to discuss an incident that occurred when she was running in the Good Citizens Charity Summer Classic 10K. After reading her statement and the waiver, consider the questions that follow. Those questions will help you think about the legal issues that the incident raises and the legal authorities that you would need to research to assess any claims she might bring.

Jordan Jones's statement

My name is Jordan Jones. I was a runner for about 10 years. When I was running, I typically ran a 10K once a month, and two half-marathons per year. Now, I am not sure that I will ever run again. About six weeks ago, I participated in a 10K organized by Good Citizens Charity Fund that provides grants for local charities and nonprofits. There was no pre-registration for the race. I registered on race day, received a T-shirt and a number, and signed the waiver below:

Liability Waiver and Image Release

I know that running/walking in a foot race is a potentially hazardous activity. I should not enter and run/walk unless I am medically able and properly trained. I agree to abide by any decision of a race official relative to my ability to safely complete the run/walk. I assume all risks associated with running/walking in this event, including, but not limited to, falls, contacts with other participants, the effects of the weather including high heat and/or humidity, low temperature, traffic, and conditions of the road or trail, all risks being known and appreciated by me.

Having read this release and knowing these facts and in consideration of your accepting my entry, I, for myself and anyone entitled to act on my behalf or on behalf of my estate, waive and release Good Citizens Charities, Inc. and all sponsors of the race, any other persons or companies assisting with the race, the officers, Board, Board members, agents, servants, employees, and their successors and assigns of each and every of the above from all claims or liabilities of any kind arising out of my participation in the run/walk, even though the liability may arise out of negligence or carelessness on the part of the persons referred to in this waiver.

I also grant permission for the use of any photographs, motion pictures, recordings, or any other record of my participation in this event for any legitimate purpose. I understand that if the race is canceled because of circumstances beyond the control of the race committee and sponsors, including, but not limited to, unsafe weather conditions or governmental ban, my entry fee will not be refunded.

Because it had been so hot, I asked about the heat index at the registration desk. The volunteer told me there been some discussion of having hoses and fans with cool mist to help out the runners, but there was just no budget to purchase those items and no one offered to donate them. Due to the heat, I knew that I would have to make sure to stay hydrated during the race. I was told there would be water stops along the route. We started out, and we got to the first water stop, but there was no

---

5. Adapted from teaching materials created by Professor Kate Irwin-Smiler, Wake Forest University School of Law.

water. I found a police officer who was helping out with the race, and he said he was told that a local supplier had agreed to donate the water but hadn't shown up with it. It was about this time that I started feeling dizzy. I walked for a bit. I began sweating profusely. Suddenly, I started seeing stars in my eyes and things started to go black. I stopped and sat down on a bench in the U.S. Veterans' park. The next thing I remember was a big crowd around me and someone was calling 911.

I understand now that I had passed out, and the first responders had a difficult time trying to rouse me to consciousness. I was taken to the local hospital where I was given IV fluids. I was in intensive care for two days. I have a tremendous amount of medical bills, daily panic attacks, and I feel depressed all the time. It is affecting my job performance and my marriage.

Questions:

1. What additional questions would you want to ask Jordan before considering whether you want to file a lawsuit?

_____

_____

_____

_____

_____

_____

2. What additional facts would you want to research? How might you go about doing so?

_____

_____

_____

_____

_____

_____

3. What sources of law would you want to research before deciding whether you would want to file a lawsuit?

_____

_____

_____

_____

_____

_____

4. Do you think the waiver Jordan signed constitutes a defense to the lawsuit? If so, what are the best arguments supporting the waiver being a defense? What are the best counter-arguments?

_____

_____

_____

_____

_____

_____

Chapter 3
Preparing for the Deep Read

 As a lawyer, you will need to read, understand, and carefully examine the boundaries of numerous legal authorities. This chapter will give you practice reading, understanding, and carefully examining two key sources of legal authorities lawyers rely on frequently: statutes and cases. Then, this chapter will provide practice on how to work with the information you gain from deep reading.

Although no two legal authorities are the same, you can follow the same three steps to read, understand, and explore a legal authority. Those three steps are:

- Get context;
- Skim the text; and
- Read the text critically and question it.

Chapters 3.1, *Reading Statutes*; 3.2, *Reading Cases*; and 3.3, *Preparing Case Briefs* will help you critically read statutes and case law for your use in the classroom and beyond, when you are working with clients.

Patrick J. Coffy

Chapter 3.1
Reading Statutes

I. Using the Three-Step Process for Reading Comprehension
II. Exercises

To read a statute, you need to first understand how they are structured. Example 3.1.A shows how statutes are generally organized when published:

Example 3.1.A: The Structure of a Statute

Title or Chapter	A group of statutes organized by topic. Within titles or chapters there may be subtitles and subchapters as well.
Articles or Parts	Titles or Chapters are then broken down into Articles or Parts, which may also be further broken down.
Section(s)	While some statutes contain only one section, most have several sections. Some sections also have subsections.

Substantive statutory sections are the controlling law in the jurisdiction. Sometimes, within a title or chapter, any terms used in those statutory sections are first defined at the beginning of that title or chapter and applied throughout each statute in the article or section. Example 3.1.B sets forth three statutory provisions: § 140.00 (definitions), § 140.25 (second degree), and §140.20 (third degree). Section 140.00 provides definitions for the other burglary statutes in that statutory section. Section 140.25 then provides details on what behaviors constitute second- and third-degree burglary in New York. As you read through the two sections, ask yourself which of the words used in sections 140.25 and 140.20 might have special definitions as set forth in section 140.00.

Example 3.1.B: Example of a Definitional Statutory Provision[1]

New York Penal Law § 140.00
Criminal trespass and burglary; definitions of terms

The following definitions are applicable to this article:

1. "Premises" includes the term "building," as defined herein, and any real property.

2. "Building," in addition to its ordinary meaning, includes any structure, vehicle or watercraft used for overnight lodging of persons, or used by persons for carrying on business therein, or used as an elementary or secondary school, or an enclosed motor truck, or an enclosed motor truck trailer. Where a building consists of two or more units separately secured or occupied, each unit shall be deemed both a separate building in itself and a part of the main building.

3. "Dwelling" means a building, which is usually occupied by a person lodging therein at night.

Example 3.1.C: Example of Substantive Statutory Provisions

New York Penal Law § 140.25
Burglary in the second degree

A person is guilty of burglary in the second degree when he knowingly enters or remains unlawfully in a building with intent to commit a crime therein, and when:

1. In effecting entry or while in the building or in immediate flight therefrom, he or another participant in the crime:

    (a) Is armed with explosives or a deadly weapon; or
    (b) Causes physical injury to any person who is not a participant in the crime;
    or
    (c) Uses or threatens the immediate use of a dangerous instrument;
    or
    (d) Displays what appears to be a pistol, revolver, rifle, shotgun, machine gun or other firearm; or

2. The building is a dwelling.

New York Penal Law § 140.20
Burglary in the third degree

A person is guilty of burglary in the third degree when he knowingly enters or remains unlawfully in a building with intent to commit a crime therein.

---

1. These burglary statutes and hypotheticals were adapted from teaching materials at St. John's University School of Law.

Questions:

1. Which terms defined in § 140.00 are used in § 140.25 (second-degree burglary) and § 140.20 (third-degree burglary)?

Building and dwelling.

2. What do you think are the differences between the two statutory sections?

Whether or not someone does it with intent, either knowingly or unknowingly.

I. Using the Three-Step Process for Reading Comprehension

Step 1: Get context

- Typically, to respond to a client's question you will focus on one or two statutory sections; however, those sections must be read in the context of the whole statutory scheme. You can generally get a quick overview of the statutory scheme by reviewing the table of contents or quickly flipping or scrolling through the statute as a whole to get a sense of where the statute you are analyzing fits.

- For example, consider the National Motor Vehicle Theft Act that you will be reading more about in Chapter 3.2. Like the examples above, that act is made of multiple statutory sections, one of which is below:

Example 3.1.D: Example of a Definitional Statutory Sub-section

National Motor Vehicle Theft Act, 18 U.S.C. § 408 (1930).

The term "motor vehicle" when used in this section shall include an automobile, automobile truck, automobile wagon, motorcycle, or any other self-propelled vehicle not designed for running on rails.

To get context, you may want to consider the name of the act and the statutory citation:

National Motor Vehicle Theft Act, 18 U.S.C. § 408 (1930).

Name of Act   **Volume**   **Code**   **Section**   **Year enacted**

- Based on the name of the act and the citation to the United States Code, we know that it is a federal criminal statute enacted in 1930 that provides criminal penalties to punish an individual who steals a motor vehicle and transports it across state lines.

Step 2: Skim the pertinent statutory sections

- Skimming will provide you with an initial understanding of how the statute works, what the relationships may be between the sections, as well as whether the statute is comprised of factors, elements, lists, or a combination thereof, or whether there are cross-references to any statutes or statutory provisions.
- Example 3.1.D shows you how, after skimming this short statute, you will know that it contains a listing of vehicles that, if stolen, are subject to criminal penalties set forth in the Act.

Step 3: Read the statute carefully and question it

- First, read the statute slowly and carefully, noting every significant word. Consider the plain language of the statute because if it is clear and unambiguous, the plain meaning will control as you apply the statute to your client's facts.
- If you need to interpret the language because it is ambiguous, you may need to use statutory interpretation tools such as **intrinsic aids, canons of construction**, and **extrinsic aids**. We will focus on statutory interpretation in depth in Chapter 12, *Statutory Interpretation*, but we introduce some of the concepts here as they may arise in cases you are reading for your classes. Figure 3.1.E provides you with further information about intrinsic aids, canons of construction, and extrinsic aids.

Figure 3.1.E: Common Tools Used to Interpret Statutes

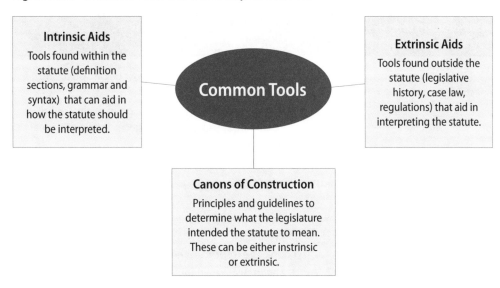

Sometimes, legislators provide an express statement of purpose in a statute. For example, in May 2018, Congress passed "The Trickett Wendler, Frank Mongiello, Jordan McLinn and Matthew Bellina Right to Try Act of 2017," which has language that expressly states that its **purpose** is "[t]o authorize the use of unapproved medical products by patients diagnosed with a terminal disease." If an express purpose is not stated, questioning your broad understanding of the statute's purpose is always helpful in gaining insights about what you are reading. (You may also want to go back and research the legislative history to help determine why the legislators felt there was a need for the law.) For example, if a statute is designed to remedy a societal problem, it should be construed broadly so as to positively affect more individuals. Thus, a workers' compensation statute is typically construed in favor of the employee. If a statute is designed to punish, such as a criminal statute, it should be construed narrowly so as to be applied only to individuals who violate the specific act prohibited.

The National Motor Vehicle Theft Act's purpose is to prevent and punish motor vehicle theft. Because our criminal law needs to be clear on what type of behavior is subject to penalty or imprisonment, we would construe the language narrowly. To examine the structure of any statute, you should group the terms into elements, factors, or lists (so you understand what standard needs to be satisfied) and search for any **red flag words** that limit, prohibit, dictate, allow, or restrict certain actions. Table 3.1.F provides definitions and examples of both.

Table 3.1.F: Questioning the Structure of a Statute

Questioning the Structure of the Statute	Definitions/Examples
Does it contain elements, factors, or lists?	• Element—a condition that must be proved to show that a standard is met • Factor—a condition that is weighed against another condition. The factors are judged on their individual or cumulative strength. • List—a number of connected items.
Does it contain a term or phrase that limits, prohibits, dictates, allows or restricts certain actions?	• And—must have all elements and factors present • Or/Either—only one element or factor need be present • Unless/except/if . . . then—creates an exception • Shall/must—mandates conduct • Shall not/must not/ may not—prohibits conduct • Provided that/Regardless of—creates an exception or adds an additional requirement

Similarly, canons of construction also look at the structure of a statute—the choice and placement of words and the grammar and syntax of words—to discern what the legislature intended. Canons of construction are not mandatory rules that must be followed but instead are common principles that you can use to guide how words or phrases in a statute should be understood. Lawyers and courts may use many different canons of construction to help interpret statutes—far too many than can be set forth here. You'll learn more about theses cannons of construction and different methodologies for statutory interpretation in Chapter 12, *Statutory Interpretation*.

II.   Exercises

The exercises below will help you to interpret and apply statutes. Try your hand at reviewing the statutes and applying them to your client's facts.

Exercise 3.1.1: Applying a Simple Statute

Consider the following fact scenario:

Polly Walker was strolling down the street when she encountered a small white poodle named "Doodles" that was in her neighbor's yard. She stepped into the yard and bent down to pet Doodles. Doodles started yipping and bit Polly in the ankle. She had to go to the hospital for treatment and would like for Doodle's owner, Debbie Dunn, to pay for her expenses. Polly asks you to look into the law and let her know whether she is likely to recover from Dunn.

You research this issue and find the following statute. Read through the statute and respond to the questions below.

Michigan Comp. Laws § 287.351 (2019)

If a dog bites a person, without provocation while the person is on public property, or lawfully on private property, including the property of the owner of the dog, the owner of the dog shall be liable for any damages suffered by the person bitten, regardless of the former viciousness of the dog or the owner's knowledge of such viciousness.

1. **How does this statute apply in the context of your client's situation?**

She was on the owner's property.

2. **As you read through the statute and question it, do you see terms that may be applicable to your client's situation that are unclear or ambiguous? If so, identify those below:**

lawfully.

3. **Are there any terms that warrant further research before responding to the client?**

lawfully.

Exercise 3.1.2: Applying a More Complex Statute

For purposes of this exercise, you work as an assistant district attorney in a jurisdiction that has experienced a rash of factual scenarios that could constitute kidnapping under state law. The kidnapping statute reads as follows:

12 State § 3201 (2019)

Whoever seizes, confines, inveigles, decoys, abducts or carries away and holds for ransom or reward or <u>otherwise</u> any person, except in the case of a minor by a parent, shall be punished by imprisonment for a term of 25 years to life.

The district attorney would like for you to consider the following fact scenarios in the context of the kidnapping statute. To help her determine whether to prosecute these situations, she would like you to respond to the questions that follow each fact scenario.[2]

Fact Scenario 1:

On July 26, Alicia Miller (who is twenty-one years old) was arrested for car theft and kidnapping. Ms. Miller's mother is terminally ill. Ms. Miller learned her mother's health insurance refused to cover the experimental treatment that the doctor had recommended. Without the expensive experimental treatment, the doctors did not expect her mother to live beyond the end of the month. This news was a severe blow to Ms. Miller, who was feeling quite desperate.

Ms. Miller noticed a person in an expensive Land Rover pull into the pharmacy next to the Dairy King, where Ms. Miller had stopped for a snack. The driver left the car running and ran into the store. Ms. Miller decided to try to steal the car and sell it to a friend "who dealt in these kinds of matters" to help raise money for her mother's treatments.

Just as she was crossing the bridge to leave town, she noticed in the rear view mirror that there was a man asleep in the backseat. Ms. Miller panicked. She pulled into a gas station and abandoned the car. A police officer happened to be in the gas station and saw Ms. Miller leave the car and run. The police officer caught Ms. Miller, who confessed to stealing the car but explained to the officer that she was unaware that a man was asleep in the backseat. The district attorney wants to know if she should prosecute Ms. Miller under the kidnapping statute.

Questions:

1. **How does the statute apply in the context of your client's legal issue?**

   She may have seized or abducted that person.

---

2. These hypotheticals were adapted from teaching materials created by various legal writing professors at Wake Forest University School of Law.

_____

_____

2. As you skim the statute, do you notice any specific statutory provisions that are likely to apply to Ms. Miller's situation?

___*or Otherwise*_____

_____

_____

_____

_____

3. As you read the statute carefully and question it in light of Ms. Miller's case, describe which terms you think are ambiguous.

___*Seize, abduct*_____

_____

_____

_____

_____

4. Highlight any "red flag words" (words that contain a term or phrase that limit, prohibit, dictate, allow or restrict certain actions) the statute contains. What do those red flag words signify?

___*or, except*_____

_____

_____

_____

_____

5. Examining the phrase "ransom or reward or otherwise," what arguments can you make that Ms. Miller should not be charged with kidnapping?

___*She didn't make any demands*_____

immediately informed law enforcement

_____

_____

_____

Fact Scenario 2:

Brad and Susan Simko are the maternal grandparents of minors Sophia Ann Berry and Emily Grace Berry. The Simkos' daughter, Karla, was married to Jack Berry, but Karla died several years ago from breast cancer. Following Karla's death, the children lived with their father, Jack, but Jack was severely injured after sustaining a fall at work. Due to his injuries, he is no longer able to work.

Jack asked if the Simkos could care for their grandchildren during the school year. This change would allow the children to attend one of the best public schools in the state. The Simkos agreed, and the children moved in with them in August. No official guardianship or custody papers were ever prepared.

The children thrived while living with the Simkos. They made good grades and were involved in sports and extracurricular activities. They visited nearby relatives frequently and became close with their cousins, who attended the same school. During the time they stayed with the Simkos, Jack fell into a deep depression. The Simkos noticed Jack had started drinking and was intoxicated during a visit. They stopped the visits.

Near the end of the school year, Jack called the Simkos and told them that he wanted the girls to come back to live with him. The girls told the Simkos they did not want to disappoint their dad, but they wanted to stay with them. The Simkos filed a lawsuit to obtain custody.

On the last day of school, Jack drove to the girls' school and told the guidance counselor that Mrs. Simko had an accident and he needed to take the girls to the hospital. Once in the car, Jack took the girls' smart phones and drove the girls to a hotel. The Simkos contacted the police. Several hours later, the police were able to trace the girls to the hotel, where they were scared but unharmed. Jack was drunk and passed out on the bed. Should the district attorney prosecute Jack for kidnapping?

6. Does the exception in this statute apply to Jack?

Yes.

7. What arguments support that Jack is a parent?

The kids are his.
creates the plans to be temporary.

8. **What arguments might you make that Jack should not be considered a parent?**

Relinquished Custody.
The kids didn't want to go back
to his custody.

Exercise 3.1.3: Applying Multiple Statutory Sections

Assume you are working as an Assistant District Attorney in Rochester, New York. Your supervisor asks you to research whether the fraternity house at Big State University constituted a "dwelling." Assume the prosecution can establish the other elements. Read through the fact pattern below, examine the statutory sections provided above in Example 3.1.B (New York Penal Law §§ 140.00, 140.25, 140.20), and respond to the questions that follow the fact pattern.

On the morning of January 1, defendant Tom Locker broke into a fraternity house for Big State University, located in Rochester, New York. He stole numerous items of school and personal property. He was apprehended when his vehicle broke down on a road near campus. A state trooper stopped to investigate, and Locker confessed when asked about items piled up in the backseat under a blanket. Locker was indicted for burglary in the second degree and petit larceny and found guilty as charged following a jury trial. Locker now brings an appeal claiming that the fraternity house was not a "dwelling," and that the lower court erred in declining to charge the jury with burglary in the third degree (as a lesser included offense of burglary in the second degree).

Testimony at trial established that the fraternity house from which Locker stole property was vacant for the semester break. However, the house was fully furnished with personal and household belongings; its occupants intended to return in the second semester. The utilities were intact. The defendant argues on appeal that the students had vacated the premises for the holidays, and thus, it did not constitute a "dwelling." Also, the house was not stocked with food.

1. **How do these three statutory provisions apply in the context of Tom's situation?**

Dwelling is defined by them.

2. List any terms that may be applicable to the fact scenario and which terms may be in controversy.

_____

_____

_____

_____

_____

_____

3. Are any red flag words (words that contain a term or phrase that limit, prohibit, dictate, allow or restrict certain actions) relevant to Tom's situation? If so, what do they signify?

_____

_____

_____

_____

_____

_____

4. Based on your reading of these statutory provisions, do you think the fraternity house was a dwelling on January 1?

_____

_____

_____

_____

_____

_____

Chapter 3.2

Reading Cases

Before jumping into reading a case, you must first develop vocabulary to discuss a case. After all, you can't think about **how** to read a case until you understand its components. Thus, the first section of this chapter quickly addresses case law vocabulary. Once you are familiar with what a case looks like and the parts that it contains, then you'll be ready to think about how to read a case.

To read a case, you must ask yourself why are you reading this case (or legal authority). You may need to adjust how you read a legal authority based on your purpose for reading it. At this point in your career, you will likely have one of two purposes for reading a case: either you are preparing for a law school class or you are preparing to analyze a client's case.

I. Diagramming the Parts of a Case

When dealing with cases, the first words you should be familiar with are all the words used to refer to a case. Those words include **opinion, decision, judicial opinion, judicial decision**, and **precedent**.

No matter what a lawyer might call it, each case has basically the same parts as every other case. Figure 3.2.A identifies the parts of a case, and the text that follows the case excerpt explains the role that these parts play.

Figure 3.2.A: The Parts of a Case[1]

(1) (2)

McBOYLE v UNITED STATES.

No. 213.

(3) Circuit Court of Appeals, Tenth Circuit.

(4) Aug. 18, 1930.

1. **Automobiles** ⟵341.

(5) Statute defining "motor vehicle" as including automobile trucks, motorcycles, "or any other self-propelled motor vehicle not designed for running on rails," includes airplanes (National Motor Vehicle Theft Act [18 USCA § 408]).

*****

7. **Criminal law** ⟵402(1).

(6) Copies of telegram were competent evidence where identified by addressee and where telegraph operators testified that originals had been destroyed.

8. **Criminal law** ⟵1156(I).

Ruling on motion for new trial will not be disturbed on appeal, in absence of abuse of discretion.

(7) COTTERAL, Circuit Judge, dissenting. 43 F.(2d)—18

(8) Appeal from the District Court of the United States for the Western District of Oklahoma.

William W. McBoyle was convicted of violation of the National Motor Vehicle Theft Act, and he appeals. **(9)**

Affirmed. **(10)**

Harry F. Brown, of Guthrie, Okl. (Frank Dale and Mr. Robert W. Hoyland, both of Guthrie, Okl., on the brief), for appellant.

Roy St. Lewis, U. S. Atty., of Oklahoma City, Okl. (Fred A. Wagoner and William Earl Wiles, Asst. U. S. Attys., both of Oklahoma City, Okl., on the brief), for appellee.

Before COTTERAL, PHILLIPS, and McDERMOTT, Circuit Judges.

PHILLIPS, Circuit Judge.

William W. McBoyle was convicted and sentenced for an alleged violation of the National Motor Vehicle Theft Act, section 408, title 18, U. S. Code (18 USCA § 408). The indictment charged that on October 10, 1926 McBoyle caused to be transported in interstate commerce from Ottawa, Ill., to Guymon, Okl., one Waco airplane, motor No. 6124, serial No. 256, which was the property of the United States Aircraft Corporation and which had theretofore been stolen; and that McBoyle then and there knew it had been stolen.

The evidence of the government established the following facts: During the year 1926, McBoyle operated a commercial airport at Galena, Ill. On July 2, 1926, McBoyle hired A. J. Lacey as an aviator for a period of six months. In October 1926, McBoyle induced Lacey to go to the field of the Aircraft Corporation at Ottawa, Ill., and steal such Waco airplane from the Aircraft Corporation. Lacey went to Ottawa, stole the airplane, and flew it to Galena, arriving here October 6th. McBoyle inquired of Lacey if anyone knew the latter had taken the airplane at Ottawa. Lacey replied in the negative. Thereupon, McBoyle changed the serial number to No. 249, and painted it over in order to conceal the alteration. McBoyle and Lacey serviced the airplane and supplied it with gas and oil. McBoyle gave Lacey $150 for expense money and instructed Lacey to fly the airplane to Amarillo, Tex., and there lease an airport for them to operate during the winter months. McBoyle arranged with Lacey to communicate with him en route by telegraphic code under the name of Pat Sullivan. Lacey left McBoyle's airport at Galena, Ill., on October 6th and flew the airplane to Guymon, Okl., stopping en route at St. Joseph, Mo., and Garden City, Kan. At Guymon, they communicated with each other by telegraph and McBoyle instructed Lacey to sell or store the stolen airplane and come back to Galena. Thereupon, Lacey returned for expenses and instructed Lacey to take an airplane of the same kind and make belonging to McBoyle back to Guymon and substitute it for the stolen airplane. The purpose was to deceive the officers when they found the Waco plane at Guymon. Lacey started back to Guymon with the second airplane but crashed near Inman, Kan. Thereupon, Lacey returned to Galena and continued to work for McBoyle until the following December.

(11)

McBoyle denied all of the facts incriminating him except the sending and receiving of the telegrams. He testified that the telegrams did not refer to the airplane but **(12)** to liquor which Lacey was supposed to have had in his possession in the airplane.

[1] The primary question is whether an airplane comes **(13)** within the purview of the National Motor Vehicle Theft Act. This act defines the term "motor vehicle," as follows:

"The term 'motor vehicle' when used in this section shall include an automobile, automobile truck, automobile wagon, motor cycle, or any other self-propelled vehicle not designed for running on rails."

Counsel for McBoyle contend that the word "vehicle" includes only conveyances that travel on the ground; that an airplane is not a vehicle but a ship; and that, under the doctrine of ejusdem generis the phrase "any other self-propelled vehicle" cannot be construed to include an airplane.

The Century Dictionary gives the derivation of the word "vehicle" as follows: "F. Vehicule, L. Vehiculum," meaning a "conveyance, carriage, *ship*." It defines the word

---

1. Adapted from teaching materials created by various professors at Wake Forest University School of Law.

as "Any receptacle, or means of transport, in which something is carried or conveyed, or *travels*." (Italics ours.)

It will be noted that the Latin word "vehiculum" means a ship as well as a carriage.

Webster defines the word "vehicle" as follows:

"(1) That in or on which any person or thing is or may be carried, esp. on land, as a coach, wagon, car, bicycle, etc.; a means of conveyance.

(2) That which is used as the instrument of conveyance or communication."

Corpus Juris, vol. 42, p. 609, § 1, defines a motor vehicle, as follows:

"A 'motor vehicle' is a vehicle operated by .a power developed within itself and used for the purpose of carrying passengers or materials; and as the term is used in the different statutes regulating such vehicles, it is generally defined as including all vehicles propelled by any power other than muscular power, except traction engines, road rollers, and such motor vehicles as run only upon rails or tracks."

Both the derivation and the definition of the word "vehicle" indicate that it is sufficiently broad to include any means or device by which persons or things are carried or transported, and it is not limited to instrumentalities used for traveling on land, although the latter may be the limited or special meaning of the word. We do not think it would be inaccurate to say that a ship or vessel is a vehicle of commerce.

An airplane is self-propelled, by means of a gasoline motor. It is designed to carry passengers and freight from place to place. It runs partly on the ground but principally in the air. It furnishes a rapid means for transportation of persons and comparatively light articles of freight and express. It therefore serves the same general purpose as an automobile, automobile truck, or motorcycle. It is of the same general kind or class as the motor vehicles specifically enumerated in the statutory definition and, therefore, construing an airplane to come within the general term, "any other self propelled vehicle," does not offend against the maxim of ejusdem generis.

Furthermore, some meaning must be ascribed to the general phrase "any other self propelled vehicle," which Congress wrote into the act. It specifically enumerated, all of the known self-propelled vehicles designed for running on land. It used the word "automobile," a generic term, which includes all self-propelled motor vehicles that travel on land and are used for the transportation of passengers, except those designed for running on rails. 42 C. J. p. 609, § 2.

We conclude that the phrase, "any other self propelled vehicle," includes an airplane, a motorboat, and any other like means of conveyance or transportation which is self-propelled, and is of the same general class as an automobile and a motorcycle.

* * * *

The judgment is therefore affirmed.

COTTERAL, Circuit Judge (dissenting).

I feel bound to dissent on the ground that the National Motor Vehicle Theft Act should not be construed as relating to the transportation of airplanes.

A prevailing rule is that a penal statute is to be construed strictly against an offender and it must state clearly the persons and acts denounced. 25 R. C. L. pp. 1081–1084; First Nat. Bank of Anamoose v. United States (C. C. A.) 206 F. 374, 46 L. R. A. (N. S.) 1139.

It would have been a simple matter in enacting the statute to insert, as descriptive words, airplanes, aircraft, or flying machines. If they had been in the legislative mind, the language would not have been expressed in such uncertainty as "any other self-propelled vehicle not designed for running on rails." The omission to definitely mention airplanes requires a construction that they were not included. Furthermore, by excepting vehicles running on rails, the meaning of the act is clarified. These words indicate it was meant to be confined to vehicles that *run*, but not on rails, and it did not extend to those that *fly*. Is it not an unreasonable view that airplanes fall within the description of self-propelled vehicles that do not run on rails? The question is its own answer.

The rule of ejusdem generis has special application to this statute. General words following a particular designation are usually presumed to be restricted so as to include only things or persons of the same kind, class, or nature, unless there is a clear manifestation of a contrary purpose. 25 R. C. L. pp. 996, 997. The general description in this statute refers to vehicles of the same general class as those enumerated. We may assume an airplane is a vehicle, in being a means of transportation. And it has its own motive power. But is an airplane classified generally with "an automobile, automobile truck, automobile wagon, or motor cycle?" Are airplanes regarded as *other types of automobiles* and the like? A moment's reflection demonstrates the contrary.

* * * *

It is familiar knowledge that the theft of automobiles had then become a public menace, but that airplanes had been rarely stolen if at all, and it is a most-uncommon thing even at this date. The prevailing mischief sought to be corrected is an aid in the construction of a statute. 25 R. C. L. 1016. I am constrained to hold that airplanes were not meant to be embraced in the designation of motor vehicles, and that the indictment charged no offense against the defendant.

We will explain each numbered section in more detail, but first, let's look at the case citation:

Court opinions are compiled in series of books called reporters. The first number refers to the volume of the reporter, volume 43. "F.2d" refers to the Federal Reporter, second series. Federal cases arising from the thirteen United States Circuit Courts of Appeals are reported in the Federal Reporter. The final number, 273, refers to the page in volume 43 of F.2d where the opinion begins. Thus, the full cite includes the name of the case, the reporter volume, the page, the court, and year of the decision.

McBoyle v. United States, 43 F. 2d 273 (10th Cir. 1930)

Parties to the case   Volume   Reporter   Page   Court   Year

A. Caption

1 **Case name.** The name of this case is *McBoyle v. United States*. Most published cases are appellate cases. Here, since McBoyle lost at trial below and brought the appeal, he is the **appellant** and is listed first. The United States is the **appellee**.

2 **Docket number.** The number 213 is the appellate docket number and is assigned by the circuit court as an identifier. You generally do not need this number, unless you need to go the appellate clerk of court to look at the file of the case.

3 **Deciding court.** This case was decided by the Tenth Circuit Court of Appeals.

4 **Date of decision.** The Tenth Circuit Court of Appeals issued its opinion on August 18, 1930.

B. Publisher's Enhancements

5 & **6** **Headnotes.** Headnotes are written by an editor, specifically from the West Publishing Company in the case above, and are not part of the opinion. Headnotes summarize many of the issues discussed in an opinion. You will find that headnotes are important research tools, but remember not to rely on them since they are not the court's own words—you must always go to the court's opinion as the primary source.

"Automobiles 🗝 341" is a key number. The key number, which includes both the word and the number, is part of the West Publishing Company research system. This number permits you to research the same issue in many different jurisdictions and in a variety of West publications. Lexis, another major legal publisher, has its own system of headnotes for cases it publishes.[2]

7 **Judges.** Judge Phillips wrote the majority opinion, and Judge Cotteral dissented from the majority opinion.

8 **Court below.** McBoyle appeals the decision of the United States District Court of the Western District of Oklahoma.

9 **Information about the appeal.** McBoyle was convicted under the National Motor Vehicle Theft Act, and he appeals.

---

2. Some opinions have summaries of the case before the headnotes. These summaries are not part of the opinion and cannot be relied upon or quoted, but they are useful research tools when you are looking for case law.

10 **Disposition.** This is the judgment of this court. The Tenth Circuit affirmed the trial court's conviction of McBoyle. The result here is that the trial court verdict and sentence will remain unchanged. This judgment can also be found at the end of the case.

11 **Attorneys representing McBoyle.** Harry F. Brown, Frank Dale, and Robert W. Hoyland represented McBoyle, defendant-appellant.

12 **Attorneys representing the U.S. government.** Roy St. Lewis, Fred A. Wagoner, and William Earl Wiles represented the United States, petitioner-appellee.

13 **Panel members.** Appeals are typically decided by a panel of three appellate judges. This appeal was decided by a three-judge panel made up of Judges Cotteral, Phillips, and McDermott.

C. The Body of the Opinion

14 **Parts of the opinion.** While some judicial opinions may differ a bit in structure, the body of most judicial opinions contain the following parts:

- Facts
- Issue or question presented
- Holding
- Reasoning
- Judgment or disposition
- Concurring and/or dissenting opinions, if any

II. The Three-Step Process for Deep Reading

Now that you have a picture of the typical parts of a case, you can begin reading. You can follow the three-step process for reading comprehension outlined in the introduction to this chapter for reading cases: (1) get context, (2) skim the case, and (3) read the case closely. Let's look at each step.

A. Get Context

Novice students—to their detriment—skip this step. However, context is very important. A case represents one legal principle within a larger system of rules. To understand where this one case—and the principle that it represents—fits, you must have a sense of the larger system of rules.

You can get a sense of the larger system of rules in several ways. First, if the cite is part of a casebook for a course, you can review the table of contents. The table of contents will usually list the major legal concepts covered in each chapter. By locating the chapter within which the case appears, you will already know which legal concept relates to the case.

A second way to get context is by reading the relevant portion of a treatise or commercial outline about the course subject matter. Once you know (by reviewing the table of contents) which legal concept the case relates to, you can read about that area of law in more detail in a treatise or a commercial outline. Doing so will provide you more detail about the area of law that the case will address. In other words, you will have a sense of the forest before examining an individual tree—the case itself.

Once you have a framework for the legal system within which this case resides, you are ready to read the case.

B. Skim the Case

To read a case effectively, begin by skimming the surface of the case. Skimming will not only provide you with a framework for the case, but it will ultimately save you time. When you skim a case, look for the big concepts outlined below. Simply note where each part exists within the case, but avoid getting bogged down in the details. Doing so will allow you to see how the case is organized. Once you understand the organization and the big concepts of the case, you can slow down on the second read and focus on the details.

C. Read the Case Closely

Once you have outlined the structure of the case and the big concepts within it, you are now ready to read the case more closely. As you do, identify the following:

- Specific legal issue the court is deciding
- Relevant facts (those facts that led to the holding)
- Holding in this case
- Additional reasoning or rationale that connects the facts to the holding
- Disposition
- Any concurring or dissenting opinions

III. Exercises

The exercises below will help you to identify and work with the different parts of judicial opinions. They will also help you develop skills for critically reading cases.

Exercise 3.2.1: Dissecting the Parts of a Case

Reread the *McBoyle* case (above) and respond to the questions below:

1. What were the relevant facts of the case?

_____

_____

_____

_____

_____

_____

2. What was the issue before the court?

_____

_____

_____

_____

_____

_____

3. What did McBoyle's lawyers argue the term "vehicle" should include?

only vehicles that travel on the ground.

_____

_____

_____

_____

4. What did the government argue the term "vehicle" should include?

An airplane.

_____

_____

_____

_____

_____

5. Which argument did the court find to be more convincing, and why?

The government, because it fit the definition and the statute was broad.

_____

_____

_____

_____

6. What was the basis for the dissenting opinion?

_____

_____

_____

_____

_____

_____

7. **Do you agree more with the majority or the dissent? Why?**

_____

_____

_____

_____

_____

_____

Exercise 3.2.2: Identifying a Holding

Marietta Title Insurance Company v. Rath,
State Court (2016)

Plaintiff Marietta Title Insurance Co., with offices in Park County, brings this action against Paul Rath asserting breach of a noncompete covenant. Plaintiff seeks injunctive relief and asks that this Court permanently enjoin defendant from working in the title insurance business in the state of Utopia for two years. Plaintiff grounds its case upon the assertion that Rath's services were unique and, therefore, he should not be permitted to work for a competitor.

Marietta hired Rath in 2012 as Senior Vice President in charge of several major sales accounts. On the first day of his employment, Rath signed a covenant not to compete, restricting him from working for another title insurance company for two years following his termination of employment services from Marietta. However, in August 2014, Rath abruptly terminated his employment with Marietta and signed on as senior vice president of a competitor, Charles Schwartz Title Co., also based in Park County. At the hearing, evidence was produced indicating that Rath had relationships with specific customers of his assigned accounts and that these customers would engage only Rath for Marietta business. Rath had a special knowledge of a computer program that was helpful for his customers' business. Rath had frequent contact with his customers. Rath's territory was limited to Park County. The accounts he oversaw were limited in the same geographic locales.

In the state of Utopia, assuming a covenant by an employee not to compete is reasonable in time and geographic scope, enforcement will be granted to the extent necessary: (1) to prevent an employee's solicitation or disclosure of trade secrets; (2) to prevent an employee's release of confidential information regarding the employer's customers; or (3) in those cases where the employee's services to the employer are deemed special or unique. In a case where (1) is met, but not (2), Utopia courts have granted injunctions to enforce covenants not to compete based upon the unique services of the defendants. In *Matheson Savings Bank v. Jonas*, the state court found that the former employee's relationships with the clients were special and qualified as unique services. The *Jonas* court deemed these relationships unique because of the highly competitive banking industry and the rare talent that rose to the top of the banking world. In addition, the *Matheson* clients had regular contact with Jonas. Thus, the court granted injunctive relief.

In analyzing whether an employee's services are unique, the focus is less on the uniqueness of the individual person and more on the employee's relationship to the employer's business and the clients.

Here, facts produced at the hearing indicate that Rath's services were, and continue to be, unique. Therefore, this Court grants plaintiff's permanent injunction; however, defendant Rath is restricted from working for title insurance companies having offices within the geographic parameters of Park County only.

1. According to the court, when are non-compete covenants enforced?

> 1. to prevent an employees solicitation
> or disclosure of trade secrets.

2. What happened in the *Jonas* case?

3. What do you think the holding is in *Rath*? What facts does the court rely on in its holding?

Chapter 3.3
Preparing Case Briefs

To read cases assigned for a law school course, you must first step back and understand the purpose of a doctrinal law school class. A doctrinal law school class is one that teaches "doctrine." The word "doctrine" refers to a system of principles. In most law school classrooms, you learn the doctrine—or system of principles—that relate to a particular area of law, such as the principles that relate to torts, criminal law, constitutional law, or civil procedure. (By contrast, other classes, such as Legal Research & Writing or Trial Practice, do not focus on a single area of law; rather, they focus on developing legal analysis and related skills through understanding doctrinal theory and providing opportunities for practice.)

For most of your 1L classes, you will be reading from a casebook. This section provides you with an overview of what a casebook is—and is not—and how to get the most out of reading cases from your casebook to prepare for class.

I. Casebooks

A casebook is a legal textbook that uses actual edited appellate court cases and other legal documents to teach legal principles. In law school, virtually all professors teaching core doctrinal classes do so by using casebooks. Learning how these books work will help you get the most out of them as you do your weekly readings and prepare for class discussion.

Casebooks contain the edited appellate cases, along with statutes, codes, and regulations that have led up to the development of modern legal doctrines. However, no two casebooks are alike, and different casebooks include different kinds of material in their pages and for different reasons. Figure 3.3.A, below, provides some advice to get the most out of your casebooks.

Figure 3.3.A: Advice for Using Casebooks Effectively

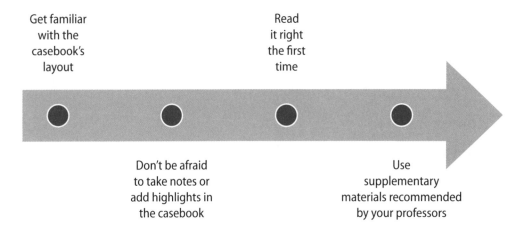

Let's examine each one:

- **Get familiar with the casebook's layout:** Each book looks different, and some of those differences may change the way you read and relate to your book. Study the Table of Contents—it will tell you where you are and where you are going during the semester. The very placement of the case within the Table of Contents can help you target the relevant doctrine that the case illustrates; knowing why you are reading something will be just as beneficial to you as remembering the details of what you are reading.

- **Don't be afraid to take notes or add highlights in the casebook:** As you get deeper into the text, it will become easier to get lost or miss key details. Having a method to identify material that is important—whether that be making notes in the margins, highlighting key passages, or taking notes on a separate sheet of paper—will help you make sense of the text.

- **Read it right the first time:** Using the reading for comprehension steps discussed in Chapter 3.2, *Reading Cases*, will help you read efficiently and effectively. While it may take a bit longer the first few times, putting in the time or effort necessary to learn what is important will help you better understand the material. It will also save you time before exams, as that initial effort will make reviewing much easier.

- **Use supplementary materials recommended by your professors:** Some of your professors have listed other supplementary books and materials to go along with your casebook. While it may seem like an extra chore, you should read these materials. Supplementary materials will help illuminate key concepts or summarize principles in different ways from the casebook, which will help you understand and absorb the concepts more effectively.

In a casebook class (think property, criminal law, or torts), the overarching goal for the semester is to learn the rules (or principles) that govern that area of law. To that end, each case that you will read will represent a legal principle. As you read a case, your goal will be to extract the legal principle represented in that case.

Law professors have other goals for the class. Those goals may include teaching students how to:

- identify the different parts of the case;
- apply the rule from the case to a set of facts;
- understand the principles of law represented in the case;

- understand policies underlying the law;
- identify the parties and the arguments being made;
- distinguish between relevant and irrelevant facts; and
- understand the implications of the court's holding on future cases.

Thus, when reading a case to prepare for a law school class, you will need to prepare for the major goal—understanding the legal principle that the case represents—and prepare for other educational goals your professor may have.

To that end, many students "brief" cases to prepare for class. Preparing a case brief is a form of note taking. The case brief will help you remember the key points of a case and respond to your professor's questions during class. Putting in too much information will weigh you down and keep you from remembering the important or salient facts. Conversely, you cannot ignore key facts just to save space or shorten the briefing process. It's a process that depends on the complexity of the case. As a rule of thumb, your case brief may range anywhere from half a page to over a page long. Going any longer may mean that you have included too many superfluous details.

II. Format of a Case Brief

No one perfect format exists for briefing cases.[1] Each professor will want you to remember different kinds of details for that professor's course, so what works best in one class may not work well in another. Modify the format as you need to satisfy the demands of each professor. You may find that considering the following suggestions is a good place to start:

A. Typical Parts of a Case Brief

1. **Name of the case.** The heading identifies the case, helps you locate it quickly and refreshes your memory. Begin with the name of the case. Then, designate the parties (1) as they were in the trial court, (2) their status on appeal, and (3) the relationship that gave rise to the controversy.

Lowell v. Trent

P/Π/Appellant/Landlord v. D/Δ/Appellee/Tenant

   The name of the case tells us that Lowell (the landlord) is suing Trent (the tenant). At the trial level, Lowell was the plaintiff (P, π) and Trent was the defendant (D, Δ). Trent won the case, and Lowell appealed. Lowell is thus the appellant (or petitioner). Trent responded to the appeal, and is the appellee (or respondent).

   Courts may refer to the parties either by the designation below (plaintiff, defendant), by their designation on appeal (appellant/petitioner, appellee/respondent) or both, which may be confusing. Do whatever you find helpful to keep track of the parties. It may be useful to identify the parties by their relationship (landlord/tenant; employer/employee; automobile driver/accident victim) both to help you keep track of them and to quickly refresh your memory as to the facts of the case.

2. **Court.** You will find it helpful to note which court decided the case and whether it is a trial, an intermediate, or the highest court. Also note whether it is a federal or state court.

---

1. Much information in this chapter had its origins in a handout, *Navigating Your 1L Year*, based on materials from the LWI Idea Bank and various LWI conferences.

3. **Year of decision**. This provides historical context.

4. **Facts**. Include events that led one party to initiate legal proceedings against the other. Briefly summarize the facts as they appeared at trial, and include only relevant or key facts—specifically, those that relate to the problem at hand. One guide to identifying relevant facts is to ask: If this fact were changed, would the court reach a different conclusion? To help you get started, and to check your understanding of the facts, ask yourself:

   - What happened between the parties?
   - What cause of action (legal theory, claim, charge, argument) does the plaintiff have?
   - What facts are relevant to plaintiff's claim?
   - How did the defendant respond?
   - Did the defendant assert defenses or claims against the plaintiff?
   - What does the plaintiff/appellant want the court to do?
   - What facts are most relevant to the defense's arguments?

   If the professor asks, "What are the facts of this case?" or "What happened in this case?" you should not answer, "Plaintiff is suing the defendant." Begin, instead, in a way that identifies the plaintiff, the salient facts, and the cause of action. For example: A landlord (Jones) is suing her tenant (Smith) for breach of contract due to the tenant's failure to pay rent.

5. **Procedural history**. The procedural history is the history of the case as it developed through litigation up to the current point in time. When summarizing the procedural history, trace the stages of litigation until you reach the present court's decision. You may want to check whether any of the questions below apply to the case you are reading:

   - What is the plaintiff claiming?
   - What happened in the court(s) below?
   - Was the original action tried before a jury or before a judge alone?
   - Was summary judgment or a directed verdict granted for one party?
   - Which party was successful?
   - What was the final disposition of the case in the trial court?

   Remember to consider only those facts or issues that are most salient or relevant. Detailing every document or motion filed with the district court will not help you understand the basic events that occurred in the litigation process.

6. **Issue**. The issue is the question (or questions) the court is called upon to decide in order to resolve the dispute between the parties. Since you will be primarily reading appellate court cases, concentrate on the issue or issues in controversy **on appeal** rather than those already handled at the district court level. Learning to spot and correctly state the issue takes time and practice, and it is a major reason why briefing cases is so important. A good statement of the issue or question presented considers whether a particular law, rule, or definition requires a particular outcome or finding when it is applied to the facts of the case. Start by asking the broadest legal question first:

   - Did the defendant have the intent to cause injury, as required for a second-degree burglary?

- Did the advertisement constitute an offer under contract law?

Then, incorporate the key facts. You should also phrase the question in a way that suggests what the outcome might be.

- Did the defendant have the intent to cause injury, as required for a second-degree burglary, when, as he fled from the complainant's apartment, he let out a karate yell and threw her to the ground?
- Did the advertisement for a one-day-only sale for one genuine lapin stole, worth $26, for $1 constitute an offer under contract law?

7. **Holding**. The holding is the answer to the question asked in the issue. The holding may include a one-word answer (yes or no), but should also include the key facts that led to the decision. A holding may be stated narrowly or broadly, and that may depend upon the court's intention. A court does not have to answer every issue presented to it. It may only need to reach a conclusion on one issue to dispose of the case. The holding only answers the questions asked, and it has precedential value only on those points (and only within that jurisdiction). When considering the holding, ask yourself what actually happened to the case and to the parties involved when the court issued its ruling. Below are some questions that may help:

- After the court answered the question presented, what happened?
- Did it affirm the lower court, reverse its decision, or remand (send the case back) for further proceedings?
- Did the court award damages? If so, to whom, for what, and how much?
- Did the court issue an injunction, order a hearing, impose a prison term, or require some other action to take place?

8. **Rationale or reasoning**. In this section, you must try to identify the court's explanation and justification for its holding. DO NOT merely quote from the court's opinion. Force yourself to state in your own words what you think the court's reasons are for deciding the case the way it did. Given the common law decisional process, a court can follow precedent or it can develop a new rule. This can result in a wide range of possible outcomes.

If the decision follows precedent, the reasoning will justify applying the existing rule. The court may compare the present case to the precedent case and conclude that the significant facts are identical, thereby requiring the application of the precedent rule. It could also conclude that, although the facts are not identical, they are sufficiently similar to justify the same result. Alternatively, the court could conclude that the significant facts are not sufficiently similar to justify the same result, and the court could distinguish or limit the precedent to its facts and thereby refuse to follow it. Or a court can decide not to follow a lower court decision, stating policy considerations. You may want to ask yourself the following questions:

- What are the stated grounds for the court's decision?
- Do the stated grounds seem to be the real reasons for the decision?
- Does the case follow or depart from precedent?
- If the case involved a statute, did the court consider the legislative intent? Did the court uphold or strike down the statute?

9. **Separate Opinions and Dissents.** Sometimes, especially in cases dealing with controversial subjects, the judges considering the case will not agree on the appropriate outcome. In these cases, judges may write additional opinions explaining their own point of view. Separate opinions generally agree with the majority, either entirely or in part, and dissents generally disagree either in whole or in part.

Because they do not express the majority will of the court, separate opinions and dissents are not binding as legal precedent. However, they can still have some persuasive value for scholars and for judges as they are considering future cases. When a case contains a separate opinion or a dissent, note what it is in the court's opinion that prompted the separate opinion. Pay special attention to dissenting opinions, as they may foreshadow alternative approaches, identify relevant political and legal controversies, or signal a future shift in a legal rule.

10. **Public policy.** Courts do not always provide policy, but when they do, it will be stated in terms of what is best for the public at large. Public policy may be phrased as why a rulemaking body intended a certain result. Alternatively, this can be included in the rationale since it likely affected why the court reached its decision.

11. **Takeaway rule from this case.** This important part of the case brief will be critical for your course outlines for exam preparation. For legal writing, it will help you with understanding how to apply this precedent case to your client's facts.[2] You may want to ask yourself questions such as:

- Does this case follow the general rule?
- Does this case extend the general rule to cover new facts?
- Does this case distinguish or narrow the rule so that it does not apply to the facts of the case at bar?
- Does this case justify overruling the old general rule and instead adopt a more modern rule?

12. **Disposition.** This is what the court's ultimate decision was in the case. For example, did the court affirm, reverse, remand, or vacate the decision below? Did the court grant a motion?

13. **Dicta.** You will want to note, if present, reasons given by the court on tangential matters other than the facts or issue before the court. Dicta is not present in every case, and it is not binding on future courts.

B. Sample Case Brief

In Exercise 3.2.2 for Chapter 3.2, *Reading Cases*, you read through the case of *Marietta Title Insurance Company v. Rath* to understand how to extract an implied holding from a case. Let's look at that case again, this time in the context of a case brief:

Sample Case Brief for *Marietta Title Ins. Co. v. Rath*

Name of the case: Marietta Title Insurance Co. v. Rath
Court: State Court
Year of Decision: 2016

---

2. For study purposes, extracting this "takeaway" rule is very useful to your case reading. Later in the semester, incorporate this takeaway rule into your course outlines to study for law school exams.

Parties: Plaintiff Marietta Title—an insurance company; Defendant is
former employee—Rath

Procedural History: In trial court, Plaintiff seeks to enjoin Defendant

Facts:

1. P hired D as Senior VP, and D signed a covenant-not-to-compete agreement, restricting him from working for another title insurance co. for two years following termination.

2. D terminated employment and signed on with competitor, also in same city.

3. Evidence revealed D had relationships with specific customers assigned to his accounts and they would engage only him.

4. Also, D had knowledge of computer programs relating to clients' accounts and D had frequent contact with clients.

Issue: Whether D's services were sufficiently unique so that the court would grant P's request for an injunction to prevent D from violating the terms of the covenant not to compete.

Holding:

Rath's services were similarly unique; therefore, P's request for injunction should be granted. The court doesn't explicitly state why it held this way but considered evidence that Rath had relationships with specific customers of his assigned accounts and that these customers would engage only Rath for Marietta business. Furthermore, Rath had knowledge of computer programs that benefited the customers, and Rath had frequent contact with his customers.

Reasoning:

1. Courts have granted injunctions to enforce covenants not to compete based upon the unique services of the defendants, provided that the restrictive covenant was reasonable.

2. In *Matheson*, the court found that the former employee's relationships with the clients were special and qualified as unique services. Relationships were unique because of the highly competitive banking industry and rare talent.

3. Also relevant in *Matheson* was that clients had regular contact with the employee.

Disposition:

P's request for injunctive relief granted, and D is restricted from working with competitor.

Takeaway Rule:

In Utopia, covenants not to compete will be enforced when the former employee had unique services such as relationships with clients, frequent contact with clients, and when the employee possessed rare talents, such as having a special knowledge of a computer program useful to clients.

Remember, case briefs are yours and need to be suited to your learning style. Although many case briefs include the above parts, the format differs from person to person. Some people will type up a case brief on a separate piece of paper. Some will highlight their casebook with different colors representing the different parts. Others will draw pictures or a flow chart. The format of a case brief does not matter. What is important is that your case brief—no matter the format—helps you understand the case and how it fits within the larger legal landscape.

III. Exercises

The exercises below will give you practice dissecting the parts of a case and preparing for class discussion. The exercises enable you to evaluate different types and forms of case briefs so you can determine which will be most helpful to you.

Exercise 3.3.1: Evaluating the Content of Case Briefs

Review the two sample case briefs below, which are based on the *McBoyle v. United States* case that you examined in Chapter 3.2, *Reading Cases*. Then, evaluate whether you believe case brief 1 or 2 would best help you respond to questions in class. Indicate your thoughts by answering the questions that follow the sample case briefs.

Case Brief 1

McBoyle v. United States
Appellant/Defendant v. Appellee/Plaintiff

Decided: August 18, 1930
U.S. Court of Appeals for the 10th Circuit
Judge Phillips

Facts:
- On July 2, 1926, Defendant hired Lacey to work at his commercial airport in Galena, Illinois.
- In October 1926, at Defendant's request, Lacey went to Ottawa, Illinois, to steal a Waco airplane from Aircraft Corporation.
- Lacey flew the stolen plane to Galena and arrived on October 6, 1926.
- On October 6, 1926, Lacey flew the airplane to Guymon, Oklahoma, per McBoyle's instructions.
- While in Guymon, McBoyle instructed Lacey to sell or store the stolen airplane and come back to Galena. They communicated with each other via telegraph.
- When Lacey returned to Galena, McBoyle instructed him to take to Guymon one of his airplanes (a Waco airplane of the same make and model as the stolen airplane).
- McBoyle claimed that the telegraph referred to liquor in the airplane, not the airplane itself.

Procedural History:
- Defendant was convicted and sentenced for violation of the National Motor Vehicle Theft Act, 18 U.S.C. § 408, in the U.S. District Court for the Western District of Oklahoma.
- In the indictment, Defendant was charged with causing the transport of in-

terstate commerce from Ottawa, Illinois to Guymon, Oklahoma. The interstate commerce was a stolen Waco airplane, property of the U.S. Aircraft Corp.

Issue:

- Whether the Waco airplane is classified as a "motor vehicle" as it is defined in the National Motor Vehicle Theft Act, which states: "the term 'motor vehicle' when used in this section shall include an automobile, motor cycle, or any other self-propelled vehicle not designated for running on rails."

Holding:

- "Any other self-propelled vehicle" in the National Motor Vehicle Theft Act includes an airplane and any other like means of conveyance or transportation self-propelled and is of the same general class as an automobile and a motorcycle.

Reasoning:

The Court looked to the derivation of "vehicle" and the definition of "vehicle" to reach its holding. In the Century Dictionary, a "vehicle" is "any receptacle, or means of transport, in which something is carried or conveyed, or travels." In Webster's Dictionary, a vehicle is a means of conveyance, especially on land. Corpus Juris defined a vehicle as a self-powered vehicle used for carrying passengers or materials. "Vehicle" is derived from the Latin "vehiculum," which means ship or carriage.

The Court adopted a broad definition of "vehicle" to include an airplane. It reached this conclusion because an airplane is self-propelled, as required by the statute, and designed to carry passengers and cargo from one place to another. Additionally, the Court analogized an airplane to an automobile because both serve the same general purpose and it is of the same kind and class of the enumerated motor vehicles.

Although Defendant contended that a "vehicle" only includes modes of transportation on the ground under the doctrine of *ejusdem generis*, the Court did not agree. Because the statute included the phrase "any other self-propelled vehicle," the Court reached its broad definition.

Separate Opinions and Dissents:

Judge Cotteral, dissenting.

The judge agreed with the Defendant and applied the rule of *ejusdem generis*. Under the doctrine, although an airplane is self-propelled, and it is a vehicle, it is not classified with an automobile or motorcycle. Additionally, while automobiles were commonly stolen, airplanes were not. The judge reasoned that Congress sought to draft a statute to deter automobile theft, and not airplane theft, because it was not a common problem.

Case Brief 2

Case Brief for *McBoyle v. United States*

Facts:

- McBoyle (D) operated a commercial airline out of Galena, Illinois, in 1926.
- D hired Lacey as an aviator in 1926.
- D induced Lacey to steal a Waco airplane from the Aircraft Corporation in Ottawa, Illinois, and fly it back to Galena, where D changed the serial number of the plane to conceal its identity.

- D then instructed Lacey to fly the plane to Amarillo, Texas, and lease an airport there for them to operate during the winter of 1926.
- Lacey flew the plane to Guymon, Oklahoma, stopping en route in Missouri and Kansas.
- Once in Guymon, D instructed Lacey to leave the plane there and return to Galena.
- D then instructed Lacey to take an airplane of the same kind and make belonging to D and substitute it for the stolen plane in order to deceive officers when they found the Waco plane in Guymon.
- On the way to Guymon, Lacey crashed and thereafter returned to Galena where he remained employed with D until the following year.
- D was charged and convicted of an alleged violation of the National Motor Vehicle Theft Act (18 U.S.C. § 408).
- The indictment charged that D caused to be transported across state lines a stolen airplane, which D knew was stolen.

Issue:

- Does the National Motor Vehicle Theft Act apply to the theft of an airplane?

Holding:

- An airplane does come within the purview of the National Motor Vehicle Theft Act.

Analysis:

- Definition of a motor vehicle within the National Motor Vehicle Theft Act includes an automobile, automobile truck, automobile wagon, motor cycle, or any other self-propelled vehicle not designed for running on rails.
- Court looked at common dictionary definitions for "vehicle" to determine whether it could be understood that "airplane" fit within that definition or should be considered a separate form of transportation other than a "vehicle."
- The Court determined, through looking at dictionary definitions, that an airplane was a vehicle because vehicles can refer to any means of transportation, whether on land or sea (but will not include transportation by rail for the purpose of this statute since such transportation is expressly excluded).
- Under the maxim of *ejusdem generis*, the Court found that "airplane" was consistent with the general statutory term of "any other self-propelled vehicle" and thus should be understood to be under the purview of the National Motor Vehicle Act.
- Since Congress expressly excluded transportation by rail, if Congress had similarly wanted to exclude transportation by airplane, it would have expressly excluded airplane transportation from the National Motor Vehicle Theft Act, but Congress did not do so.

Dissent:

- Disagreed with the Court's reading of the National Motor Vehicle Theft Act to include an airplane within the purview of the National Motor Vehicle Theft Act.
- Dissent believes that Congress's failure to expressly include airplanes within the National Motor Vehicle Theft Act indicated that airplanes were not within the contemplation of the National Motor Vehicle Theft Act, as a reference to

air travel would have been included in the National Motor Vehicle Theft Act had Congress contemplated that method of travel.

- The maxim of *ejusdem generis* requires airplane travel to be excluded because the National Motor Vehicle Theft Act generally refers to vehicles that run on land, and in constructing the statute, the maxim requires that only similar things or persons of the same kind, class, or nature be included in a reading of the general language.
- Dissent argues that airplanes are not generally considered "automobiles," and thus, a reading of the National Motor Vehicle Theft Act's language referring to "other types of automobiles" should not be understood to include airplanes.
- Legislative context indicates that Congress was concerned with putting a stop to the increased theft of automobiles when enacting the statute and was not concerned with airplane thefts, which were extremely rare.

1. Which case brief would you prefer to have with you in class?

_____

_____

_____

_____

_____

2. Which parts of case brief 1 are most helpful? Why?

_____

_____

_____

_____

_____

_____

3. Which parts of case brief 2 are most helpful? Why?

_____

_____

_____

_____

_____

_____

4. How could each brief be improved?

_____

_____

_____

_____

_____

_____

Exercise 3.3.2: Briefing a Case

What is an advertisement? A solicitation to consumers (such as that in a newspaper or radio announcement), paid for by a store or manufacturer that is designed to induce customers to purchase their products or shop in their stores. One general rule of contract law is that advertisements are not offers. The case of _Lefkowitz v. Great Minneapolis Surplus Store, Inc._, pronounced an exception to the general rule that advertisements are not offers. Read the case and answer the questions that follow.

Supreme Court of Minnesota.

Morris LEFKOWITZ, Respondent,

v.

GREAT MINNEAPOLIS SURPLUS STORE, Inc., Appellant.

251 Minn. 188 (1957)

Syllabus by the Court [This section provides a summary but is not part of the official opinion]

1. Where one offers for sale by newspaper advertisement a certain article of definite value at a quoted price, which offer is clear, definite, and explicit and leaves nothing open for negotiation, it constitutes an offer, acceptance of which may complete the contract.

2. While an advertiser has the right at any time before acceptance to modify his offer, he does not have the right, after acceptance, to impose new or arbitrary conditions not contained in the published offer.

Opinion

MURPHY, Justice.

This is an appeal from an order of the Municipal Court of Minneapolis denying the motion of the defendant for amended findings of fact, or, in the alternative, for a new trial. The order for judgment awarded the plaintiff the sum of $138.50 as damages for breach of contract.

This case grows out of the alleged refusal of the defendant to sell to the plaintiff a certain fur piece, which it had offered for sale in a newspaper advertisement. It appears from the record that on April 6, 1956, the defendant published the following advertisement in a Minneapolis newspaper:

Saturday 9 A.M. Sharp
3 Brand New Fur Coats Worth to $100.00
First Come First Served $1 Each

On April 13, the defendant again published an advertisement in the same newspaper as follows:

Saturday 9 A.M.
2 Brand New Pastel Mink 3-Skin Scarfs Selling for $89.50
Out they go Saturday. Each . . . $1.00
1 Black Lapin Stole Beautiful, worth $139.50 . . . $1.00
First Come First Served

The record supports the findings of the court that on each of the Saturdays following the publication of the above-described ads the plaintiff was the first to present himself at the appropriate counter in the defendant's store and on each occasion demanded the coat and the stole so advertised and indicated his readiness to pay the sale price of $1. On both occasions, the defendant refused to sell the merchandise to the plaintiff, stating on the first occasion that by a "house rule" the offer was intended for women only and sales would not be made to men, and on the second visit that plaintiff knew defendant's house rules.

The trial court properly disallowed plaintiff's claim for the value of the fur coats since the value of these articles was speculative and uncertain. The only evidence of value was the advertisement itself to the effect that the coats were "Worth to $100.00," how much less being speculative especially in view of the price for which they were offered for sale. With reference to the offer of the defendant on April 13, 1956, to sell the "1 Black Lapin Stole * * * worth $139.50 * * *" the trial court held that the value of this article was established and granted judgment in favor of the plaintiff for that amount less the $1 quoted purchase price.

1. The defendant contends that a newspaper advertisement offering items of merchandise for sale at a named price is a "unilateral offer" which may be withdrawn without notice. He relies upon authorities which hold that, where an advertiser publishes in a newspaper that he has a certain quantity or quality of goods which he wants to dispose of at certain prices and on certain terms, such advertisements are not offers which become contracts as soon as any person to whose notice they may come signifies his acceptance by notifying the other that he will take a certain quantity of them. Such advertisements have been construed as an invitation for an offer of sale on the terms stated, which offer, when received, may be accepted or rejected and which therefore does not become a contract of sale until accepted by the seller; and until a contract has been so made, the seller may modify or revoke such prices or terms. *Montgomery Ward & Co. v. Johnson*, 95 N.E. 290 (Mass. 1911); Annotation, 157 A.L.R. 746.

The defendant relies principally on *Craft v. Elder & Johnston Co.*, 38 N.E.2d 416 (Ohio Ct. App. 1941). In that case, the court discussed the legal effect of an advertisement offering for sale, as a one-day special, an electric sewing machine at a named price. The view was expressed that the advertisement was "not an offer made to any specific person but was made to the public generally. Thereby it would be properly designated as a unilateral offer, and not being supported by any consideration, could be withdrawn at will and without notice." It is true that such an offer may be withdrawn before acceptance. Since all offers are by their nature unilateral because they are necessarily made by one party or on one side in the negotiation of a contract, the distinction made in that decision between a unilateral offer and a unilateral contract is not clear. On the facts before us we are concerned with whether the advertisement constituted an offer, and, if so, whether the plaintiff's conduct constituted an acceptance.

There are numerous authorities, which hold that a particular advertisement in a newspaper or circular letter relating to a sale of articles may be construed by the court as constituting an offer, acceptance of which would complete a contract. *J. E. Pinkham Lumber Co. v. C. W. Griffin & Co.*, 102 So. 689 (Ala. 1901).

The test of whether a binding obligation may originate in advertisements addressed to the general public is "whether the facts show that some performance was promised in positive terms in return for something requested." 1 Samuel Williston & George J. Thompson, A Treatise on the Law of Contracts (Rev. ed.) § 27.

The authorities above cited emphasize that, where the offer is clear, definite, and explicit, and leaves nothing open for negotiation, it constitutes an offer, acceptance of which will complete the contract. The most recent case on the subject is *Johnson v. Capital City Ford Co.*, 85 So. 2d 75 (La. App. 1956), in which the court pointed out that a newspaper advertisement relating to the purchase and sale of automobiles may constitute an offer, acceptance of which will consummate a contract and create an obligation in the offeror to perform according to the terms of the published offer.

Whether in any individual instance a newspaper advertisement is an offer rather than an invitation to make an offer depends on the legal intention of the parties and the surrounding circumstances. 17 C.J.S., Contracts, § 389. We are of the view on the facts before us that the offer by the defendant of the sale of the Lapin fur was clear, definite, and explicit, and left nothing open for negotiation. The plaintiff having successful [sic] managed to be the first one to appear at the seller's place of business to be served, as requested by the advertisement, and having offered the stated purchase price of the article, he was entitled to performance on the part of the defendant. We think the trial court was correct in holding that there was in the conduct of the parties a sufficient mutuality of obligation to constitute a contract of sale.

The defendant contends that the offer was modified by a "house rule" to the effect that only women were qualified to receive the bargains advertised. The advertisement contained no such restriction. This objection may be disposed of briefly by stating that, while an advertiser has the right at any time before acceptance to modify his offer, he does not have the right, after acceptance, to impose new or arbitrary conditions not contained in the published offer.

Affirmed.

1. Identify the Appellant and the Respondent.

_____

_____

2. Identify the court that decided the case and the year the case was decided.

_____

3. Describe the procedural history.

_____

_____

_____

_____

_____

_____

4. What were the facts of the case?

_____

_____

_____

_____

_____

_____

5. What legal issue was the court deciding?

_____

_____

_____

_____

_____

_____

6. What was the court's holding?

_____

_____

_____

_____

_____

_____

7. What was the court's reasoning?

_____

_____

_____

_____

_____

_____

Exercise 3.3.3: Briefing a Case

Prepare a case brief for *Reaver v. Martin Theatres*. Do not copy all of the words verbatim, but decide how to paraphrase facts using the relevant categories in the case brief format discussed above.

Reaver, et al. v. Martin Theatres,

52 So. 2d 682

Supreme Court of Florida

(1951)

ROBERTS, Justice.

The plaintiff-appellant has owned and operated a small private airport in Panama City for four years. The defendant-appellee recently purchased a tract of land north of plaintiff's airport, a portion of which (some 160 feet) is contiguous to the northern terminus of plaintiff's landing strip, for the purpose of constructing a drive-in theatre. Upon learning of defendant's intention, the plaintiff filed suit to enjoin the defendant from constructing the theatre, on the ground that it would constitute a nuisance and hazard to the plaintiff and to the public generally. The defendant answered, alleging that the operation of a drive-in theatre was a legitimate use of its property, that its proposed construction would not violate any of the regulations of the Civil Aeronautics Administration respecting hazards near an airport. Trial was had before the Court, and final decree was entered in favor of defendant, from which plaintiff has appealed.

The general question of whether the owner of an airport can enjoin an adjoining landowner from using his property in a manner hazardous to the operation of the airport, but which use would not be hazardous to the operation of any other business, has not been presented to this court.

Under the familiar maxim "*Sic utere tuo ut alienum non laedas*," it is well settled that a property owner may put his own property to any reasonable and lawful use, so long as he does not thereby deprive the adjoining landowner of any right of enjoyment of his property which is recognized and protected by law, and so long as his use is not such a one as the law will pronounce a nuisance. 39 Am. Jur., Nuisances; *Cason v. Florida Power Company*, 76 So. 535 (Fla.). The "reasonableness" of such use must be determined according to the circumstances of each case, and in accordance with established legal and equitable principles. *Cason v. Florida Power Co.*

The operation of a drive-in theatre is not, per se, a nuisance; it is as legal a use of his premises by the defendant as is the operation of an airport by the plaintiff. There is no physical invasion of the plaintiff's premises by the defendant. In fact, the "invasion," if any, is of the defendant's premises by the plaintiff, although it appears to be established that the operator of an airplane is "privileged" to enter the airspace above land in the possession of another, so long as he does so in a reasonable manner, at such a height as is in conformity with legislative requirements, and without interfering unreasonably with the possessor's enjoyment of the surface of the earth and the airspace above it. *See* Restatement of Torts.

Counsel for plaintiff has cited no case, and our independent research has revealed none, where the "privilege" of an airplane to invade the airspace above land in the possession of another has been held superior to the lawful and reasonable use of such airspace by the owner of the land. It appears that their rights are generally held to be co-equal, with the balance, if any, in favor of the landowner.

In *Smith v. New England Aircraft Co.*, it was stated that "Aerial navigation, important as it may be, has no inherent superiority over the landowner where their rights and claims are in actual conflict." 170 N.E. 385 (Mass. 1930). See also *Air Terminal Properties v. City of New York*, 172 Misc. 945, 16 N.Y.S.2d 629 (Sup. Ct. Queens Ctny. 1939), where the court denied an injunction seeking to restrain the planting of trees on a city street adjacent to the plaintiff's airport on the ground that the trees would interfere to some extent with the operation of the airport; and *Capitol Airways v. Indianapolis Power & Light Co.*, 18 N.E.2d 776 (Ind. 1939), in which the owner of an airport was denied the right to recover damages for the alleged interference with and destruction of his established business caused by the defendant's constructing a power line, consisting of steel towers about 90 feet in height and electric wires, along the boundary of the airport.

While the placing of obstructions near the property line of an airport solely for the purpose of harassing the owner thereof, and without relation to any reasonable use which the adjoining landowner might wish to make of his property, might well be held to be a nuisance, that is not the case here. It is unquestioned that the defendant intends to use its premises for a drive-in theatre, which is a legitimate business, and one which is permitted in that area of Panama City where the defendant intends to operate it.

Moreover, aside from the legal question involved, this case also presented questions of fact, which could properly have been resolved against the plaintiff. There was ample evidence to prove that the construction of a screen by defendant would not measurably add to the hazards which already existed; that the lights to be used by defendant in operating its theatre would not unreasonably interfere with the operation of the airport by plaintiff; and that the traffic problem created by the ingress and egress of patrons of the theatre would not constitute a public nuisance.

No error having been made to appear, the final decree of dismissal should be and it is hereby.

Affirmed.

SEBRING, C. J., and CHAPMAN and ADAMS, JJ., concur.

1. Identify the Appellant and the Appellee.

_____

_____

2. Identify the court that decided the case and the year the case was decided.

_____

3. Describe the procedural history.

_____

_____

_____

_____

_____

_____

4. What were the facts of the case?

_____

_____

_____

_____

_____

_____

5. What legal issue was the court deciding?

_____

_____

_____

_____

_____

_____

6. What was the court's holding? (Hint: The holding is implied—can you explain what it is?)

_____

_____

_____

_____

_____

_____

7. What was the court's reasoning?

_____

_____

_____

_____

_____

_____

8. Describe the "takeaway rule" from this case.

_____

_____

_____

_____

_____

Chapter 4

Finding Your Argument

I. Rules Generally

In the Chapter 3 exercises, we examined holdings—the court's response to a particular legal issue in a case. In this chapter, we will start to look more at rules. A **rule** is a standard that tells people what they must or can do, what they must not or should not do, what they are entitled to under certain conditions, and what consequences exist for violating the rule. The rule is the legal principle the case will stand for in the future. In a case, the **holding** is a statement describing how the court decided the legal issue, that is, how the court applied the rule to the particular facts of the case.

As we discussed in the earlier chapters, as you work to master the art of legal analysis, you must first identify your client's issue. Once you identify the issue, finding the overarching legal principle that applies—also called the **governing rule**—will help determine the structure your analysis will need to take. The focus of this chapter is learning to identify a governing rule and to understand how a governing rule may work. Sometimes it may be quite easy to identify a governing rule because the rule will be explicitly stated, as in a statute or a regulation, or even in some cases. Other times rules can be implicit and will need to be extracted from a case.

Many times, after you express the governing rule, you will need to inventory the rule by breaking it down into the relevant elements, factor, or components. The ability to break down the governing rule will enable you to have a deeper understanding of how the legal concept may apply to your client's problem. It may help identify the primary rules and sub-rules you will need to analyze. It will also provide an initial structure for your analysis.

II. Explicit Rules

Many rules are stated explicitly within primary authority when the legislature or court specifies the legal standard that permits, limits, or prohibits conduct. These rules are termed **explicit rules**. Statutes, regulations, and code provisions, such as the Uniform Commercial Code (UCC), are examples of explicit rules.

In addition, courts also explicitly set out the legal standard that they want individuals to comply with in the future. Many times this rule will also be the court's **holding**—the court's decision on the legal issue it is analyzing. Table 4.A below shows examples of explicit rules from a statute, a regulation, and a case:

Table 4.A: Examples of Explicit Rules

Source	Example
An explicit rule in a statute	If a dog bites a person, without provocation while the person is on public property, or lawfully on private property, including the property of the owner of the dog, the owner of the dog shall be liable for any damages suffered by the person bitten, regardless of the former viciousness of the dog or the owner's knowledge of such viciousness. Michigan Comp. Laws § 287.351
An explicit rule in a regulation	Any dog or cat that, while in quarantine, has bitten any person or animal shall be examined by a government veterinarian and placed under post-bite rabies observation for ten (10) days. The biting dog or cat shall be removed from its assigned kennel and placed in isolation during the observation period. 9 Guam R. & Regs. § 3232
An explicit rule in a case	The common law protects a licensee on private property who is bitten by a dog of known viciousness even where that dog is restrained by a leash. *Jones v. Manhart*, 585 P.2d 1250, 1252 (Ariz. 1978)

III. Implicit Rules

Some cases have rules that are not clearly set forth in text. For example, the rule for intentional infliction of emotional distress prohibits "extreme and outrageous" behavior, but the court's rule may not specify what kind of behavior meets that standard. In that instance, you need to examine what the court is saying about the rule and how the court is using the rule in the context of your client's situation. Figure 4.B illustrates the process to extract an implicit rule from a case and make it explicit (and therefore usable in your legal analysis):

Figure 4.B: Steps in Extracting an Implicit Rule

IV. Using the Rule to Structure Your Analysis

Once you have identified which rule will govern the legal issue, you will use that rule to create the backbone or structure for your argument—the manner in which you present the rule creates the structural foundation for your analysis and every component of the analysis stems from the governing rule.

After identifying the governing rule through one of the processes described above, create the structural organization for your legal analysis by taking an inventory of the different parts of the rule and analyzing each part. To do this, see first whether the rules can be broken down into **elements,** in which case each condition must be met, or **factors,** in which case the different conditions are weighed against each other, as shown in Table 4.C below.

Table 4.C: Elements and Factors

Term	Definition	Example	Organization
Element	A condition that must be proved to establish that a standard is met.	To support a claim of intentional infliction of emotional distress, a plaintiff must prove the following elements: (1) extreme and outrageous conduct; (2) which is intended to cause severe emotional distress; and (3) does cause severe emotional distress. *Dickens v. Puryear*, 276 S.E.2d 325, 335 (N.C. 1983)	You analyze each element, usually following the same order in which the element was described in the governing rule.
Factor	A condition weighed against another condition.	In making a custody determination, the court analyzes what is in the best interest of the child. *Priddy v. Chamberlin*, 352 S.E. 2d 475 (N.C. 1999)	You analyze which factors apply to the facts of your client's case, such as the child's preference, relationships between parent and child, parents' mental and physical health, etc.

When breaking down a rule into any component parts, make sure to note any **red flag words** that identify how the different parts of the rule operate in relation to one another. For example, the word "and" in a rule means that all components may need to be proven, but the word "or" usually means the opposite. Likewise, if you see the term "unless," you are likely looking at an exception to the general rule.

Table 4.D, below, provides some examples concerning how to inventory and break down a rule to frame your analysis.

Table 4.D: Breaking Down a Rule

Governing Rules	Governing Rule Broken Down Into Component Parts
Battery. An individual commits a battery if he acts intentionally either to cause a harmful or offensive touching of another person.[1]	1. Intent; 2. Harmful or offensive; 3. Touching of another person; and 4. Causation.

Municipal liability. Notwithstanding any other provision of law, the city shall not be liable for any injury to property or personal injury, including death, proximately caused by the failure to maintain sidewalks (other than sidewalks abutting one-, two-, or three-family residential real property that is (i) in whole or in part owner occupied, and (ii) used exclusively for residential purposes) in a reasonably safe condition.	1. City not liable for personal injury or property caused by failure to maintain sidewalks in a reasonably safe condition,
	2. OTHER THAN sidewalks abutting one- , two-, or three-family residential structures that are
	  a. Owner occupied, AND
	  b. Used exclusively for residential purposes

V. Exercises

The exercises below will help you to critique different rule statements to determine which sample most effectively describes the rule for your legal reader. The exercises will also help you to describe explicit rules, extract implicit rules, and inventory rules by breaking them down into their component parts.

Exercise 4.1: Evaluating Rule Statements

In Chapter 3.1, *Reading Statutes*, we reviewed some of the provisions from the New York Burglary statutes, along with a set of client facts from *People v. Locker*. Let's review those facts again:

> On the morning of January 1, defendant Tom Locker broke into a fraternity house for Rochester College, located in Rochester, New York. He stole numerous items of school and personal property. He was apprehended when his vehicle broke down on a road near campus. A State Trooper stopped to investigate, and Locker confessed when asked about items piled up in the backseat under a blanket. Locker was indicted on burglary in the second degree and petit larceny, and he was found guilty as charged following a jury trial. Locker now brings an appeal claiming that the fraternity house was not a "dwelling," and that the lower court erred in declining to charge the jury with burglary in the third degree (as a lesser included offense of burglary in the second degree).
>
> Testimony at trial established that the fraternity house from which Locker stole property was vacant for the semester break. However, the house was fully fur-

---

1. *See* Steven I. Friedland, *100 Rules to Know for Passing the Multistate Bar Exam* 105 (2d ed. 2012). In Exercise 4.4, we use two additional examples of causes of action from Professor Friedland's book. *Id.* at 104, 107.

nished with personal and household belongings; its occupants intended to return in the second semester. The utilities were intact. The defendant argues on appeal that the students had vacated the premises for the holidays, and thus the fraternity house did not constitute a "dwelling." Also, the house was not stocked with food.

Examine the rules set out in the three memo samples below. (The citations have been omitted.) If you are a supervisor in the district attorney's office deciding whether the fraternity house at issue constituted a "dwelling," which of the following three drafts do you think most effectively describes the governing rule?

Sample Memo 1

Burglary in the Second Degree is defined as:

A person is guilty of burglary in the second degree when he knowingly enters or remains unlawfully in a building with intent to commit a crime therein, and when:

In effecting entry or while in the building or in immediate flight therefrom, he or another participant in the crime:

    (a) Is armed with explosives or a deadly weapon; or

    (b) Causes physical injury to any person who is not a participant in the crime; or

    (c) Uses or threatens the immediate use of a dangerous instrument; or

    (d) Displays what appears to be a pistol, revolver, rifle, shotgun, machine gun or other firearm; or

(3) The building is a dwelling.

The term "building" is defined as:

[I]n addition to its ordinary meaning, includes any structure, vehicle or watercraft used for overnight lodging of persons, or used by persons for carrying on business therein, or used as an elementary or secondary school, or an enclosed motor truck, or an enclosed motor truck trailer. Where a building consists of two or more units separately secured or occupied, each unit shall be deemed both a separate building in itself and a part of the main building. The term "dwelling" is defined as meaning "a building which is usually occupied by a person lodging therein at night."

Sample Memo 2

The state statute for Burglary defines "dwelling" as "occupied by a person lodging therein at night."

Sample Memo 3

Burglary in the Second Degree applies when a person "knowingly enters" a "building with the intent to commit a crime therein" and when "[t]he building is a dwelling." The term "building" is defined as having its ordinary meaning. The term "dwelling" is defined as meaning "a building which is usually occupied by a person lodging therein at night."

1. Which memo most effectively describes the governing rule and why?

The third memo because it says all of the relevant information w/o additional info that isn't being asked for.

Exercise 4.2: Using a Code Provision to Describe an Explicit Rule

Your client, Jennifer of Jennifer's Interiors, asks your advice about a problem she is having with a customer.

Harry Homeowner was renovating his home kitchen and went to Jennifer's shop asking that the design team create a granite countertop of a rare color of purple that would fit the dimensions for his kitchen counters. He did not ask for a receipt. Because the salesperson at the store knew Harry—he was a longtime customer—she gave him a verbal assurance that the store would have the countertop custom made to his specifications in a week's time for a cost of $1,000. When Jennifer called Harry and told him that the countertop was ready for delivery, Harry said he changed his mind and refused to accept delivery. Jennifer claims she cannot find another buyer for a purple granite countertop of these dimensions. She wants to know if she will win in a breach of contract action against Harry Homeowner.

You find the Uniform Commercial Code and the relevant provisions in U.C.C. § 2-201, also known as the Statute of Frauds.

New York's Uniform Commercial Code,
§ 2-201. Formal Requirements; Statute of Frauds:

(1) Except as otherwise provided in this section, a contract for the sale of goods for the price of $500 or more is not enforceable by way of action or defense unless there is some writing sufficient to indicate that a contract for sale has been made between the parties and signed by the party against whom enforcement is sought or by his authorized agent or broker. A writing is not insufficient because it omits or incorrectly states a term agreed upon but the contract is not enforceable under this paragraph beyond the quantity of goods shown in such writing.

(2) Between merchants if within a reasonable time a writing in confirmation of the contract is received and the party receiving it has reason to know its contents, it satisfies the requirements of subsection (1) against such party unless written notice of objection to its contents is given within ten days after it is received.

(3) A contract which does not satisfy the requirements of subsection (1) but which is valid in other respects is enforceable

(a) if the goods are to be specially manufactured for the buyer and are not suitable for sale to others in the ordinary course of the seller's business and the seller, before notice of repudiation is received and under circumstances which reasonably indicate that the goods are for the buyer, has made either a substantial beginning of their manufacture or commitments for their procurement; or

(b) if the party against whom enforcement is sought admits in his pleading, testimony or otherwise in court that a contract for sale was made, but the contract is not enforceable under this provision beyond the quantity of goods admitted; or

(c) with respect to goods for which payment has been made and accepted or which have been received and accepted.

Questions:

1. Using the relevant language from this code provision (you should quote in part and paraphrase in part), how would you identify the rule in a memorandum of law to your supervising attorney?

Sec. 2-201 of New York's UCC Provides that (1)... a contract for the sale of goods for the Price of $500 or more is not enforceable by way of action or defense unless there is something writing Sufficient... (3) (a)

2. How might you inventory your rule or break it down to analyze it part-by-part?

1.) writing sufficient to indicate contract of sale. 2) goods that are specially Manufactured.

Exercise 4.3: Extracting an Implicit Rule from a Common Law Case

Consider the hypothetical[2] below:

> Suzy Maudiere was excited to visit the historic sites of Boston. Upon arriving in the city, Suzy went immediately to Faneuil Hall, even though it was 4:30 on Monday morning. Suzy went to the main entrance, saw that the shops were closed, but wandered around the building, gazing and pondering the meaning of history. Suzy then slipped and fell on the cobblestones. Although in great pain, Suzy looked around and spotted a brown, leathery banana peel, six inches in length, lying on the gray, stone floor.
>
> Custodians employed by Faneuil Hall are responsible for sweeping up every night after the businesses close at 9:00 p.m. (6:00 p.m. on Sundays). Suzy comes to your firm asking whether she will be able to recover damages sustained from her fall at Faneuil Hall.

Your research uncovers the *Scaccia* case, an excerpt of which is below.

Scaccia v. Boston Elevated Railway Co., 57 N.E.2d 761 (Mass. 1944)

LUMMUS, Justice.

This action of tort for personal injuries, resulting from slipping on a banana peel which was on the floor of a motor bus operated by the defendant in which the plaintiff was a passenger, was tried before a judge of the Superior Court, sitting without jury, upon an "agreed statement of facts" submitted as evidence.

* * *

We now come to the merits of the ruling. When the plaintiff boarded the defendant's motor bus at Cleary Square in the Hyde Park section of Boston at noon on October 2, 1934, on the floor in the aisle, near the front of the bus, a banana peel lay "four inches long, all black, all pressed down, dirty, covered with sand and gravel, dry and gritty looking." When the plaintiff left the bus nine minutes later, she slipped and fell on the banana peel, which remained in the same position. Only three passengers were in the bus during the trip. It could have been found that Cleary Square was one terminus of the line, and that the bus remained there without passengers in it for "a minute or two" at least. The bus was operated by one man.

The question is whether the foregoing basic facts warrant an inference of negligence on the part of the defendant or its operator. No one would be likely to enter the bus except servants of the defendant and passengers. In the ordinary course of events, no passenger would carry into the bus a banana peel, or a banana, in the condition shown by the agreed facts. Such a condition naturally would result from laying a considerable time on the floor. We think that it could be found that the peel had remained on the floor of the bus so long that in the exercise of due care the defendant should have discovered and removed it. *Anjou v. Boston Elevated R. Co.*, 94 N.E. 386 (Mass. 1911).

---

2. Adapted with permission from Paul Figley, *Teaching Rule Synthesis with Real Cases*, 61 J. Leg. Ed. 245 (2011).

A number of cases in which the unexplained presence on floors or stairs of discarded parts of fruit was held insufficient evidence of negligence may be distinguished. In *Goddard v. Boston & M. R. R.*, 60 N.E. 486 (Mass. 1901), the banana peel did not appear to be other than fresh. In *Mascary v. Boston Elevated R. Co.*, 155 N.E. 637 (Mass. 1927), where a banana peel was much like that described in the *Anjou* case, it lay on stairs leading from the street, and might have been recently thrown there by a child in play. In *McBreen v. Collins*, 284 Mass. 253, 187 N.E. 591 (Mass. 1933), the plaintiff fell on a lemon or orange peel that showed no marks of age comparable to those in the present case. In other cases, the cause of the injury was an apple core or other fruit which would become discolored sooner than a banana peel would become in the condition described in the evidence in the present case. *See, e.g., O'Neill v. Boston Elevated R. Co.*, 142 N.E. 904 (Mass. 1924).

In accordance with the terms of the report, judgment is to be entered for the plaintiff a finding for $750.

1. **How does the *Scaccia* court describe the rule?**

   The presence of discarded parts of fruits
   on floors or stairs that cause injury
   is negligent if the peel should
   have been thrown away or discarded of
   by workers.

2. **Do you see any similarities or differences between Scaccia's claims and Suzy's claims?**

   The age indicates the peel had been there
   a while

3. **After considering your client's facts, how would you describe your take-away rule from *Scaccia*?**

Exercise 4.4: Breaking Down a Rule to Understand Its Component Parts

Read the rule on the left. Then, as we did in Table 4.D above, inventory the rule by breaking it down into its component parts.

Rule	Rule broken down into elements, factors, or other components
If a dog bites a person, without provocation while the person is on public property, or lawfully on private property, including the property of the owner of the dog, the owner of the dog shall be liable for any damages suffered by the person bitten, regardless of the former viciousness of the dog or the owner's knowledge of such viciousness. Michigan Comp. Laws § 287.351 (2015).	Dog bites Without Provocation Public or Private

Contracts. A clear, definite, and explicit offer of sale by defendant that leaves nothing open for negotiation is an offer, acceptance of which will complete the contract.
 	
Lefkowitz v. Great Minneapolis Surplus Store, 251 Minn. 188 (1957).
	Offer acceptance
	  Clear
	  definite
	  explicit
	  not open
	  for negotiation

Conversion. Where the defendant intentionally and substantially interferes with another's personal or otherwise tangible property, defendant is liable for damage or loss of the property.	
Attractive nuisance. The offending condition, circumstance or contrivance although apparently dangerous to adults of discretion, is nevertheless so enticing and alluring as to be calculated to excite the curiosity of children of tender years to the extent of inducing them to utilize the instrumentality in some childish endeavor, the inherent danger of which the child is incapable of comprehending.	
Nuisance. A property owner may put his own property to any reasonable and lawful use, so long as he does not thereby deprive the adjoining landowner of any right of enjoyment of his property, which is recognized and protected by law, and so long as the owner's use is not such a one as the law will pronounce a nuisance. *Reaver v. Martin Theatres*, 52 So. 2d 682 (Fla. 1951).	

Chapter 5

Organizing Legal Authority

I. Charts

II. Outlines

III. Exercises

This chapter provides information and exercises to help you organize your legal authorities so that the writing process is more efficient and effective. Organizing your authorities allows you to see trends in the law and helps you avoid gaps in your analysis. Like research, organizing your authorities is a recursive process that you may continue to do throughout the writing process as you refine your analysis. While you can organize your authorities in many ways, this chapter focuses on charting and outlining.

I. Charts

Organizing and consolidating the important aspects of your research into a chart allows you to visually analyze the law as a whole for each legal issue. Charts can help you to understand the relationships among the cases, see similarities and differences, visualize how the authorities fit together, and identify patterns or trends in the law. And case charting has the added benefit of helping you to identify which authorities would be best to use in your memo. Example 5.A shows one way to organize authorities in a case chart.

Example 5.A: Organizing Your Authorities in a Case Chart[1]

Case Name	Facts	Holding	Reasoning
State v. Merritt, 463 S.E.2d 590 (N.C. Ct. App. 1995).	Sorority house attached, but separate apartment used by house director and family. Defendant appeals his conviction of first-degree burglary arguing that the sorority house was not a dwelling.	Because the common areas of the sorority house were contiguous to the house director's apartment, and the main portion of the sorority house contributed to the comfort or convenience of the director, the court held that it was a dwelling.	The director's apartment was under the same roof, with entrances into the sorority common area. The main dwelling contributed in a meaningful way to the comfort and conveniences of the director's apartment by providing storage access for family bikes, clothing, etc.
State v. Fields, 337 S.E.2d 518 (N.C. 1985)	Defendant broke into a tool shed, stole tools, and then shot neighbor. Shed was 45 feet away from the home. Defendant argued that the shed was not within the curtilage of the dwelling house and that the burglary charge in the second degree should have been quashed.	The outbuilding did not immediately serve the comfort and convenience of those who inhabited the house because it was used to keep and secure tools and other personal property. Court reversed the judgment upon the conviction of burglary in the second degree. Furthermore, the defendant's conviction for felony murder committed during the perpetration of that felony was vacated.	Curtilage is the land around a dwelling house upon which the outbuildings lie and are commonly used with the dwelling house. The question of whether a building was part of the dwelling rests upon whether it served the comfort and convenience of the dwelling. This outbuilding was used sporadically and was far enough away from the home that the defendant's entering activity did not disturb the repose of the owners. The law of burglary is to protect people, not property.
State v. Green, 290 S.E.2d 625 (N.C. 1982)	Defendant broke into the storage room that attached to the bedroom. Stole a motorcycle from the storage room.	The storage room, which could be reached through the bedroom window, was appurtenant to the house, and therefore the burglary was of a dwelling.	Definition of "dwelling house" is not limited to the house proper. The storage room was "appurtenant" to the dwelling. The storage room could be entered through the outside door or through the window to the house.

Although the case chart in Example 5.A is organized around the different parts of the case, you can organize a case chart in whatever manner works best for the legal issue you are analyzing. Below are some other organizations you may want to consider:

- By elements, factors, or components of the governing rule
- In chronological order (or reverse chronological order) to see a trend in the law
- By level of authority—charting binding authority first, followed by persuasive authority
- Cases that support your client's position and that can be analogized, followed by cases that should be distinguished

The bottom line is that each case chart may be organized differently. You will need to determine which organization makes the most sense for your particular inquiry.

---

1. Adapted from teaching materials created by Prof. Liz Johnson, Wake Forest University School of Law.

II. Outlines

Once you've organized your research in a case chart, the next most efficient step is to outline. Outlining is an important step because it allows you to evaluate your analytical points, and the structure in which those points should be present, before you commit your valuable time and effort to actual writing. Outlining makes the writing process more efficient by allowing you to organize around major points of law. Once you have your structure, you can specifically consider how the authorities you found in your research support those major points, which authorities best support your assertions, and how the authorities should be arranged.

> Do not feel constrained to use the conventional Roman outline format—unless it works for you. For students who are more visual thinkers and learners, other formats might be more useful. For example, some students use a "mind map" outline, in which the various points of the discussion are represented graphically and spatially. Other students use flowcharts to see their analysis. The goal is to find a method that helps you organize your discussion logically and effectively.

Like case charts, outlines come in different forms and are tailored to your client's legal question. However, keep this rule of thumb in mind: Outlines should be organized around different legal principles or points of law, rather than around different cases. As you review Chapters 6, 7, 8, and 9, you will learn more details about organizing your analysis around legal principles. This knowledge will, in turn, improve your ability to create an effective outline.

One approach to outlining the discussion of the memo is to use bullet points (or the equivalent) to note the important points you need to cover, the key authorities you plan to use to cover them, and the facts from your case that are relevant to those points. Do not feel constrained to use the old Roman outline format—unless it is compatible with your learning style or preferences. For now, the key is to develop an outline that allows you to sort and logically arrange legal arguments.

III. Exercises

These exercises are designed to assist you not only in preparing a case chart but also in thinking beyond the case chart toward outlining the information. The exercises require you to dissect cases and categorize information. The exercises increase in complexity. You will first complete a simple, traditional case chart then move on to organizing multiple cases construing an element of a common law claim. In the last exercise you will organize information according to a statute's requirements and relevant case law.

Exercise 5.1: Creating a Case Chart and Preparing to Outline

Consider the following hypothetical, then review the case excerpts below:

> Brooke Arndt and Jane Lopez are celebrity TV show co-hosts of a morning program. They were friends on and off the air. One day when Brooke was spending time at Jane's house, she walked through the house to use the bathroom and did not see a pair of Jane's pricey vintage tennis shoes left in the middle of the hallway floor. She tripped over the shoes and landed so hard on the marble floor that she broke her leg and dislocated her shoulder.

> Since Brooke was due to leave their morning show and star in a movie the next week, this little mishap cost her major bucks. Brooke filed suit against Jane (telling her, "Sorry sweetie, the tabloids loved us together, but business is business."). Jane has contacted your firm and wants to know if this klutzy ex-friend of hers has a chance of getting her mitts on any of Jane's hard-earned money.

You have found two relevant authorities that are set forth below. Using the authorities below,[2] create a case chart and a potential outline for your analysis.

Case 1

Price v. Denton,
California Intermediate Court (2009)

Ms. Kathy Price was a social worker for Los Angeles County in California. She worked for the school system and was given the task of visiting the homes of truant students. One sunny morning this past spring, she was asked to visit the home of Rick Denton who had been absent for 22 days during the previous quarter. The house was a small ranch style house located in a suburb outside L.A.

She parked her car on the street in front of the house and walked up the short driveway to the front steps. She climbed the steps, approached the front door, and knocked. An obviously annoyed man opened the door and, in response to Ms. Price, identified himself as Rick's father, Andy Denton. When Ms. Price told Mr. Denton why she was visiting the home, he became irate. He began yelling at her, using profanities and gesturing wildly with his arms. He said that it was the mother's fault, not his, that Rick was skipping school and he resented being questioned by someone from the government about something that was not his fault. Denton finished by telling her to leave and not bother him again.

Price realized she was going to get nowhere with Denton—she felt it was wise to leave the property as soon as possible given Denton's anger toward her. She turned, went down the steps, and started walking briskly across the yard toward her car. As she crossed the grass, she tripped over a five-foot rake that had been left in the yard. The rake had black tines and a long red handle. Price broke her arm in two places and missed two months of work. She sued Denton, alleging that he had failed to keep his property safe and had failed to warn her of the dangerous condition.

The trial court concluded that Price's claim should be dismissed. The court stated, and this Court agrees:

> Generally, a landowner has a duty to keep his premises in a safe condition and to warn guests of a hazardous condition. However, where the hazardous condition is apparent to anyone looking, the landowner has no duty to warn of its presence and cannot be held responsible for any injuries suffered by a guest as a result of the condition. Even when on another's property, an individual has a duty to use ordinary care to prevent injury to himself. This includes a duty to keep a proper lookout. Here, we do not doubt that the plaintiff failed to see the rake. However, any person using ordinary care and keeping a proper lookout would have undoubtedly seen the rake, given its size and color. Consequently, we cannot hold the landowner responsible for plaintiff's injuries.

---

2. Adapted from teaching materials initially created by Prof. Linda Rogers, Wake Forest University School of Law.

Case 2

Partner v. Dagon,
California Intermediate Court (2019)

Dagon held an election fundraiser in his house for Wilmer Judge, who was running for a position on the local school board. The fundraiser was held at 7:00 p.m., and it was dark outside. Dagon had invited about 100 people, including Sally Partner. The fundraiser was a success—everyone showed up and guests were very generous. After meeting the candidate and hearing her speak, Partner went to leave. She said her goodbyes to Dagon and asked if there was a quicker way to get to her car than going around the block. Dagon said she could go through the backyard but she should be careful because he was putting in a new deck.

Partner went outside and fell into a recently dug trench that did not have any construction tape around it. She broke her leg and cracked three ribs. She missed three weeks of work and did not get to run in the Boston Marathon, for which she had recently qualified. Partner brought an action against Dagon. The trial court dismissed the claim. The Court of Appeals, however, reversed stating:

> Generally, a landowner has a duty to keep his premises in a safe condition and to warn guests of a hazardous condition. However, where the hazardous condition is apparent to anyone looking, the landowner has no duty to warn of its presence and cannot be held responsible for any injuries suffered by a guest as a result of the condition. Even when on another's property, an individual has a duty to use ordinary care to prevent injury to himself. This includes a duty to keep a proper lookout. Here, the homeowner told the guest to use the back steps but to "be careful." Because he did not mention the trench or place construction tape around it, we doubt that plaintiff would have been able to see the trench, even using ordinary care and keeping a proper lookout. Consequently, the landowner can be responsible for plaintiff's injuries. We remand this case back to the trial court to make findings consistent with this opinion.

1. **Prepare a case chart using the chart below:**

Case/Court/Year	Facts	Holding—was owner liable for injuries?	Court's reasoning
Price v. Denton, California Intermediate Court (2009)	Social worker tripped over rake in front yard and broke her arm.	No	Hazard condition was apparent. P has duty to use ordinary care
Partner v. Dagon, California Intermediate Court (2019)	Tripped in unmarked ditch. Home owner warned her to be careful because of construction	~~No~~ Yes	warning was not sufficient because ditch wasn't apparent.

2. Using your case chart to inform your decision, if you were to draft a legal analysis, in what order would you discuss the cases? Why?

> The first one because she wasn't given warning - and it was a case where she should have but ordinary case.

Exercise 5.2: Preparing a Case Chart for a Legal Issue with Multiple Elements

Our client is Dr. Monica Young, who is an OB/GYN. She practices with Jackson County Physicians For Women in Sparta, North Carolina ("PFW"). Dr. Young alleges the other three doctors in the practice, who are male, treat her poorly. She believes they are jealous of her rapport and popularity with patients.

Dr. Young says that PFW discourages her from providing free medical care to indigent people in the county area. She wants to start her own practice. PFW is the only physician group that provides OB/GYN care in the county. While one other male OB/GYN practices in the county, he practices alone. He appears to be in his sixties and she thinks he may retire before long, though she has nothing specific to back that up.

Dr. Young's legal concern is that she signed an employment agreement with PFW that includes a non-compete covenant with PFW prohibiting her from providing OB-GYN services in Jackson County or any other of the five counties contiguous to Jackson County (approximately a fifty-mile radius from the clinic) for thirty-six months. This five-county area represents much of Western North Carolina. Dr. Young came to us to find out if the non-compete provision will be enforceable.

Another associate did some initial research for us. For PFW to enforce the covenant against Dr. Young, it will need to show that the covenant is: (1) in writing, (2) entered into at the time and as part of the contract of employment, (3) based upon reasonable consideration, (4) reasonable both as to time and territory, and (5) not against public policy.

We want to examine whether the non-compete is reasonable as to time and territory. We have found several cases, which are summarized below, that may be relevant. Read through the case excerpts below and complete the case chart; next, determine whether we may have a basis to argue the non-compete agreement is unreasonable with respect to length of time and geography, and is, therefore, not enforceable:

Manpower of Guilford County v. Hedgecock, 257 S.E.2d 109 (N.C. 1979)

The plaintiff sued the defendant for breach of a non-compete, which precluded the defendant from competing with the plaintiff for one year within a twenty-five mile radius of any of the many cities where plaintiff kept an office. The court found that a one-year restriction was reasonable; however, a restriction that potentially covered a 25-mile radius of any city in the country where plaintiff kept an office was more extensive than necessary to protect the plaintiff's legitimate business interests.

Jewel Box Stores Corp. v. Morrow, 158 S.E.2d 840 (N.C. 1968)

The defendant (Morrow), the owner of a jewelry store, sold his business in Morganton, North Carolina to the plaintiff buyer and granted the buyer all interest in his trade name. In exchange, seller Morrow agreed not to compete with the buyer for a period of ten years in Morganton and within ten miles of the Morganton city limits. Buyer ran notices that it would be selling merchandise at discount prices. The seller opened a gift shop across the street from its former store, which competed with its former merchandise. The buyer instituted this action to restrain defendant seller from selling retail jewelry items and from engaging in the jewelry business in Morganton and within ten miles of its city limits. Reasoning that the buyer would not have entered into this contract without the restrictive covenant from the seller, the court explained that time and territory restrictions need to be considered in tandem when determining the reasonableness of each component. The court found the covenant enforceable, stating that a longer period of time was reasonable when the area of competition was relatively small. In this case, the court found that the restriction was reasonable because there were only four or five other jewelry stores in the area, and it could take the plaintiff buyer that long to establish confidence and a good reputation with the townspeople. Held for plaintiff.

Electrical South, Inc. v. Lewis, 385 S.E.2d 352 (N.C. Ct. App. 1989)

An employee who repaired industrial electronic equipment signed a non-compete agreement that prohibited him from working for two years with any company that competed directly or indirectly with the employer, Electrical South, within a 200-mile radius from the employee's current branch in Greensboro, North Carolina. The employee ultimately quit his job in the Greensboro location and took a job with a competitor in South Carolina where he began performing repairs on industrial electronic equipment. The court held that the covenant was not reasonable because the restriction was not limited to customers within the 200-mile radius but also included customers that had a link, no matter how slender, to any competitor of Electrical South. This restriction, the court explained, had the practical effect of making the clause a worldwide restriction if the employee indirectly competed with the Greensboro office. Therefore, the non-compete agreement was too broad.

Kennedy v. Kennedy, 584 S.E.2d 328 (N.C. Ct. App. 2003)

Dr. Kennedy owned a dental practice and sold the practice to his nephew (also Dr. Kennedy). The parties agreed upon the sale that the uncle would not open a new dental practice within fifteen miles of the old dental practice for a period of three years. The uncle ultimately opened a new office that was within fifteen miles of the old office. The Court of Appeals reversed the trial court and found the covenant reasonable, noting that a fifteen-mile radius for three years was well within the limits allowed by the courts in the past.

Case	Duration	Geographic Scope	Enforceable?
Manpower v Hedgecock	1 year ✓	25 mile radius ✗	NO
Jewel box v Mondow	10 yrs	10 mile radius	Yes
Electrical south v. Lewis	2 yrs	200 mile radius	NO, indirect competition too broad
Kennedy v Kennedy	3 yrs	15 miles	Yes

1. Based on your case chart, do you think the court will find the time restriction to be reasonable?

Yes

2. Based on your case chart, do you think the court will find the geographic restriction to be reasonable?

NO, restrictions based on neighboring counties

will likely be to broad to protect legitimate business interest.

3. What do you consider to be the take-away rule for considering time and territory in the context of a non-compete in this jurisdiction?

4. What is your initial prediction of whether the court will consider the restriction on time and territory in Dr. Young's case to be reasonable?

Maybe, better argument is public policy.

Exercise 5.3: Preparing a Case Chart and Moving Toward an Outline

We have recently been retained by a new client, Andrea Perkins.[3] On July 30, Detective Simpson of the Huntsville Police Department placed Ms. Perkins under arrest for robbery. We need to get a handle on the theft of property charge. As of this date, the District Attorney's Office has not yet made a charging decision against Ms. Perkins.

The D.A. will seek to charge her with the highest degree crime that the evidence will

3. This problem was adapted from teaching materials created by Professor Lucy Jewell, University of Tennessee.

support under Alabama law. What you should find out is whether she can be charged with First Degree Robbery because she used a "dangerous instrument."

Ms. Perkins is an honors student at Apollo University, studying fashion merchandising. Because of a conditional "morals clause" connected to her college scholarship, Ms. Perkins stands to lose a great deal if she serves even a single day in jail for these incidents. Here are the relevant facts from the police report:

> On July 28, Mr. Davon Miller said he called the police because Ms. Perkins had taken his personal belongings from his home. He stated that he was the sole owner of the residence, but that Ms. Perkins and he had lived together for the last two years in that residence.
>
> One week prior to that night, on July 21, he had ended his relationship with Ms. Perkins. On that day, he had informed Ms. Perkins that he had fallen in love with his long-term friend, Callen Klein, and that he wanted Ms. Perkins to pack her things and leave his house. He stated that Ms. Perkins began to cry and ran out of the restaurant where they had been eating lunch.
>
> Mr. Miller did not see or speak to Ms. Perkins again until approximately 10:30 p.m. the evening of July 28 when Ms. Perkins texted Mr. Miller and asked if she could come over to reach "closure" that evening. Mr. Miller told her that "yes, she could come over" to discuss the end of their relationship.
>
> Ms. Perkins came to Mr. Miller's home at 10:30 p.m., and they shared a drink together in his living room. Ms. Perkins excused herself to use the bathroom in his bedroom. When she did not return, Mr. Miller stepped inside his bedroom where he saw Ms. Perkins inside his bathroom's large walk in closet, with her back turned to him.
>
> Ms. Perkins then turned around and Mr. Miller noticed she was holding a Cartier jewelry box containing a diamond necklace that he had hidden in the closet, planning to present the necklace to Ms. Klein in the near future. Mr. Miller was standing just outside the closet doorway when Ms. Perkins turned around and saw him. She stated, "I remembered you bought that necklace last month—I was wondering if it had been delivered yet."
>
> Ms. Perkins then grabbed Mr. Miller's metal-pronged track cleat. He could see the sharp sole of the cleat as she pointed the heel toward his chest. Mr. Miller asked her, "What are you doing?" Ms. Perkins then screamed at him, "I'm leaving, and I'm taking this necklace!" Ms. Perkins screamed, "Get out of my way or else . . .!" She drew back her right hand that had the shoe in it and pointed the cleat upwards, toward his face. Ms. Perkins then walked quickly toward the closet door. As Ms. Perkins continued to move forward quickly, she brushed Mr. Miller's shoulder and lightly grazed his arm with the shoe's cleat as she passed him. However, no scratch marks were visible on Mr. Miller's arm. A few hours later, the police found the Cartier jewelry box with the necklace in Ms. Perkins' car.
>
> Mr. Miller is 6 foot 2 inches and weighs 190 pounds. Ms. Perkins is 5 feet tall and weighs about 115 pounds.

We need an objective opinion as to what crime the prosecution can charge her with so that we can conduct the preliminary conversations and plea negotiations with the D.A. Our specific question is whether she can be charged with First Degree Robbery for using the shoe as a "dangerous instrument." To start the process, organize the relevant legal authority, prepare a case chart, and respond to the questions that follow the case briefs below.

Alabama Code § 13A-8-41, Robbery in the First Degree:

(a) A person commits the crime of robbery in the first degree if he violates Section 13A-8-43 and he:

　(1) Is armed with a deadly weapon or dangerous instrument; or
　(2) Causes serious physical injury to another.

(b) Possession then and there of an article used or fashioned in a manner to lead any person who is present reasonably to believe it to be a deadly weapon or dangerous instrument, or any verbal or other representation by the defendant that he is then and there so armed, is prima facie evidence under subsection (a) of this section that he was so armed.

The relevant case excerpts are below:

Breedlove v. State, 482 So. 2d 1277 (Ala. Crim. App. 1975)

Defendant was properly charged with first degree robbery when he told the cab driver to pull over, stuck an object into the driver's side, and told the driver that if he "tried to do anything" he would "blow him away." The court upheld the conviction and said it was not necessary that the defendant actually have a gun to sustain the conviction of first degree robbery.

Ex Parte Williams, 780 So. 2d 673 (Ala. 2000)

The defendant repeatedly hit the storeowner with a can of beans/peas while the co-defendant stole money from the cash register. The court held that the can of vegetables could constitute a "dangerous instrument" within the scope of first degree robbery.

Goodwin v. State, 641 So. 2d 1289 (Ala. Crim. App. 1994)

The defendant was convicted of first degree robbery when he threatened two men with a stick during the course of stealing their radio at a swimming hole and said, "Is your life worth $40?" Because the victim believed the defendant was holding a gun (even if the victim was mistaken) the test to be applied is a subjective one, which focuses on the "reaction of the victim to the threats of the robber." The court held that a jury could have reasonably believed that the defendant threatened the imminent use of force with the intent to compel the victim to give up the radio and that the conviction was therefore proper.

Cook v. State, 582 So. 2d 592 (Ala. Crim. App. 1991)

The defendant who robbed a convenience store threatened the cashier with a steak knife but did not physically injure the cashier. The court held that the first-degree robbery charge was proper because first-degree robbery does not require that actual force be used to commit theft; evidence of threatened or imminent force is sufficient.

Using the case excerpts above, complete the chart on the next page. (Hint: Not all case excerpts contain information relevant to each box.)

Case Chart Assessing First Degree Robbery Elements

Case	Used Dangerous Instrument	Possessed article that made victim reasonably believe article was a dangerous instrument	Holding: Did facts meet standard for first degree robbery?
Breedlove v. State	NO	Yes	Yes, not necessary to actually have gun.
Ex Parte Williams			
Goodwin v. State			
Cock v. State			

1. Based on your case chart, do you predict the cleat will be considered a dangerous instrument or deadly weapon?

Yes,

2. Do you see any way that your case chart can assist with creating a broad outline for your legal analysis?

People v. Carter, 53 N.Y. 2d 113 (1981)

Id. at 116. stuff about dif case. Carter 53 N.Y. 2d at 116

Chapter 6

One Legal Argument

I. **Using Templates**

II. **The Components of a Legal Argument**

III. **Exercises**

A governing rule may be composed of a single legal argument, or multiple legal arguments, particularly if the client's question requires analysis of multiple elements or factors. Each legal argument that an attorney builds will have the same components. Those components are

- A statement identifying the legal issue to be addressed.
- The rule governing the legal issue and, where needed, an explanation of the relevant authorities or cases supporting that rule.
- An application of the law to the facts of your client's case.
- A final conclusion or prediction about how a court might rule on the legal issue.

Although the depth of analysis and the length of each single legal argument may vary, you will need to include each component in the legal argument that you build. Attorneys often use common templates as helpful reminders of these essential components when building a legal argument. This chapter explains several templates and provides examples to help you identify the components of a legal argument.

I. Using Templates

Example 6.A describes some of the templates attorneys commonly use, and how they match up with the essential components set forth above.

Example 6.A: Table of Commonly Used Templates and How They Relate to Objective Analysis

Template	How Components Relate to the Multi-step Process of Objective Analysis
IRAC	• I → A statement identifying the legal issue • R → An explanation of the governing rule, which may include an illustration of the relevant cases • A → An application of the law to the client's facts • C → A conclusion or prediction about the legal issue
TREAC	• T → A thesis statement about the legal issue • R → An explanation of the governing rule, which may include the relevant cases • E → An explanation of the rule, which may include an illustration of the relevant cases • A → An application of the law to the client's facts • C → A conclusion or prediction about the legal issue
CREAC	• C → A conclusion about the legal issue • R → An explanation of the governing rule • E → An explanation of the rule, which may include an illustration of the relevant cases • A → An application of the law to the client's facts • C → A conclusion or prediction about the legal issue
CRExAC	• C → A conclusion about the legal issue • R → An explanation of the governing rule • Ex → An explanation of the rule, which may include an illustration of the relevant cases • A → An application of the law to the client's facts • C → A conclusion or prediction about the legal issue
CRRPAP	• C → A conclusion about the legal issue • R → An explanation of the governing rule • RP → An explanation of the rule, which may include an illustration of the relevant cases that prove how the rule has functioned in past cases • A → An application of the law to the client's facts • P → A prediction about the legal issue

II. The Components of a Legal Argument

No matter which template you choose, the various components ensure that your analysis of the legal issue is sound. By using a template, you can present your sound legal analysis in a way that your reader will expect and understand. Of all components, the heart of your client's question will be the legal rules that apply and the key facts on which those rules turn.

- **Issue/Thesis/Conclusion**

The first component identifies the legal issue that will be addressed in the legal argument. This component can be framed in one of three ways: as a statement of the issue; as a thesis—that is, an assertion; or as a conclusion or prediction of how the court will decide legal issue.

- **Rule**

Once the legal question you are analyzing has been identified, set forth the governing rule that addresses the issue. The rule may come from a statute, a regulation, a case, a series of cases, or a combination of sources.

- **Explanation: Case Illustration or Rule Proof**

Rules stripped of their context often become unclear; consequently, you will likely need to show, or to prove, how the rule works. To prove how the rule works, you may need to add relevant sub-rules that further explain or support the rule. Most of the time, however, you will prove how the rule works by illustrating how the rule worked in a previous fact situation. The most common rule explanation is the case illustration (setting forth the relevant facts, holding, and reasoning of a prior case) or "rule proof" (that is, showing the reader how the rule has functioned in a past case; thereby proving the rule). The case illustration or rule proof sets forth the relevant facts, holding, and reasoning from a precedent case to illustrate or prove the rule.

- **Application**

After you have identified the specific issue or principle you need to resolve, set forth the governing rule, and have explained how the rule has functioned in the past, you are ready to apply the rule to your client's facts. We apply the law by using rule-based reasoning, analogical reasoning, or a combination of both.

- **Conclusion**

By the time you reach the conclusion, you have done all of the hard work. Now, all that remains is to state (or restate, because you may have started the legal analysis with a conclusion) the prediction you have drawn from the governing rule, the way that you explained or proved the governing rule, and your application of the law to your client's facts.

III. Exercises

The following exercises will help you to dissect and identify the various components of a legal argument. You will also see a process for drafting a single legal argument. Finally, you will continue to evaluate and identify the components of a legal argument by practicing with a variety of sentences.

Exercise 6.1: Identifying Components of a Legal Argument

Read through the following facts, and examples of analysis, and answer the questions that follow:

> Ralph Singh is a part-time actor who is friends with Vanessa Redgave, the creator and co-producer of a hit television show called "Let's Be Real." Ralph admits to you that he is not a household name and that he is just starting out in show business. "Let's Be Real" is a reality show in which the host interviews celebrities about their lifestyle, shopping and dining choices, vacation spots, and other personal topics. The host for "Let's Be Real" is Martin Cheen. Ralph and Martin both have outgoing personalities, a good sense of humor, and comedic timing. Both Ralph and Martin have previously done stand-up comedy in prior shows. Ralph feels slighted that Vanessa chose Martin over him for the host spot. He also feels that

Martin is trying to imitate Ralph's persona by dressing like him and using some of his mannerisms and speech patterns. Martin's name on the show is "Marty." Martin and Vanessa tell Ralph that Marty's persona is unique and that it was created by Martin and Vanessa.

Ralph seeks your advice, as his attorney, about whether he has a cause of action against the show's producers. The filming is taking place in New York. You've done your research and found that there is no common law cause of action in New York. However, one statute is on point, the Civil Rights Law, particularly sections 50 and 51.

As Ralph's attorney, you write the following analysis in a letter:

Dear Mr. Singh:

You have asked whether you are entitled to damages or injunctive relief against the producers of the hit reality television show, "Let's Be Real." You have told me that you observe similarities between yourself and the show's host, played by Martin Cheen. After researching the law in this state, my conclusion is that you would not have a cause of action based upon these facts.

According to Section 50 of the New York Civil Rights Law, a person or corporation is prohibited from using for "purposes of trade, the name, portrait or picture of any living person without having first obtained the written consent of such person." N.Y. Civ. Rights Law § 50 (Westlaw 2019). Under Section 51, the plaintiff is entitled to an equitable remedy (such as an injunction) or damages. N.Y. Civ. Rights Law § 51 (Westlaw 2019).

The New York courts have not recognized a viable cause of action under this statute for situations where real life inspires works of art. *Hampton v. Guare*, 195 A.D.2d 366, 366, 600 N.Y.S.2d 57, 58 (1st Dep't 1993). In *Hampton*, the intermediate court held that an individual who claimed that his real life criminal acts inspired a hit Broadway play did not have a cause of action. In that case, the plaintiff was an aspiring actor who had been convicted of attempted burglary, impersonation, and other charges when he pretended to be someone he was not and scammed victims for money. Later, the award-winning play was created, "Six Degrees of Separation," which was inspired by these true crimes. At the center of the play was a con artist who pretended to be the son of the famous actor Sidney Poitier, and convinced people to give him money. The *Hampton* court reasoned that, "works of fiction and satire do not fall within the narrow scope of the statutory phrases 'advertising' and 'trade.'" *Id.* (quoting sections 50 and 51).

Similarly, courts have held that plaintiffs do not have a cause of action when the subject matter is a work of fiction. *Costanza v. Seinfeld*, 269 A.D.2d 255, 255, 719 N.Y.S.2d 29, 30 (1st Dep't 2001). In *Costanza*, an acquaintance of the creators of the television sitcom "Seinfeld" claimed that defendants used his name and persona to create a television character for the hit television series. The court reasoned, "defendants have never used plaintiff's actual name, or filmed plaintiff himself or made use of a photograph of plaintiff, in any form." *Id.* The court held that the television series was a work of fiction and, therefore, any potential resemblance to the plaintiff did not violate the statute. *Id.*

In applying the reasoning of the *Hampton* and *Costanza* courts to the issue presented, a court would likely conclude that Marty does not actually depict you in the show, thus precluding recovery against the creator and producers of "Let's Be Real." Similar to the events with Hampton's crimes that inspired the play, your persona may have inspired Marty's clothing choices, mannerisms, and speech patterns, but you are not actually portrayed on the show. Furthermore, applying similar reasoning from the *Costanza* case, none of the following occurred: your actual name was not used, you were not filmed in the show, nor was your photograph used.

Although "Let's Be Real" is based upon real-life celebrities, as opposed to fictional stories in the precedent cases, nonetheless, your true life is not portrayed in the show. Even if Marty's dress, mannerisms, and speech patterns are similar to yours, you as an individual are not identifiable to the viewing audience. As you have explained to me, your prior work as a stand-up comedian has not materialized into your stage presence being known by the general public. Like in *Hampton*, where the events depicted in the show were inspired by real life but extremely exaggerated and meant to entertain, Marty's persona, whether similar to you or not, is probably too extenuated for the audience to draw a connection to you.

In conclusion, a court would likely determine that you do not have a claim for violation of Civil Rights Law Sections 50 and 51 against the producers of the television show "Let's Be Real." Although the show is based upon the lives of actual people, the show did not use your name, portrait, or picture for purposes of trade.

Questions:

1. **Describe the issue being addressed in the client letter.**

   Can Ralph recover for ~~producers~~ simila

   _____

   _____

   _____

   _____

   _____

2. **Can you identify the governing rule for the legal issue being addressed?**

   _____

   _____

   _____

   _____

   _____

   _____

3. **Identify the relevant facts, holding, and reasoning of the *Hampton* case.**

   _____

   _____

   _____

   _____

4. Identify the relevant facts, holding, and reasoning of the *Costanza* case.

_____

_____

_____

_____

_____

_____

5. Identify how Mr. Singh's claim is similar to or different from the plaintiff in *Hampton*.

_____

_____

_____

_____

_____

_____

6. Identify how Mr. Singh's claim is similar to or different from the plaintiff's claim in *Costanza*.

_____

_____

_____

_____

_____

_____

7. What are the primary reasons why the writer predicts Mr. Singh will not recover?

_____

_____

_____

_____

_____

Exercise 6.2: Identifying the Components of a Legal Argument

Exercise 6.2 sets forth a single legal argument concerning one element of the tort of "alienation of affection."[1] In this case, Russ Price is suing David DeAngelo. Russ alleges that David's pursuit of Lana Price, while she was married to Russ, was the "controlling or effective cause" of their divorce. Read through the argument and identify the following components in the margin beside the exercise: Issue, Governing Rule, Case Illustration, Application, and Conclusion. After you have identified the components of the legal argument, answer the questions that follow.

The critical issue in David's case is whether his active and unwelcome pursuit of Lana during her marriage was a "controlling or effective cause" of the break-up of her marriage to Russ. A defendant may be the "controlling or effective cause" of the alienation of affections, even if other causes also contributed to the alienation. *Hutelmyer v. Cox*, 514 S.E.2d 554, 559 (N.C. Ct. App. 1999). For example, it is sufficient if there is "active participation, initiative or encouragement on the part of the defendant in causing one spouse's loss of the other spouse's affections." *Id.* In *Hutelmyer*, the defendant paramour flirted openly with the plaintiff's husband, allowed him to stay overnight in her home, and had a sexual relationship with him. *Id.* As the plaintiff's husband began to spend more time with the defendant, he began to spend less time with his family, and his sexual relationship with his wife deteriorated. *Id.* Ultimately, the plaintiff's husband left the marital home and moved in with the defendant. *Id.* at 557–58. The court observed that even though other causes might have contributed to the breakdown of the plaintiff's marriage, it was not until the plaintiff's husband began to spend time alone with the defendant, at the defendant's urging, that the plaintiff's marriage began to deteriorate. *Id.* Therefore, the court held that a jury could find that the defendant was a "controlling or effective cause" of the alienation of affections. *Id.*

Here, the evidence is also sufficient for a jury to conclude that David was the controlling or effective cause of Lana's alienation of affection. First, like the defendant in *Hutelmyer*, whose conduct encouraged the plaintiff's husband to ignore his family, David initiated a course of conduct aimed at causing Lana to leave Russ. Second, just as the defendant in *Hutelmyer* openly flirted with the plaintiff's husband, David publicly professed his desire for Lana, even in front of Russ. Third, in both cases, the defendant ignored requests that the couple be left alone. The defendant in *Hutelmyer* ignored the husband's statements that he wished to work things out with his wife. Similarly, David at first ignored Lana's repeated pleas for him to leave her alone.

It is insignificant that David did eventually stop pursuing Lana, unlike the defendant in *Hutelmyer;* this distinction is not controlling. Lana's own journal confirms that she had a growing obsession with David, which led to the break-up of her marriage. Most likely this obsession would not have developed if David had not been so persistent in his earlier efforts to win her affections. Therefore, Russ can probably establish that David was a "controlling or effective cause" of the alienation of affections between him and Lana.

---

1. Adapted from teaching materials created by Prof. Laura Graham, Director of Legal Analysis, Writing, and Research at Wake Forest University School of Law.

1. What is the governing rule? Is it written in the present or past tense?

_____

_____

_____

_____

_____

_____

2. Can you identify any sub-rules that may show how the governing rule works?

_____

_____

_____

_____

_____

_____

3. What is the purpose of the *Hutelmyer* case illustration in this legal argument?

_____

_____

_____

_____

_____

_____

4. Does the writer analogize Hutelmyer or distinguish it?

_____

_____

_____

_____

_____

_____

_____

5. The writer makes three analytic points in the application. What are they? What technique does the writer use to let the reader know she is making three separate points?

_____

_____

_____

_____

_____

_____

6. Does the argument contain a counter-argument? If so, what is it?

_____

_____

_____

_____

_____

7. What is the writer's prediction as to the outcome of the legal issue?

_____

_____

_____

_____

_____

Exercise 6.3: Evaluating the Components of a Legal Argument

Evaluate the following excerpts from an objective memorandum of law to a supervising attorney.[2] Then, identify whether the statement is an issue, rule, case illustration, application of law to fact, or conclusion. A list of each of these terms follows each excerpt. Circle the appropriate term that describes the excerpt.

1. **An owner has no duty to protect or assist an invitee unless the owner placed the invitee in peril or the invitee is helpless.** *Osterlind v. Hill,* 160 N.E. 301, 302 (Mass. 1928).

    Circle the term that best describes the above excerpt:

    - Issue
    - Rule
    - Case Illustration
    - Application
    - Conclusion

2. **Like the canoe in** *Osterlind,* **which was not alleged to be out of repair or unsafe, there is no indication that the raft rented by Clark was faulty. Similar to the invitee in** *Osterlind,* **who was able to hang onto the canoe for one-half hour and call loudly for assistance, Clark handled the raft for most of the rafting trip, showing he was not helpless. He also assured Eddie, the guide, that he was fine after Eddie noticed he was limping and warned him that the rapids were rough in certain areas.**

    Circle the term that best describes the above excerpt:

    - Issue
    - Rule
    - Case Illustration
    - Application
    - Conclusion

3. **Because Rafts-R-US placed Clark in a perilous situation and because Clark's injuries rendered him helpless, as seen by Clark's dizziness and inability to swim, Clark can most likely establish that Rafts-R-US had a duty to protect and assist him.**

    Circle the term that best describes the above excerpt:

    - Issue
    - Rule
    - Case Illustration
    - Application
    - Conclusion

---

2. Adapted from teaching materials created by Prof. Laura Graham, Director of Legal Analysis, Writing, and Research at Wake Forest University School of Law.

4. The issue in this case is whether Eddie, the owner of Rafts-R-Us, had a duty to protect Clark, an invitee, by refusing to let him ride the raft due to his severely twisted ankle, or to assist Clark, when the rapids became extremely rough.

Circle the term that best describes the above excerpt:

- Issue

- Rule

- Case Illustration

- Application

- Conclusion

5. In *Osterlind*, the defendant, Hill, rented a canoe to the plaintiff's son, Osterlind, who was intoxicated at the time. *Id.* at 301. The canoe overturned, and Osterlind held onto the side for about thirty minutes while loudly calling for assistance. His loud cries went unanswered by Hill. *Id.* The court held that there was no duty on the part of Hill to either refuse rental or offer assistance, since Osterlind was not helpless, nor was Hill responsible for placing Osterlind in a perilous situation.

Circle the term that best describes the above excerpt:

- Issue

- Rule

- Case Illustration

- Application

- Conclusion

Chapter 7

Explaining the Law: Introduction

 To conduct an objective analysis of a legal issue, you will need to identify the law that will govern the predicted result of your client's legal question. The first step in constructing the predicted result is to provide your legal reader with an explanation of the law—that is, a cohesive account of the law as it pertains to your client's legal issue. This explanation may involve:

- Synthesizing the relevant law to construct a rule (whether from a sub-rule, element, factor, or other component) that applies to your client's situation
- Illustrating how the rule applies by discussing relevant cases that have applied the rules in the past

Chapter 7.1 will provide instruction and exercises to help you craft rules and synthesize rules. Then, Chapter 7.2 will provide an overview and exercises that focus on using cases to illustrate how the legal rules work.

Chapter 7.1
Explaining the Law: Rule Synthesis

I. Techniques for Drafting Rules
II. Rule Synthesis
III. Exercises

The first step in drafting your explanation of the law is to craft the rule. A **rule** is a legal standard that is usually derived from a primary authority such as a statute, a regulation, or a case. In this chapter, we examine (1) techniques for effectively crafting rules when drafting a legal analysis and (2) how to craft rules from a series of cases and authorities.

I. Techniques for Drafting Rules

When you sit down to construct a rule or rule paragraph for your legal analysis, consider the following techniques:

- Generally, lead with the statute before discussing any case law, if there is a statute on point.
- If you are using an explicit rule from a statute, case, or a line of cases, you will want to quote relevant portions or make sure to use verbatim any specific terms of art.
- When drafting a rule paragraph, describe the broad rules first and then the narrower legal principles.
- Because you are framing the rule to predict what a future court may do, state the rule in the present tense.
- Do not describe the historical development of the rule—these details are too difficult for your reader to digest and retain.
- Always consider relevant counter-arguments. If you have two competing rules, generally discuss the rule you predict the court will use first (the primary rule), before discussing the opposing or secondary rule.

II. Rule Synthesis

Sometimes the rule for a given legal issue is consistent and static. In such a case, you can use the rule as stated by the prior authorities. In other cases, however, you may need to blend or combine parts of rules from the prior authorities to extract the rule. Synthesis is a method for building a rule that can explain a legal doctrine.[1]

So, how do you synthesize a series of cases? The first step is to dissect the authorities to recognize patterns by asking questions such as:

- Has the rule been broadened over time to cover more circumstances?
- Has the rule been more narrowly interpreted to cover fewer circumstances?
- Are there new exceptions to the rule?
- Are there new or expanded policy considerations?
- Is the reasoning in the cases consistent, even if the outcome is inconsistent?
- Have the courts added/eliminated factors, prongs, tests, or possibly elements needed to satisfy the rule?

Table 7.1.A provides an example of synthesizing a rule through a series of cases, looking at the extreme and outrageous conduct element of the intentional infliction of emotion distress tort.

Table 7.1.A: An Example of Synthesizing a Rule Using a Series of Cases

Case	Facts	Was the conduct extreme & outrageous?
Woodruff v. Miller, 307 S.E.2d 176, 178 (N.C. Ct. App. 1983)	After filing two unsuccessful lawsuits against a school superintendent (Plaintiff), Defendant posted copies of warrants on a wanted board to create the false impression that Plaintiff had broken the law and had not been punished.	Yes. Conduct was extreme and outrageous because Defendant purposely was trying to ruin Plaintiff's reputation, and Defendant continued his offensive conduct.
Briggs v. Rosenthal, 327 S.E.2d 308, 311 (N.C. Ct. App. 1985)	A newspaper editor wrote an unflattering obituary, stating that deceased was a heavy drinker but also a solid citizen.	No. Conduct was not extreme and outrageous because comments were unflattering, perhaps insulting, but sincere and a matter of opinion.
West v. King's Dep't Store, Inc., 365 S.E.2d 621, 623–25 (N.C. 1988)	A store manager repeatedly and loudly accused innocent customers of shoplifting in the presence of other store patrons.	Yes. Conduct was extreme and outrageous where Defendant's conduct was offensive and continuous.

From the chart, you can determine that in the *Woodruff* and *West* cases, each court found the behavior extreme and outrageous where (1) the defendant made public accusations, and (2) the defendant accused plaintiff of socially unacceptable behavior. However, the *Briggs* case adds the caveat that to be actionable, public accusations must be more than mere insults.

---

1. Steven I. Friedland, *100 Rules to Know for Passing the Multistate Bar Exam* ix (2d ed. 2012).

So, in light of these factors, you may process the following rule as in Figure 7.1.B:

Figure 7.1.B: Processing Factors from Cases to Synthesize a Rule

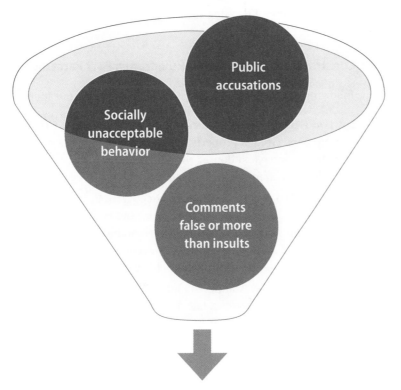

Possible synthesized rule: A defendant's conduct is extreme and outrageous when the defendant persistently makes false public statements about the plaintiff, *Woodruff*, or where the behavior was publicly offensive and continuous, *West*.

In the above example, the writer was able to synthesize the prior cases into a one-sentence rule statement. When the best construction of a rule is one that necessitates a blending or combining of authorities, lawyers call it **rule synthesis**.

Sometimes you will need more than one sentence to accurately capture the prior authorities in a comprehensive manner. In that case, you will need to create a **rule synthesis paragraph.** Thus, rather than combining or blending parts of rules to create one statement that explains the doctrine, you will start with the broadest statement of the rule (many times the language of the statute, regulation, or other explicit rule) and continue to add sub-rules that help explain the nuances (likely found in the case law).

Example 7.1.C: An Example of a Rule Synthesis Paragraph

One can be charged with civil contempt for "[d]isobedience or resistance" to a court order. 18 U.S.C. § 401 (2002). A court has discretion in whether to hold a party in contempt for disregarding the court's orders. *In re Crystal Palace*, 817 F.2d 1361 (9th Cir. 1987). However, where a party acts in "'good faith and [with] reasonable interpretation of [the court's order],'" the party would not be held in contempt. *Vertex Distribut., Inc. v. Falcon Foam Plastics, Inc.*, 689 F.2d 885, 889 (9th Cir. 1982) (quoting *Rinehart v. Brewer*, 483 F. Supp. 165, 171 (S.D. Iowa 1980)).

III. Exercises

The following exercises are designed to help you practice skills involved with rule synthesis, while honing techniques for drafting rules.

Exercise 7.1.1: Constructing a Synthesized Rule from a Fact Pattern

Consider the following non-legal hypothetical[2] and respond to the questions that follow:

> On Sunday, two neighborhood children, Andrea Spartis and Corey Campbell, Jr., snuck onto Mrs. Gregg's property to taunt Mrs. Gregg's dog with sticks. Mrs. Gregg came to the porch and doused the children with water from the garden hose, yelling, "You kids get off my lawn or I'll call your parents!" The youths ran away.

> On Monday, Akilah Jackson nodded to Mrs. Gregg from the sidewalk, and Mrs. Gregg waved her over, calling, "Akilah Jackson, come out of the sun for a spell and have some lemonade with me on the porch." Akilah ambled up the driveway past the "Keep Out" signs and sat and talked with Mrs. Gregg, nodding repeatedly as Mrs. Gregg regaled Akilah with details of her battle with poison ivy.

> On Tuesday, Trudy Dewey wandered onto Mrs. Gregg's property to pick mint leaves from her garden for a cocktail she was making called a "mint julep." Mrs. Gregg sprang from behind the bushes with the garden hose, spraying Trudy and ruining her freshly blown-out hairstyle. Mrs. Gregg shouted, "Trudy Dewey, are you making those potent cocktails again? Well, you had better get off my lawn before I knock you in the head!" Trudy scrambled off Mrs. Gregg's property, empty-handed.

> On Wednesday, Strongsville had its annual Founders Day Parade. Sam Aquilino was dressed as Abe Lincoln in a top hat and was walking down the street on stilts when suddenly a pig escaped from one of the 4-H cages, knocking Sam over and onto Mrs. Gregg's property. Having seen the incident, Mrs. Gregg came over, dusted Sam off and offered him some lemonade.

> On Thursday, Eli King was being chased by a swarm of hornets, so he ran onto Mrs. Gregg's property and dove into the pond in the backyard. Mrs. Gregg saw the whole incident and laughed so hard, she fell off her porch chair. She didn't bother with the garden hose.

> On Friday, Corey Campbell, Jr. was chased onto Mrs. Gregg's property by Elisa McKeown, who was wielding a croquet club and threatening to pummel Henry for using her best dress to keep his prize-winning piglets warm. In running from Elisa, Henry trampled Mrs. Gregg's patch of cucumbers (which she intended to sell at the county fair) and damaged the gate to Mrs. Gregg's chicken coop. Mrs. Gregg did not spray Henry with water, but she immediately called his parents and demanded that they reimburse her for the damaged cucumbers and chicken coop.

---

2. Adapted with permission from Paul Figley, *Teaching Rule Synthesis with Real Cases*, 61 J. Leg. Ed. 245 (2011).

Questions:

1. **What is the rule from Sunday?**

Use water hole on Kids who sneak onto Property and taunt dog.

2. **What is the rule from Monday?**

Keep out sign does not apply to people invited onto the Property.

3. **What is the rule from Tuesday?**

Use Waterhose on People who are on the Property but not invited.

4. **What is the rule from Wednesday?**

People on the Property w/o Permission but are there by accident are ok.

5. **What is the rule from Thursday?**

or extenuating circumstances.

6. **What is the rule from Friday?**

except when they cause damage.

7. **Now use the rules from above and see if you can you can combine them into a single rule that may predict Mrs. Gregg's behavior in future cases.**

Being on the Property is only ok when given explicit Permission or by accident due to extenuating circumstances.

Exercise 7.1.2: Evaluating Rule Statements for Effectiveness

Compare the two examples below extracted from two interoffice memoranda. Assume that an associate was asked to predict whether a court would find that a business partner's blog statements met the element of extreme and outrageous conduct for the tort of Intentional Infliction of Emotional Distress.

Version A:

The business partner's statements in his blog were likely extreme and outrageous conduct. A defendant's conduct is extreme and outrageous if the conduct exceeds "all bounds usually tolerated by decent society." *Stanback v. Stanback*, 254 S.E.2d 611, 622 (N.C. 1979). A public accusation of socially unacceptable behavior is evidence of extreme and outrageous conduct. *West v. King's Dep't Store, Inc.*, 365 S.E.2d 621 (N.C. 1988).

Version B:

The business partner's statements in his blog were likely extreme and outrageous conduct. A defendant's conduct is extreme and outrageous if the conduct exceeds "all bounds usually tolerated by decent society." *Stanback v. Stanback*, 254 S.E.2d 611, 622 (N.C. 1979). In *Woodruff v. Miller*, 307 S.E.2d 176, 178 (N.C. Ct. App. 1983), the Court of Appeals held that extreme and outrageous conduct existed when the defendant publicly accused the plaintiff of breaking the law. Several years later, in *West v. King's Dep't Store*, 365 S.E.2d 621, 623 (N.C. 1988), the Supreme Court, following *Woodruff*, held that the defendant's conduct was extreme and outrageous because he made a public accusation of illegal behavior in the presence of others. These cases suggest that public accusations of illegal behavior are evidence of extreme and outrageous conduct. *See Woodruff*, 307 S.E.2d at 178; *West*, 365 S.E.2d at 625.

1. Which rule statement is more effective and why?

   Version B.

Exercise 7.1.3: Creating a Rule Synthesis Paragraph

In this exercise, you are provided with facts and two case summaries. Read the facts, then the first case summary, and provide responses to the guided questions. Then read the next case summary, and again, follow the prompts.

You are working as a public defender in Queens, New York, and representing indigent clients in criminal matters. Your client, James Clark, was arrested for drug possession. In reviewing the facts of the case, you read that the arresting police officer observed what looked like a buy and sell of drugs on a street corner. One of the two suspects ran away, but your client did not run until the officer yelled at him to stand still. When your client began to run, he tossed aside a backpack and flung it approximately 10 feet away. Momentarily, the officer caught him, handcuffed and frisked him, and then walked over to where the backpack was lying on the ground (12 feet away from defendant) and searched it. Illegal drugs were found in the backpack, for which your client was charged. You now get ready to write a motion to suppress the drugs on the theory that the officer did not have probable cause for the warrantless search of the closed container (backpack).

Your research reveals that although the State Constitution protects citizens from unlawful searches, the case law provides facts and holdings that you can use for the suppression motion. You wish to construct a rule synthesis paragraph that weaves together the holdings, rules, and some key facts. Thereafter, you will hone in on a case or two for illustration (next chapter), but for now you are working on an overview. Construct a rule synthesis paragraph from these case summaries, starting first with the leading case in New York:

People v. Gokey, 457 N.E.2d 723 (N.Y. 1983)[3]

A duffel bag that is within the immediate control or "grabbable area" of a suspect at the time of his arrest may not be subjected to a warrantless search incident to the arrest, unless the circumstances leading to the arrest support a reasonable belief that the suspect may gain possession of a weapon or be able to destroy evidence located in the bag. There being no such exigency present at the time police searched defendant's bag, the motion to suppress should have been granted.

Having received a tip from an informant that defendant possessed marijuana and hashish in his possession, five police officers waited at the bus terminal for defendant's arrival. With them was a dog specially trained to detect marijuana. Defendant was observed to be carrying a duffel bag when he disembarked from the bus. Officers approached defendant and informed him that he was under arrest. Defendant was then ordered to place his hands against the wall and to spread his feet so that he could be frisked. When led to the duffel bag, which lay on the ground between defendant's feet, the dog's reaction indicated the presence of marijuana. Defendant was then handcuffed. An officer searched the duffel bag and found approximately 11 ounces of marijuana.

Under the State Constitution, an individual's right of privacy in his or her effects dictates that a warrantless search incident to arrest be deemed unreasonable unless justified by the presence of exigent circumstances. When an individual subjected to arrest has a privacy interest in property within his or her immediate

---

3. The New York Court of Appeals is the state's highest court.

control or "grabbable area," this court has identified two interests that may justify the warrantless search of that property incident to a lawful arrest: the safety of the public and the arresting officer; and the protection of evidence from destruction or concealment.

The People have not asserted the presence of any exigency to justify the warrantless search of defendant's duffel bag. The police sought defendant's arrest for two nonviolent crimes and the People concede that the defendant was not armed. The police permitted defendant to keep the bag between his legs while he was frisked.

Furthermore, the police have not asserted that the search was justified by the need to preserve evidence located in the bag. The presence of any exigency is belied by the police officers' failure to seize the bag immediately upon encountering defendant. By the time the search was undertaken, defendant's hands were handcuffed behind his back, and several police officers and their dogs surrounded him. Therefore, because the police did not fear for their safety, and because they could not have reasonably believed that the search of the bag was necessary to preserve any evidence that might have been located in it, the warrantless search of the bag was invalid.

Fill in the blanks:

You begin to write a rule synthesis paragraph for the rule regarding searching of closed containers (such as the duffel bag in the *Gokey* case). You start to write, and your mind is prompting you to make the following word choices:

A citizen has a privacy interest in his personal effects. In *People v. Gokey*, the Court [~~suppressed~~ or did not suppress (circle one)] evidence stemming from the search of the defendant's backpack when it was found [insert location of the bag in proximity to defendant] __in the immediate area__.

The Court ruled that warrantless searches of closed containers within grab~~bable areas are permissible only when~~ *the safety of*

exigent circumstances __the public or arresting officer and in the interest of preserving the evidence.__

_____

_____

_____

Although *Gokey* is the leading case in the state, your research further reveals that a significant number of cases have facts and holdings that favor the prosecution. To give a balanced rule in your paragraph, you read the following case:

People v. Alvarado, 126 A.D.3d 803, 5 N.Y.S.3d 271 (2d Dep't 2015)[4]

Appeal by the defendant from a judgment of the trial court convicting him of criminal possession of a weapon. The trial court properly denied defendant's motion to suppress physical evidence recovered incident to his arrest. Under the State Constitution, an individual's right of privacy in his or her effects dictates that a warrantless search incident to arrest be deemed unreasonable unless justified by the presence of exigent circumstances. *People v. Gokey,* 457 N.E.2d 723 (N.Y. 1983). For compelling reasons, including the safety of the officers or the public, a search not significantly divorced in time or place from the arrest may be conducted even though the arrested person has been subdued and his closed container is within the exclusive control of the police.

Here, the police officer who arrested the defendant testified that he received a radio report of a shooting at a private house, when he saw the defendant walking on a street approximately five blocks from the subject house. He regularly patrolled the neighborhood and knew the defendant lived at the subject house. He saw that the defendant wore a backpack, and had blood on his pants, his shirt, and his hands. Based on the radio report of a shooting and the defendant's appearance, the officer had reason to believe that he was faced with a dangerous situation.

The officer took the backpack from the defendant and put it on the hood of a nearby car, searched the defendant for weapons, and handcuffed the defendant approximately three feet from the backpack. As soon as the defendant was hand-cuffed, he said that his brother was just shot and that the guns were in the bag. At that point, the officer had probable cause to arrest the defendant for criminal possession of a weapon. The arresting officer properly searched the defendant's backpack incident to the lawful arrest. The People presented evidence establishing exigent circumstances at the time of the arrest that would justify the search. The circumstances supported a reasonable belief that the backpack contained a weapon. The judgment of conviction is affirmed.

Fill in the blanks:

Your writing of the rule synthesis paragraph continues and you wish to contrast this decision with *Gokey.* You begin to write:

In contrast, in *People v. Avarado,* the motion to suppress was [denied or granted (pick one)] by the trial court and affirmed on appeal. The arresting officer [did/did not] lawfully search defendant's backpack, which was [located/placed] on _the suspects back initially, however at the time of the search it had been placed on the hood of the car._ because _defendant told him the guns were in the bag._

_____

---

4. New York's intermediate court.

Exercise 7.1.4: Crafting a Rule from a Series of Cases

Read the facts of Suzy's slip and fall then read the following four case summaries.[5] Fill in the rule synthesis chart, and then construct a rule from your understanding of the case facts and holdings.

Suzy Maudiere was excited to visit the historic sites of Boston. Upon arriving in the city, Suzy went immediately to Faneuil Hall, even though it was 4:30 a.m. on a Monday morning. Suzy went to the main entrance, saw that the shops were closed, but wandered around the building, gazing and pondering the meaning of history. Suzy then slipped and fell on the cobblestones. Although in great pain, Suzy looked around and spotted a brown, leathery banana peel, six inches in length, lying on the floor.

Custodians employed by Faneuil Hall are responsible for sweeping up every night after the businesses close at 9:00 p.m. (6:00 p.m. on Sundays). Suzy comes to your firm asking whether she will be able to recover damages sustained from her fall at Faneuil Hall.

To predict how the court may rule, you need to read through the relevant case law from Massachusetts concerning slip and falls as a result of food left on the floor. You will extract a principle from each case, and then synthesize these principles to create a rule that will likely govern the outcome of this legal issue.

Goddard v. Boston & M. R. R. Co., 60 N.E. 486 (Mass. 1901)

Plaintiff Wilfred Goddard was a passenger on a train operated by the Defendant Boston & Maine Railroad Company. When he got to the Defendant's station in Boston, he stepped off of the train onto the platform. Unfortunately, instead of a clean platform, the plaintiff stepped on a banana peel, which caused him to slip and fall. The Court determined that Goddard could not recover from the railroad company since there were many passengers on the platform, and there was no evidence as to how long the banana peel had been on the platform.

What is the rule from *Goddard v. Boston?*

No liability when discarded peels origin is undeterminable.

and how long it had been there.

no indication

---

5. Adapted with permission from Paul Figley, *Teaching Rule Synthesis with Real Cases,* 61 J. Leg. Ed. 245 (2011).

Anjou v. Boston Elevated Railway Co., 94 N.E. 386 (Mass. 1911)

The plaintiff was a passenger on a train operated by Boston Elevated Railway Co. She arrived on a train at the Dudley Street terminal. After waiting until most of the passengers left the platform, she asked a railway employee for directions to another car. Plaintiff was following the employee along a narrow platform when she slipped and fell on a banana peel. The banana peel was described as being dry, gritty, as if it had been trampled over a good deal, flattened, and all black with no particles of yellow.

The Court explained that one of the duties of railway employees was to keep the platform clear of items that might be a safety hazard. Based on the reported condition of the banana peel, the Court determined it must have been there for a long time and, therefore, the employees of the defendant should have had plenty of time to see and remove it if they were reasonably performing their duty. The Plaintiff was allowed to recover from the railway company.

What is the rule from *Anjou v. Boston*?

When it can be deduced that pieces of discarded fruit have been there for a long time and, should have been picked up, defendant + Plaintiff can recover

Mascary v. Boston Elevated Railway Co., 155 N.E. 637 (Mass. 1927)

The plaintiff was walking down a flight of stairs at Defendant Boston Elevated Railway Co.'s Central Square Station when she slipped and fell. A piece of banana was found under her shoe and, when her husband checked the place where she fell, he found a part of a banana skin that was very black, dry, smoothed down, and soft.

While the Defendant owned and controlled the stairway, it was open to the public. Thus, the Court found that there was no evidence of negligence on the part of the Defendant in this case because the banana peel could have been dropped by a total stranger to the defendant or could have found its way onto the stairs through no fault of the Defendant. Therefore, the plaintiff was not allowed to recover from the railroad company.

What is the rule from *Mascary v. Boston Elevated Railway Company*?

evidence of how long but its origin cant be determined

Scaccia v. Boston Elevated Railway Co., 57 N.E.2d 761 (Mass. 1944)

Plaintiff boarded defendant's bus in Boston. On the floor in the aisle, near the front of the bus, a banana peel lay "four inches long, all black, all pressed down, dirty, covered with sand and gravel, dry and gritty looking." When the plaintiff left the bus nine minutes later, she slipped and fell on the banana peel, which remained in the same position. Only three passengers were in the bus during the trip.

The court found that no one was likely to enter the bus except passengers or bus employees. In the ordinary course of events, no passenger would carry into the bus a banana peel, or a banana, in the condition shown by the agreed facts. Rather, the condition of the banana would result from it laying on the floor for some time. We think that it could be found that the peel had remained on the floor of the bus so long that in the exercise of due care the defendant should have discovered and removed it. Thus the court held that the plaintiff could recover damages associated with her fall.

What is the rule from *Scaccia v. Boston Elevated Railway Company*?

Sufficient evidence that it
was there for awhile

Let's put the rules that you extracted from these cases together in the following table.

Case	Description of Rule
Goddard v. *Boston & M. R. R. Co.*	
Anjou v. *Boston Elevated Ry. Co.*	
Mascary v. *Boston Elevated Ry. Co.*	
Scaccia v. *Boston Elevated Ry. Co.*	

Based on the four rules above, can you create a synthesized rule that could apply to the facts of Suzy's potential claim?

Property owners and transit carriers are liable for when discarded fuels ~~org~~ Place and time of origin ~~can be determined~~ are of such a nature that, defendant should have reasonably performed their duty.

Chapter 7.2

Case Illustrations

I. Case Illustrations Generally
II. Choosing Which Cases to Illustrate
III. Drafting Case Illustrations Effectively
IV. Exercises

I. Case Illustrations Generally

While rules explain how courts determine whether a particular standard is met, case illustrations show how those standards were met in actual cases. As Table 7.2.A explains, case illustrations typically have the following four parts:

Table 7.2.A: Typical Parts of a Case Illustration

The legal principle	A case illustration generally starts by setting forth the legal principle for which you are using the case. This can be done by stating the rule for which you are using the case, the court's holding as to the particular legal issue you are examining, or by providing a general thesis statement as to why you are using the case.
The critical or key facts	A case illustration needs to set out the facts that were critical or key to the court's holding on the legal principle for which you are using the case. In addition, you should set out any additional facts that you deem necessary for your reader to understand the critical or key facts.
The court's holding	A case illustration should include the court's precise holding on the narrow legal issue for which you are illustrating the case.
The court's reasoning	A case illustration should include the court's explanation of why it ruled as it did.

To decide which order is most effective for your case illustrations, it is helpful to review the different functions case illustrations perform and determine whether one or more apply to the legal issue you are analyzing. As shown in the Table 7.2.B below, case illustrations perform a variety of functions.

Table 7.2.B: Functions of a Case Illustration

You will not always need to provide a case illustration in your explanation. The purpose is to help support the applicable legal rule. If the rule standing alone, with its legal citation, is sufficiently clear or no case exists that would facilitate one of the above functions, then just set forth the rule and legal citation without a case illustration.

II. Choosing Which Cases to Illustrate

When you are researching you may find many cases that represent the legal principle at issue. Consider the following guidelines when choosing which cases to illustrate:

- Does the case have similar facts to my client's case?
  - If so, consider illustrating factually analogous cases before cases that are distinguishable.
- What court issued the opinion? (state or federal; level of court)
  - Illustrate cases from the relevant jurisdiction first.
- Is this a case of first impression on my issue?
  - If so, use detailed case illustrations from cases that are the closest factual match.

- Does the opinion contain great language that would strengthen my analysis?
    - Is the holding logical, sound, and clear?
    - Is the court's reasoning sound and convincing?
    - Is the case similar to mine?
- What is the date of the decision?
    - Consider the date the case was decided in determining which order to illustrate your cases.
    - Even if the case is older, is this a landmark case that all of the other cases cite?
    - Is this case too old to be useful?
    - Has the holding been altered by later cases?
    - Is the case so new that its holding has not been tested?
- How did the panel of judges decide the case?
    - Is the holding unanimous? A plurality?
    - Was there a concurrence or dissent?

Remember, you do not need to provide an illustration of a case just because you cited a particular case for the rule. While the case you cite for the overall rule and the case illustration may indeed be the same case, sometimes a certain case is commonly cited for a legal principle, yet another case may be more factually analogous, more recent, or from a higher court and will better serve your application.

III. Drafting Case Illustrations Effectively

When drafting case illustrations, keep the following principles in mind:

- The **facts** of the principal cases are highly important. When the facts of a principal case are similar to those of your client's case, and the case is controlling in the jurisdiction, you will want to have a more detailed case illustration.
- Crop your case illustrations carefully by summarizing the case concisely, bearing in mind the busy reader, and omitting facts that are not crucial for the reader's understanding.
- Use the past tense!
- Identify parties by their role in the case instead of by litigation status or proper names. For instance, use descriptive terms such as landlord, employee, teacher, etc., rather than proper names.
- When constructing a case illustration, focus on that part of the case that is important for your analysis. If you are analyzing a legal issue with more than one element or factor, and the same case deals with both elements or factors, you can **split** the case into more than one case illustration, focusing the information in the case illustration to the element or factor you are analyzing.

IV. Exercises

The goal of these exercises is to help you craft effective case illustrations. The exercises help you to identify the necessary components of an effective case illustration, and provide you with an opportunity to practice drafting case illustrations using the tips set out above.

Exercise 7.2.1: Identifying the Parts of a Case Illustration

Our client, James Doe, was charged with burglary in the second degree.[1] He has provided us with the following facts:

> One evening, Doe had a few too many beers and climbed a neighbor's tree and entered the treehouse the neighbor had constructed for his children. The treehouse, which was approximately 10 feet off the ground, did not have electricity and was primarily used by the neighbor's children as an afternoon play space. It did have a mattress, blankets, pillows, and some folding chairs for sleepovers in the summer months from June through September. The treehouse also contained some miscellaneous items, such as flashlights and a radio.

> Doe listened to some music, and took the flashlight to help him find his way down. He also liked the radio so he put that in his coat pocket. On his way down, the neighbor's dog started barking, alerting the neighbor. Doe's neighbor called the police, and Doe was arrested.

> Doe has been charged with the crime of burglary in the second degree, which requires that the structure entered be a dwelling. The New York Penal Code defines a "dwelling" as a building that is "usually occupied by a person lodging therein at night." N.Y. Penal Law § 140.00(3) (Westlaw 2019).

You found two cases that may be relevant in determining whether the treehouse is a dwelling: *People v. Sheirod*, 124 A.D.2d 14, 510 N.Y.S.2d 945 (4th Dep't 1987), and *People v. Quattlebaum*, 698 N.E.2d 421 (N.Y. 1998). You then drafted the following two case illustrations:

> *What kind of operable utilities.*
>
> In *Sheirod*, a private residence was vacant for a year, was broken into, and a robbery suspect was arrested. In determining whether the suspect should be charged with second or third degree burglary, the court examined whether the residence was a "dwelling" when it was left furnished and with operable utilities, yet unoccupied. The court considered the following factors: (1) the nature of the structure; (2) the intent of the owner to return; and (3) whether on the date of the burglary, a person could have occupied the structure overnight. The court held that although the house was vacant, it was only a "temporary absence." The court reasoned that the structure was suitable for "overnight accommodations," and it could have been so occupied; thus, it was a dwelling.

> *Needs more reasoning why bed that sufficient*
>
> In contrast, in *Quattlebaum,* the Court came to the opposite conclusion. At issue was whether a school that had on its fifth floor two offices with a bed and a chair constituted a "dwelling" under the burglary statute in the second degree. Although the bed was used for an occasional overnight stay, the Court found that the school was not a dwelling. The Court considered the *Sheirod* factors and the nature of how the structure was "usually occupied." The Court said that neither the entire building, nor the office, had the "customary indicia of a residence and its character or attributes."

To determine whether your case illustrations are complete and provide your legal reader with all the necessary information, you examine the case illustrations and look for the following parts:

---

1. The treehouse facts were inspired by an exercise circulating at St. John's University School of Law.

- The legal principle (sometimes called the hook)
- The facts
- The courts' holdings
- The courts' reasoning
- A transition between the cases that discusses the relationship between the cases

Questions:

1. Were both case illustrations complete? If not, identify what was missing in each illustration and how the missing parts might affect a reader's ability to understand the relevance of the cases.

Not enough of a transition.

2. What does the transition "in contrast" signify to you as the reader? Was the hook in the second case illustration effective? If not, why not?

Exercise 7.2.2: Evaluating Case Illustrations for Effectiveness

You are a prosecutor representing the District Attorney's Office in a burglary case in which Destiny Dolich is charged with two separate counts of burglary. You need to determine whether Dolich's theft from Mrs. Molly Izo's "she shed" qualifies as the burglary of "an inhabited dwelling house" under Wyoming's common law burglary standard.

The relevant facts are as follows:

Molly Izo is an artist in Cheyenne, Wyoming. As a hobby, she creates digital artwork from her smart phone (mounted on either canvas or on specialty papers) and sells the artwork at area art fairs and exhibitions. Molly lives on a small, five-acre ranch with her spouse and five children. On her property is her home, a free-standing garage that is connected to the house by an enclosed breezeway, and a separate barn.

Molly also has a "tiny house" structure mounted on a trailer that she uses as both a moveable studio for her art and as a "she shed" in which she can relax and escape from her busy family. She spends several hours each day in the structure and sometimes sleeps in the structure when traveling to regional art fairs. The tiny house is not physically connected to the home, but it is situated 15 feet from the home and is accessible by a covered walkway attached to the enclosed breezeway.

Destiny Dolich broke into the Izo home and stole electronics, jewelry, and a few other small valuables while the Izos were out. During the same theft event, she broke into Molly Izo's shed and stole a computer, a Wacom digital art device, and a high-resolution printer.

For each of the hypothetical examples below, evaluate the effectiveness of the case illustration in light of the Dolich facts.

1. **The *Picaroni* court held that burglary of a garage was not burglary of an inhabited dwelling house. *People v. Picaroni*, 719 P.2d 193, 198–99 (Wyo. 1986).[2]**

Effective or **not effective**: Circle one and explain your reasoning below.

_____

_____

_____

_____

2. **In *People v. Picaroni*, 719 P.2d 193, 198–99 (Wyo. 1986), the Wyoming Supreme Court affirmed Anthony Picaroni's conviction for burglarizing the contents of a poorly lit garage, including two crates of dishes later found in his truck, and rejected Mr. Picaroni's argument that his conviction of burglarizing the garage was inconsistent with his acquittal for burglarizing the main house, because the two crimes were not identical.**

Effective or **not effective**: Circle one and explain your reasoning below.

_____

_____

_____

_____

3. **Under the Wyoming common law burglary rule, burglary of a structure that is not attached to a residence does not qualify as burglary of an inhabited dwelling house. *People v. Picaroni*, 719 P.2d 193, 198–99 (Wyo. 1986). For**

2. Excerpts of cases adapted from Legal Writing Institute materials. The original author of exercise is unknown.

example, in *Picaroni,* the Wyoming Supreme Court held that burglary of an unattached garage constituted a distinct crime from burglary of an adjacent inhabited dwelling because the garage and the house were two unconnected, adjacent buildings, separated by a cement walkway. *Id.* at 199.

Effective or **not effective**: Circle one and explain your reasoning below.

_____

_____

_____

_____

4. On the other hand, the *Cook* court held that a building, which is an attached and integral part of a house, can qualify as "an inhabited dwelling house." *People v. Cook,* 719 P.2d 193, 195 (Wyo. 1986).

Effective or **not effective**: Circle one and explain your reasoning below.

_____

_____

_____

_____

5. In *People v. Cook,* 719 P.2d 193, 195 (Wyo. 1986), the Wyoming Supreme Court affirmed Robert Cook's conviction for an early morning burglary of two chairs, a clock radio, and a tool box from the garage and patio of Michael Van Horn because the garage and patio Mr. Cook burglarized qualified as part of the inhabited dwelling house under the common law burglary rule.

Effective or **not effective**: Circle one and explain your reasoning below.

_____

_____

_____

_____

6. Wyoming common law limits burglary to theft from "an inhabited dwelling house," and the term "inhabited dwelling house" includes any structure that is an attached and integral part of a house. *People v. Cook,* 719 P.2d 193, 195 (Wyo. 1986). The Wyoming Supreme Court affirmed a burglary conviction for burglary of an inhabited dwelling house where the criminal defendant burglarized an enclosed patio and a garage attached to a house. *Id.* at 196. The court held that neither the garage nor the patio were structures separate from the main house but rather "they [were] an integral part of the [victim's]

residence." *Id.* The attached garage in particular was "simply one room of several which together compose[d] the dwelling especially where the garage can be reached through an inside door connecting it to the rest of the residence." *Id.* at 198.

Effective or **not effective**: Circle one and explain your reasoning below.

_____

_____

_____

_____

_____

Exercise 7.2.3: Crafting Case Illustrations

In this exercise, read the following case scenario and the synopses of two cases.

Dr. Young practices with Jackson Physicians For Women in Sparta, North Carolina ("PFW"). Dr. Young alleges the other three doctors in the practice, who are male, treat her poorly. She believes they are jealous of her rapport and popularity with patients.

Dr. Young says that PFW discourages her from providing free medical care to indigent people in the county area. She wants to start her own practice. PFW is the only physician group that provides OB/GYN care in the county. While one other male OB/GYN practices in the county, he practices alone. He appears to be in his sixties and she thinks he may retire before long, though she has nothing specific to back that up.

Dr. Young's legal concern is that she signed an employment agreement with PFW that includes a non-compete covenant with PFW prohibiting her from providing OB/GYN services in Jackson County or any other of the five counties contiguous to Jackson County (approximately fifty miles from the clinic) for thirty-six months. This five-county area represents much of Western North Carolina. Dr. Young came to us to find out if the non-compete provision will be enforceable.

Another associate did some initial research for us. For PFW to enforce the covenant against Dr. Young, it will need to show that the covenant is: (1) in writing, (2) entered into at the time and as part of the contract of employment, (3) based upon reasonable consideration, (4) reasonable both as to time and territory, and (5) not against public policy.

In Exercise 5.2, you organized case authorities to analyze whether the non-compete is reasonable as to time and territory. Now your supervising attorney wants you to analyze whether the non-compete agreement may violate public policy. She has some notes on the cases and asks you to create some case illustrations so that she can have the relevant law summarized for use in an objective memo or client letter. (She is not asking you to apply the cases to the facts of Dr. Young's claim at this time.)

Iredell Digestive Disease Clinic v. Petrozza, 373 S.E.2d 449 (N.C. Ct. App. 1988)

In this case, the Plaintiff, Iredell Digestive Disease Clinic (the Clinic) was a professional association that provided medical services and specialized in gastroenterology. The Clinic hired the Defendant, Dr. Petrozza, who signed a covenant not to compete. The non-compete provided that should Dr. Petrozza's employment be terminated, he would not compete for three years in a twenty mile radius of Statesville or a five-mile radius of any hospital served by the Clinic, whichever was greater. Thereafter, Dr. Petrozza and the Clinic had a disagreement over the potential partnership agreement. Dr. Petrozza resigned and then started his own practice in the Statesville area.

The Clinic sued, *inter alia,* for enforcement of the non-compete agreement. The Court found that the covenant was reasonable in terms of time and territory. The Court nonetheless invalidated it on public policy grounds because enforcing the non-compete would effectively deprive Statesville residents of necessary medical care. The Court explained that, "if ordering the covenantor to honor his contractual obligations would create a substantial question of harm to the public health, then the public interest outweighs the contract interests of the covenantee and the court may refuse to enforce the covenant. If ordering the covenantor to honor his agreement will merely inconvenience the public without causing substantial harm, then the covenantee is entitled to have the contract enforced."

The Court reasoned that if the covenant were enforced, lives could be lost as a result of the distance patients would have to travel to reach either Dr. Petrozza or another doctor with his qualifications. The Court was also concerned that if the non-compete were to be enforced, it would create a monopoly on behalf of the Clinic. A monopoly could, in turn, impact fees for the public and would leave few, if any, doctors available for emergencies. The Court emphasized that patients must have some choice in their selection of physicians.

Statesville Medical Grp., P.A. v. Dickey, 418 S.E.2d 256 (N.C. Ct. App. 1992)

In this case, the defendant, Dr. Dickey, was an endocrinologist who signed a covenant against competition when he began his employment with Statesville Medical Group (the Medical Group). The non-compete prohibited Dr. Dickey from practicing medicine in Iredell County for two years from the date of termination of employment with the Medical Group.

However, the two parties came to odds, and Dr. Dickey tendered his resignation causing the Medical Group to attempt renegotiating with him. After the negotiations fell through, Dr. Dickey told the Medical Group that his earlier resignation was still effective and opened his own practice. Dr. Dickey was the only doctor in his area with a specialty in endocrinology. After his resignation, the Medical Group contracted for a part-time doctor to perform the defendant's specialty. The court held that even though the time and territory restrictions were reasonable, enforcing the non-compete would violate public policy. The court reiterated the rule from *Petrozza:* "if ordering the covenantor to honor his contractual obligations would create a substantial question of harm to the public health, then the public interest outweighs the contract interests of the covenantee and the court may refuse to enforce the covenant. If ordering the covenantor to honor his agreement will merely inconvenience the public without causing substantial harm, then the covenantee is entitled to have the contract enforced."

The Court explained that enforcement would give the Medical Group a monopoly, thus erasing fee competition. The Court also held that patients' access to their physician of choice and ability to procure a second opinion would be impaired by enforcement. The distance to another doctor at all times, especially during an emergency, was also seen as a detriment to the public.

Draft a case illustration for each case above.

1. *Iredell Digestive Disease Clinic v. Petrozza*:

_____

_____

_____

_____

_____

_____

_____

_____

_____

_____

_____

_____

_____

_____

_____

_____

_____

_____

2. *Statesville Medical Grp., P.A. v. Dickey*:

_____

_____

_____

_____

_____

_____

_____

_____

_____

_____

_____

_____

_____

_____

_____

_____

_____

_____

_____

_____

_____

_____

_____

_____

_____

Chapter 8
Applying the Law: Introduction

One of the more critical skills a lawyer needs is the ability to apply the law to the facts. Successful application of law to fact will influence how your advice will be received by the supervising partner or, later, by a judge (when writing persuasive briefs).

Attorneys use two types of reasoning techniques in the application section: rule-based reasoning and analogical reasoning. In the first type, you will directly apply a rule to the facts. In the second type, analogical reasoning, you will compare and contrast the relevant law provided in the case explanation section with the facts of your client's case and weigh the primary and opposing arguments to predict the most likely outcome.

In either type of application, you will want to prove that your assertion is true by showing the reader how the law supports (or not) the facts of your client's case. The application section is like a geometry proof—it shows each step of the analytic process. The following subchapters will provide you with explanations and exercises to help you develop both types of reasoning.

Chapter 8.1
Rule-Based Reasoning

I. **Rule-Based Reasoning Generally**

II. **Exercises**

I. Rule-Based Reasoning Generally

Rule-based reasoning is the simplest tool an attorney can use to predict an outcome. To use rule-based reasoning, apply the language of the rule directly to the client's facts. We use rule-based reasoning when there is no ambiguity about the rule, when there is no need for detailed case explanations for term definition, or when there is no analogous case that will help illustrate how the rule has functioned in past cases.

The application section is always considered the heart of any legal analysis and requires a critical analysis of whether the rule (or any element, factor, or component of the rule) is met. When constructing a rule-based application, you will want to

- Integrate key language from the rule into the application of the client's facts.
- Describe your client's facts with **concrete and specific** detail.

Figure 8.1.A: The Process for Rule-Based Reasoning

Taking care to be precise and descriptive in your application will enable you to effectively weigh the various arguments and predict which outcome is most likely.

II. Exercises

The exercises below will help you learn how to effectively utilize rule-based application techniques.

Exercise 8.1.1: Identifying When Terms in a Statute Apply to Your Client's Facts

A long-term client of the firm, Paul Bitters, called and spoke with your senior partner, LaTonia Matthews. Mr. Bitters wants to know if he has a potential cause of action against Sunblock, Inc. for using a photograph of him in one of their advertisements without his permission. Ms. Matthews's notes regarding the phone call are set forth below:

> Paul Bitters complains that he was sunbathing on the rooftop of his apartment building in upstate New York. He placed a towel over his face and immediately went to sleep. Unfortunately, as he slept, he received a scorching sunburn. He was wearing only a bathing suit. By the afternoon, when Bitters's sunburn was quite red, a person approached him and took his picture. Bitters woke up, removed the towel, and saw the photographer as he was exiting the rooftop. A day later, Bitters saw his photograph appeared in an advertisement for Sunblock, Inc., a company that makes suntan products. The advertisement showed his full face and body, not his name, with the words on the bottom, "Smear it, Don't burn it."

After researching you find Section 51 of the New York Civil Rights Law that creates a civil cause of action for the invasion of the right of privacy.

Underline, circle, or highlight the words of the statute that may be applicable to Bitters's potential case so that you can provide an initial response.

> ### *New York Civil Rights Law,* § 51. Right of privacy—Civil Remedies
>
> Section 51 states: "Any person whose name, portrait, picture or voice is used within this state for advertising purposes or for the purpose of trade without having obtained the written consent of such person, or if a minor of his or her parent or guardian, may maintain an equitable action . . . to prevent and restrain the use thereof, and may also sue and recover damages for any injuries sustained by reason of such use."

Exercise 8.1.2: Applying the Restatement of Contracts to Your Client's Facts

In addition to statutes, rules may come from other authority, such as the Restatement, which is a scholarly treatise that courts can choose to incorporate into their jurisprudence.

> Candy and Thomas Adajian reside in Allentown, Pennsylvania and were fundraising for their favorite charity, a local hospital for children with disabilities. They were introduced to a prospective donor, Danny Warbucks. The Adajians told Warbucks that they had raised only $200,000 to date for improvements and that a new

wing, which was needed for the community, would cost $1.5 million. Warbucks promised to donate $1 million to construct a wing for the hospital, although he did not put his promise in writing. The Adajians, feeling grateful for his generosity, told Warbucks that his name would be added to a sign that will adorn the new wing: "Warbucks Wing."

In anticipation of the large donation, the Adajians contracted with an architect to develop plans. The architect got started on the project and sent them a bill for her initial work totaling twenty hours, which came to $3,000. When the Adajians reached out to Warbucks for his pledge, Warbucks said he changed his mind. He also refused to pay the architect's bill saying, "Easy come, easy dough."

The Adajians do not have the money to cover the architect's bill, and neither does the hospital, and now they come to you for advice. You find a Restatement provision that addresses the issue of promissory estoppel, along with two cases indicating that Pennsylvania has incorporated the Restatement (Second) of Contracts, section 90, into its state jurisprudence.

The relevant section of the Restatement (Second) of Contracts § 90 (Am. Law Inst. 1981):

(1) A promise which the promisor should reasonably expect to induce action or forbearance on the part of the promisee or a third person and which does induce such action or forbearance is binding if injustice can be avoided only by enforcement of the promise. The remedy granted for breach may be limited as justice requires.

Pennsylvania case law:

Crouse v. Cyclops Indus., 745 A.2d 606 (Pa. 2000)

The court stated that when there is no enforceable agreement between the parties because the agreement is not supported by consideration, the doctrine of promissory estoppel is invoked. The doctrine avoids injustice by making enforceable a promise made by one party to the other when the promisee relies on the promise and therefore changes his position to his own detriment (citing the Restatement (Second) Contracts § 90 (Am. Law Inst. 1981)). Because promissory estoppel is invoked to avoid injustice, it permits an equitable remedy to a contract dispute. Thus, because promissory estoppel makes otherwise unenforceable agreements binding, the doctrine "sounds in contract law."

Iversen Baking Co. v. Western Foods, 874 F. Supp. 96, 102 (E.D. Pa. 1995)

The court explained that in Pennsylvania, a promissory estoppel claim, based upon Restatement (Second) of Contracts, can only exist in the absence of a contract. Promissory estoppel is an equitable remedy used only when no contract exits; "it is not designed to protect parties who do not adequately memorialize their contracts in writing." The claims of breach of contract and promissory estoppel may be pleaded in the alternative, but if the court finds that a contract exists, the promissory estoppel claim will fall.

1. The cases cited above indicate that Pennsylvania courts have incorporated § 90, Promissory Estoppel, into state doctrine. Enumerate below the elements of § 90(1). (Note: A promisor is the person making the promise.)

Promissor could reasonably expect
to induce action or forbearance

does induce

injustice can't be avoided otherwise

2. How do the elements apply to the Adajians? (Hint: Apply each element one at a time.)

Could reasonably expect they would
start making plan for the wing.

They did start making the plans

Cant be avoided because P's and
hospital cant cover the bill.

Exercise 8.1.3: Evaluating the Effectiveness of Rule-Based Applications

Read through the facts of your client's case below and decide which rule-based application is effective or not effective. Explain your responses in the space provided below.

May O'Brien comes to you for advice. Her niece, Dolly Haggerty, was riding her bicycle across railroad tracks when a car struck and killed her. O'Brien lives separately from her niece but near the railroad tracks and heard the crash of a car. She ran out of her house and a few minutes after the accident occurred, May arrived at the scene, in time to witness her niece's body being covered up by a sheet.

You research and find a case on point:

Thing v. La Chusa, 771 P.2d 814 (Cal. 1989)

In this case, John Thing, a minor, was injured when struck by an automobile operated by defendant James La Chusa. John's mother, plaintiff, was nearby, but neither saw nor heard the accident. She became aware of the injury to her son when told by a daughter that John had been struck by a car. The mother sued defendant alleging that she suffered Negligent

Inflction of Emotional Distress (NIED) as a result of these events, and that the injury to John and emotional distress she suffered were proximately caused by defendant's negligence. The court stated:

> We hold that the mother cannot recover damages from the driver for NIED because she did not witness the accident. A plaintiff may recover damages for emotional distress caused by observing the negligently inflicted injury of a third person if, but only if, said plaintiff : (1) is closely related to the injury victim; (2) is present at the scene of the injury producing event at the time it occurs and is then aware that it is causing injury to the victim; and (3) as a result suffers serious emotional distress—a reaction beyond that which would be anticipated in a distinterested witness and which is not an abnormal response to the circumstances. Although we are not faced with this issue of close relations, the rule in this state is that only relatives residing in the same household, or parents, siblings, and grandparents of the victim may recover.

In an interoffice memorandum of law to a supervising attorney in your firm, which of the following is more effective in communicating the rule from *Thing v. LaChusa* and applying it to the facts of May's case?

Sample 1

To recover for NIED, the plaintiff must be a close relative to the victim and be present at the scene of the accident. Our client, May O'Brien was neither.

Sample 2

To recover for NIED, plaintiff must meet all three criteria: (1) closely related to the injury victim; (2) present at the scene of the injury producing event at the time it occurs and is then aware that it is causing injury to the victim; and (3) as a result of the injury, suffers serious emotional distress. Ms. O'Brien does not meet the first or second element.

Sample 3

To recover for NIED, plaintiff must meet all three criteria: (1) closely related to the injury victim; (2) present at the scene of the injury producing event at the time it occurs and is then aware that it is causing injury to the victim; and (3) as a result of the injury, suffers serious emotional distress. By law, Ms. O'Brien is not closely related to her niece, the victim. In *dictum*, the *Thing* court explained that only relatives residing in the same household, or parents, siblings, and grandparents of the victim may recover. Ms. O'Brien is an aunt, not any of the permitted relations. Furthermore, Ms. O'Brien was not at the scene of the accident when it occurred, the second criterion for recovery. Distinguishable from the *Thing* case is that Ms. O'Brien heard the crash, whereas the mother in *Thing* did not hear nor see the accident, leaving her without recovery. However, our client would still not recover because of the first criterion, even if she can establish the third criterion, that she suffers serious emotional distress.

Sample two.

Exercise 8.1.4: Crafting a Rule-Based Application

Consider the following set of facts and controlling law, then fill out the charts that follow.

Stacy Bold entered the First Savings Bank. She was lingering near the back table where a teller saw her writing something on a piece of paper. The teller took note of her because Bold was acting "nervous and agitated." Ten minutes later, Bold left the bank. The teller went over to where Bold had been standing and noticed a piece of paper that was crumpled up. The teller opened the piece of paper and it said the words, "Give me all the money in your cash drawer. I have a gun and I am not afraid to use it!" The teller immediately called the police. She provided them with a description of Bold and a copy of the note. The police found Bold in a nearby coffee shop and arrested her. The police found a loaded pistol in her jacket.

You work as an Assistant District Attorney in New York. The District Attorney would like to charge her with Robbery, or Attempted Robbery, and asks you to send her a short written response whether the statute applies to Bold's situation.

Read through the applicable statutory section and then complete the chart below to craft your response.

New York Penal Law
§ 160.15 Robbery in the First Degree

A person is guilty of robbery in the first degree when he forcibly steals property and when, in the course of the commission of the crime or of immediate flight therefrom, he or another participant in the crime:

1. Causes serious physical injury to any person who is not a participant in the crime; or
2. Is armed with a deadly weapon; or
3. Uses or threatens the immediate use of a dangerous instrument; or
4. Displays what appears to be a pistol, revolver, rifle, shotgun, machine gun or other firearm; except that in any prosecution under this subdivision, it is an affirmative defense that such pistol, revolver, rifle, shotgun, machine gun or other firearm was not a loaded weapon from which a shot, readily capable of producing death or other serious physical injury, could be discharged. Nothing contained in this

subdivision shall constitute a defense to a prosecution for, or preclude a conviction of, robbery in the second degree, robbery in the
third degree or any other crime.

New York Penal Law
§ 110.00 Attempt to Commit a Crime

A person is guilty of an attempt to commit a crime when, with intent to
commit a crime, he engages in conduct which tends to effect the commission of such crime.

Use the charts below to construct a rule-based application and counter-application. As
you read the statute of Robbery in the First Degree, you are certain that the charge of Robbery would not pertain to Stacy Bold. Explain below:

Step 1: Describe the potentially relevant provisions of § 160.15, First Degree Robbery.	(a) (2) (3) The potentially relevant provisions are lines (2) and (3) which focus on presence of deadly weapons and threats of immediate use
Step 2: Integrate key language from the rule with the concrete and specific facts of Bold's case to support why you believe it should not apply to Bold's situation.	Police found a loaded pistol in her jacket thus, she was armed with a deadly weapon. didn't forcibly steal was armed but didn't forcibly steal
Step 3: Describe the relevant portions of § 110, Attempt to Commit a Crime, that could be potentially applicable. (Again, here, you do not think it will be controlling given Bold's facts, but state the pertinent language.)	No attempt because she crumpled up and left the bank before acting on any of her intentions
Step 4: Describe why § 110 probably does not apply to Bold's facts.	Began: All that materialized of her attempt was a not stating her intent however,
Step 5: Set out your conclusion.	Ms. Bold's actions does not constitute ~~an attempt to commit a crime~~ first degree robbery or an attempt to commit a crime because she did not forcibly steal any property nor did she actually perpetrate the crime she ↑ take steps to begin or ~~attempt~~ to perpetrate.

Chapter 8.2
Analogical Reasoning

I. Analogical Reasoning Generally

Analogical reasoning allows lawyers to predict how the reasoning of a prior case will extend to a current legal issue by comparing the similarities and differences between the prior case and a client's case. After stating the rule in the case explanation section, you will use a case illustration to fully explain that legal rule and then you will compare that case with your own in the application section. Analogical reasoning is powered by stare decisis. If an attorney can establish that a client's case is factually similar to a binding prior case, then the court will be bound by the outcome in the prior case. On the other hand, if an attorney can distinguish a prior case, then the court would not be bound by the prior case.

II. Techniques for Effective Analogical Reasoning

You can construct an effective analogical argument with the following steps.

Figure 8.2.A: Three-Step Process for Analogical Reasoning

Sometimes you may do a separate application for each case; other times, you may discuss several cases first and construct a joint application. You may also apply the facts from a case that you believe controls the outcome, and then you may want to add a counter-argument by distinguishing a case with an opposing outcome.

Some other tips to constructing effective analogical arguments include:

- Compare or contrast facts that are directly relevant to the legal principle being analyzed.
- Compare specific facts from the prior cases to the specific facts of your client's case.
- Make sure your case illustration is sufficiently complete so that you do not need new information about the prior case in the application section.

III. Incorporating Counter-Arguments

As we have discussed in previous chapters, to fully develop an application in a legal analysis, you need to address both sides of the argument.

A. Unfavorable Authorities

When you have unfavorable authorities,[1] you may want to consider using one or more of the arguments in Table 8.2.B below, depending on whether the case is binding or persuasive.

Table 8.2.B: Ways to Use Unfavorable Authorities

Type of Authority	Argument
Binding or persuasive	• The case is inconsistent with another binding authority.
Binding or persuasive	• Materially distinguishable facts can explain the adverse result.
Binding or persuasive	• The court's holding may be adverse to your client, but on a closer reading of the law, the reasoning actually supports your client's position.
Binding	• The case has been superseded by subsequent legislation/regulation/case or other change in the law.
Persuasive	• The case is not binding because it is from another jurisdiction (or from a trial court in this jurisdiction).
Persuasive	• The case is non-precedential (for instance, an unreported decision).
Persuasive	• The case represents a minority view among courts that have resolved the issue or is against the trend in other jurisdictions.
Persuasive	• Policy argument—the case will lead to bad results in the future.

---

1. Adapted from teaching materials prepared by Professor Russell Gold and Professor John Korzen, Wake Forest University School of Law.

B. Organizational Schemes

Below are three organizational schemes you may want to consider as a starting point, depending on the type of counter-argument present (if any) in the case. You will see that these proposed organizations follow the analytic templates (IRAC, TREAC, CREAC, CRExAC, CRRPAP) we discussed in Chapter 6, *One Legal Argument*. As always, consider these proposed organizational schemes as a starting point and continue to revise until you determine the most effective organization for your analysis.

Proposed Organization # 1
(Use for analyses in which there are cases with opposing outcomes.)

Statute (or statutory sub-section or element) or case element, factor, or component

Rule Synthesis statement or paragraph, if applicable

Case 1 illustration of the relevant legal principle being analyzed using an analogous case(s)

Application of Case 1 by comparing factual similarities of precedent with client's facts

Case 2 illustration of the relevant legal principle being analyzed by distinguishing an adverse case(s)

Application of Case 2 by distinguishing facts of precedent with client's facts

Conclusion

Proposed Organization # 2
(Use for analyses in cases in which there are opposing outcomes.)

Statute (or statutory sub-section or element) or case element, factor, or component

Rule Synthesis statement or paragraph, if applicable

Case 1 illustration of the relevant legal principle being analyzed (using analogous case(s))

Case 2 illustration of the relevant legal principle being analyzed (distinguishing adverse case(s))

Application of cases 1 and 2 using analogies to and distinctions from precedent to client's facts.

Conclusion

Proposed Organization # 3

(Use for cases in which the client's facts may support both the primary and opposing arguments.)

Statute (or statutory sub-section or element) or case element, factor, or component

Rule Synthesis statement or paragraph

Case illustrations of the relevant legal principle being analyzed

Application including comparison of strong facts of client's case to facts of the precedent case(s)

Application distinguishing weak facts of client's case that differ from the precedent cases and that the opposing side may point out

Weighing the analogies and distinctions and predicting the likely outcome.

Conclusion

There are always various effective organizations for any type of legal analysis. The most effective organization will depend on the particular legal issue you are analyzing, the relevant law, and the critical facts of the client's case. So, you can alter the organizational schemes above and combine proposed structures or follow another analytic structure. The bottom line is that you should find the organization that will allow you to communicate your legal analysis in the most effective and credible manner possible.

IV. Exercises

The exercises below are designed to help you understand how to use analogical reasoning to draft effective application sections and to incorporate counter-arguments. In the first exercise, 8.2.1, you will evaluate excerpts of application to determine whether they are effective and why. In the next two exercises, you will practice drafting an application section based on a single binding case, and then practice will be expanded to drafting an application section based upon two cases. Finally, in the last exercise, you will read both a landmark case and a more recent case, and then apply the legal rule to various hypothetical facts.

Exercise 8.2.1: Evaluating Excerpts of Application Sections for Effectiveness[2]

Stuart Rich comes to our office to obtain advice on a possible lawsuit he would like to bring against Nighty-Night Motel for the actions of its employee, Hugh Gerald. Rich tells us the following story:

> In August, Rich and his family had gone on a cross-country vacation. They stopped in Mudville, Massachusetts for the night, after visiting the Twine Museum, a museum that touted having the largest ball of twine in the U.S. They checked into the Nighty-Night Motel. After checking into their room, Rich went to the bar and

---

2. Adapted from teaching materials provided by Professor Laura Graham, Wake Forest University School of Law.

had several beers. He then decided to take a swim. He took a big leap off the diving board and did a belly flop, splashing water all over the other guests.

Gerald, the pool attendant, told Rich to get out of the pool. Rich went back to the diving board and attempted to do a back flip off the diving board. Rich missed and hit his head on the board. He was able to get out of the pool on his own but felt disoriented. He walked unsteadily to Gerald and told him he needed help. He stated, "My head hurts and I am dizzy." Gerald responded, "You're drunk. Your head looks okay." Rich then responded, "I'm telling you, I don't feel good." Gerald became aggravated and said, "I suggest you go back to your room and sleep it off."

Rich started walking back to his room but passed out and fell to the ground. He shattered his right arm. The injuries required extensive surgery. He will never again have full use of his right arm.

Another associate researches the issue and determines that Rich was a business invitee of the Nighty-Night Motel when the injury occurred. He finds a case called *Osterlind v. Hill*, and he drafts an objective analysis. He asks you to critique the application section.

Here is the relevant case illustration your colleague drafted:

An owner owes a duty to assist an invitee if the invitee is helpless and the owner places the invitee in danger. *Osterlind v. Hill*, 160 N.E. 301, 302 (Mass. 1928). In *Osterlind*, the defendant, Mr. Hill, had rented a canoe to Osterlind, the invitee, who was intoxicated. *Id.* Although the canoe was not faulty, it overturned in the water, and Osterlind clung to its side for one-half hour while yelling for help. *Id.* Hill heard the cries but did not assist, and Osterlind drowned. *Id.* The Court held that Hill did not owe Osterlind a duty of care and was therefore not negligent. *Id.* The court explained that Osterlind, by hanging onto the canoe and yelling for one-half hour, was capable of exercising care for his own safety.

Below are several draft sentences from your colleague's application section. Read through each excerpt, determine whether the excerpt is effective, and explain your reasoning.

1. **Rich's case is distinguishable from the facts in *Osterlind*. In *Osterlind*, the invitee caused his own imperilment and acted to protect himself by calling for assistance, which the court viewed as an indication that the invitee was not helpless. Such was not the case here. Thus, Rich likely has a claim against the Nighty-Night Motel.**

Effective or ~~not effective~~? (Circle one and explain your reasoning below.)

Doesn't explain why Rich was actually helpless.

2. Like in *Osterlind,* where Hill did not provide help to Osterlind, Gerald, the pool attendant, made Rich leave the pool without medical attention and told him to "sleep it off," even though Rich was dizzy and disoriented.

Effective or not effective? (Circle one and explain your reasoning below.)

> In osterlind Ô Didn't need to
> Provide help, stating this would
> only work against Rich.

3. Ignoring Rich's dizziness, Gerald offered Rich substandard advice to "sleep off" a head injury. Gerald's offer of advice differs from the facts in *Osterlind*, where Hill did not provide assistance to Osterlind. Rich will argue that a reasonable person could foresee that he was walking unsteadily, thus helpless. Rich was in danger of passing out and therefore in no condition to walk home unaided.

Effective or not effective? (Circle one and explain your reasoning below.)

> No could be walking unsteadily
> because he was drunk.

4. Unlike the invitee in *Osterlind*, Rich was verbally recognized by the pool attendant to be intoxicated and was asked to leave the pool area. Rich did not heed the request, but this distinction is not controlling.

Effective or not effective? (Circle one and explain your reasoning below.)

5. Rich will likely be able to prove that he was helpless, and that Gerald had a duty to provide medical aid. Immediately after Rich hit his head, he could barely lift himself out of the pool, was disoriented from the injury, and asked Gerald for help. Unlike the *Osterlind* victim, who was able to hang on for thirty minutes, Rich needed help right away. In *Osterlind*, the court held that the victim was not helpless because he was able to hang onto a canoe for thirty minutes. In the present case, the action was much more immediate; Rich fell shortly after leaving the pool. Gerald, the pool attendant, failed to recognize Rich's helplessness and then put him in a situation of peril by making him leave immediately without medical attention when Rich was dizzy and disoriented.

Effective or **not effective?** (Circle one and explain your reasoning below.)

_____

_____

_____

_____

_____

_____

Exercise 8.2.2: Crafting an Analogical-Based Application

Your senior partner calls you into her office. She has just met with a potential new client, Ms. Nikki Hornfeck. The senior partner gives you her notes from that meeting and the relevant case authority, *Robinson v. Lindsay* (set forth below). She would like you to analyze whether, given the rule in *Robinson,* the Hornfecks may have a viable claim for negligence.

To: Joe Whang (Junior Partner)
From: Laura Thomas (Senior Partner)
Date: August 18
Re: Meeting with Ms. Nikki Hornfeck

On June 28, fifteen-year old Ted Dewey and fourteen-year old Morgan Hornfeck were hanging out at Morgan's house when Ted mentioned that he would like to go rock climbing. Ted had gone rock climbing with his father and sister on a few occasions. Ted recommended that they go to Winterfell Park to scale a 40-foot cliff called Shaky Peak. Morgan agreed, but told his mother only that the two were going to the park and did not tell her about the rock-climbing plans. Mrs. Hornfeck allowed the boys to go to Winterfell Park, but said that Morgan had to bring his younger brother, Brian, who was 13 years old.

Upon reaching Shaky Peak, Ted unpacked his gear and recommended that he and Morgan attempt a simule climb.[3] When Ted took out the gear from its packaging, both he and Morgan saw the warning label on the package saying, "For

---

3. A simule climb is a style where two climbers climb at the same time while tied to the same rope.

Expert Climbers Only!" Ted recommended this climb because he had learned it from his father, an excellent climber. Before making the climb, Ted spent about 30 minutes instructing Morgan on the proper techniques to avoid the dangers of the climb. Within the hour, the two boys successfully climbed the 40-foot peak with relative ease.

Brian, however, also wanted to climb and boasted about his tree climbing abilities. After listening to Brian's pleas, Ted said that Brian could climb alone. Although Ted had never participated in this type of climb, he had seen his father and older sister handle single climbers.

Ted told Brian how to fasten the harness. Ted proceeded to hammer the top anchor into the rock face. Although Ted had seen his father tie a double bowline knot for this type of climb, he did not know how to tie that type of knot. Because he could not tie the knot, Ted decided to put on his climbing gloves and hold the rope, figuring that he was strong enough to hold the weight of the much smaller Brian.

As Brian began to climb, he moved skillfully and did not need to rely on Ted for support. While about 30-feet from the bottom, Brian suddenly lost his footing, causing him to fall backward. This jolt took Ted by surprise and the rope slid through his hands unexpectedly. The rope slid through the anchor, and Brian went crashing to the ground. Brian broke both legs in multiple places, and he required extensive hospitalizations, surgery, physical rehabilitation, and therapy.

Brian's mother, Mrs. Hornfeck, wants to know whether she will succeed in a negligence claim against Ted (through his parents) for his role in Brian's fall. Mrs. Hornfeck said she has contacted the Deweys who stated that Ted should not be liable because a child should not be held to an adult level standard of care.

Robinson v. Lindsay, 598 P.2d 392 (Wash. 1979)[4]

An action seeking damages for personal injuries was brought on behalf of Kelly Robinson who lost full use of a thumb in a snowmobile accident when she was 11 years of age. [Being a minor, her Guardian Ad Litem brought this case against (minor) Billy Anderson and two sets of parents—the Lindsays and the Andersons).] Billy Anderson, 13 years of age at the time of the accident, was the driver of the snowmobile at issue. After a jury verdict in favor of Anderson, the trial court ordered a new trial, and defendants appealed. [Defendants are the petitioners.]

The single issue on appeal is whether a minor operating a snowmobile is to be held to an adult standard of care. The trial court failed to instruct the jury as to that standard and ordered a new trial because it believed the jury should have been so instructed. We agree and affirm the order granting a new trial. For the reasons set forth below, we hold that the minor should have been held to the standard of care expected of an adult.

In the courts' search for a uniform standard of behavior to use in determining whether or not a person's conduct has fallen below minimal acceptable standards, the law has developed a fictitious person, the "reasonable man of ordinary prudence." *Vaughan v. Menlove*, 132 Eng. Rep. 490 (1837).

Exceptions to the reasonable person standard developed when the individual whose conduct was alleged to have been negligent suffered from some physical impairment, such as blindness, deafness, or lameness. Courts also found it nec-

---

4. Language from this case has been edited and adapted for the purposes of this exercise.

essary, as a practical matter, to depart considerably from the objective standard when dealing with children's behavior. Children are traditionally encouraged to pursue childhood activities without the same burdens and responsibilities with which adults must contend. *See* Bahr, *Tort Law and the Games Kids Play*, 23 S.D.L. Rev. 725 (1978). As a result, courts evolved a special standard of care to measure a child's negligence in a particular situation.

In *Roth v. Union Depot Co.*, 43 P. 641 (Wash. 1896), Washington has joined "the overwhelming weight of authority" in distinguishing between the capacity of a child and that of an adult. As the court then stated, "[I]t would be a monstrous doctrine to hold that a child of inexperience—and experience can come only with years—should be held to the same degree of care in avoiding danger as a person of mature years and accumulated experience." *Id.* at 647.

However, this case is the first to consider the question of a child's liability for injuries sustained as a result of his or her operation of a motorized vehicle or participation in an inherently dangerous activity.

Courts in other jurisdictions have created an exception to the special child standard because of the apparent injustice that would occur if a child who caused injury while engaged in certain dangerous activities were permitted to defend himself by saying that other children similarly situated would not have exercised a degree of care higher than his, and he is, therefore, not liable for his tort. Some courts have couched the exception in terms of children engaging in an activity, which is normally one for adults only. We believe a better rationale is that when the activity a child engages in is inherently dangerous, as is the operation of powerful mechanized vehicles, the child should be held to an adult standard of care.

Such a rule protects the need of children to be children but at the same time discourages immature individuals from engaging in inherently dangerous activities. Children will still be free to enjoy traditional childhood activities without being held to an adult standard of care. Although accidents sometimes occur as the result of such activities, they are not activities generally considered capable of resulting in "grave danger to others and to the minor himself if the care used in the course of the activity drops below that care which the reasonable and prudent adult would use . . . ." *Daniels v. Evans*, 224 A.2d 63, 64 (N.H. 1966).

At the time of the accident, the 13-year-old petitioner had operated snowmobiles for about 2 years. When the injury occurred, petitioner was operating a 30-horsepower snowmobile at speeds of 10 to 20 miles per hour. The record indicates that the machine itself was capable of 65 miles per hour. Because petitioner was operating a powerful motorized vehicle, he should be held to the standard of care and conduct expected of an adult.

The order granting a new trial is affirmed.

Create a chart to help identify relevant comparisons or distinctions for your application.

	Robinson Facts	Hornfeck Facts
Possible comparisons/ analogies		
Possible contrasts/ distinctions	• Snow Mobile	• Rock climbing.

Now that you have identified the analogies and distinctions, draft a case explanation and application using the table below that has broken the process down into steps.

Step 1: Draft a statement about the legal issue of whether the standard of care applies to Ted's actions. (This statement may also be known as the "hook.")	The Rock climbing undertaken by Ted is an inherently dangerous activity, that does not afford him freedom from liability because of his age
Step 2: Identify and draft the legal rule or principle you derived from *Robinson v. Lindsay*. (Hint: Use the present tense when you draft the rule.)	~~Children~~ when undertaking normal childhood activities are not held to the same standard of care as adults. However, when a childs activity is inherently dangerous, they owe a duty to exercise the same level of reasonable care as an adult.
Step 3: Draft the relevant facts, holding, and reasoning from the *Robinson* case to explain or prove how the rule you identified in Step 2 has functioned previously. (Hint: Use the past tense when you draft the illustration.)	• ~~under took~~

Step 4: Draft the application by applying the law to your facts, making sure to explicitly identify the comparisons (analogies) or contrasts (distinctions) you see between *Robinson* and the facts of the Hornfeck matter.	Saw the warning label that said equipment was for use by expert climbers only. Didn't tell his mom because knew she would object to an inherently dangerous activity. • Always done w/ his dad, thus knew it was an adult activity
Step 5: Based on the case explanation and application above, what is your prediction as to whether the court is likely to hold Ted to an adult standard of care based on the facts of *Robinson*?	

Exercise 8.2.3: Analogizing and Distinguishing Cases in the Application

Burton Price is the co-owner of an art brokerage firm based in Boone, North Carolina and his firm represents a number of artists in the Appalachian region. He comes to our firm to see if he may have a claim against a former employee, Marcus Earle.[5] Price provides us the following facts:

About a month ago, Price fired Earle because Earle had become increasingly insubordinate to Price and Price's co-owner Carol Chan. Earle had on several occasions been "rude" to clients of the firm. In addition, Price discovered that Earle had been very active on social media, constantly tweeting controversial remarks during the workday.

Price's firing of Earle did not go smoothly. Earle was quite upset, claiming that Price and Chan were prejudiced and "out to get him." He threatened to sue them and "bring their little business down." The following week, Price attended the annual Buncombe County Arts and Crafts show, located in the Buncombe County Convention Center. Unfortunately, Earle was also at the show. Earle spotted Price talking to Bill and Maryjane Constantine about the possibility of representing them in brokering some of their art. The Constantines apparently paint religious scenes on old saw blades and other old farm tools, and had expressed some interest in hiring Price & Chan.

When Earle saw Price he shouted, "There you are, you home wrecker!" at the top of his lungs. Earle was standing about 30 feet away from Price and the Constantines. Price tried unsuccessfully to shush Earle, while Earle loudly accused Price of an extramarital affair with Chan. Earle yelled that he hoped Price would "roast" for his promiscuous ways. With that comment, Earle winked at Price and whispered, "That'll teach you!" before walking off.

---

5. This case hypothetical was adapted from a problem that was originally posted in the Legal Writing Institute's Idea Bank. The primary author is unknown.

Price was momentarily stunned by both the exchange and by the small circle of bystanders who had gathered to watch the fracas. He composed himself and returned to the Constantines' booth, but when he got there, the couple informed him rather coldly that they had customers to attend to and that they would contact him if they needed his services. Price says that the Constantines have not called him or returned his calls.

Price tells me that the remarks were false. Price also says that he knows some of the bystanders heard the entire exchange, but he does not have any way to contact them as witnesses. He does not know how much business he lost from the Constantines but says there is an increasing market for their kind of artwork.

Price wants to know whether he has a claim for slander against Earle. You research the issue and find that, to recover for slander under North Carolina law, a plaintiff must show: (1) The defendant spoke defamatory words which derogatorily affected the plaintiff's reputation; (2) the statement was false; and (3) the statement was published or communicated to and understood by a third person. You speak with your senior partner who wants you to analyze the third element—whether Earle's statements were published or communicated to and understood by a third person. You find two relevant cases, which are summarized below:

West v. King's Dep't Store, Inc., 365 S.E.2d 621 (N.C. 1988)

People being around isn't enough.

In this case, the plaintiffs, after validly purchasing items, left the store and were making their way to their car when the manager ran up to them in the parking lot. The manager accused plaintiffs of stealing the merchandise. The plaintiffs produced a receipt, which the manager ignored and repeated the accusation of stealing the merchandise. As the manager and the plaintiffs began yelling at each other, a small group of people gathered around the plaintiffs and the store manager while the altercation was taking place—a period of about twenty minutes. These onlookers were approximately ten feet from the plaintiffs and the manager. The Court said:

> This Court denies plaintiffs recovery for slander because they failed to prove the publication element. In order to provide the publication element of slander, it is not enough to show that there are people who were around who could have or might have heard the conversation. Rather, plaintiffs needed to provide actual evidence that those around at the time of the altercation actually heard and understood the allegedly slanderous terms.

Harris v. Temple, 392 S.E.2d 752 (N.C. Ct. App. 1990)

People being around is enough.

In this case, the plaintiff was accused of writing bad checks by the manager of a grocery store. The plaintiff testified that inside the grocery store, the manager was loudly accusing her of writing a bad check, while another customer was stuck behind plaintiff attempting to leave the store during the altercation. Several other patrons entered the store while the altercation was taking place, passing directly by the plaintiff and manager. Other customers were watching and there were several employees standing within three feet of the plaintiff during the altercation. The manager also made the plaintiff return her groceries before leaving the store, which involved the cashier. Individuals had heard and understood the accusations because there is nothing ambiguous about an accusation that the customer has given a worthless check for merchandise. Moreover, the plaintiff was forced to return the merchandise to the cashier. The close proximity of so many people inside the grocery store during the altercation was sufficient evidence that the publication element of slander was met.

1. **Outline the factual points between Price's case and the facts of *West* and *Harris*.**

Price's case	Relevant facts of *West*	Relevant facts of *Harris*

2. The two cases have different outcomes. Which one do you think is most controlling and why? (Hint: For this question, consider the facts of the case along with other information such as the level of court that decided the case, the date, etc.)

Harris (1990)

West

3. Which case would you illustrate first and why? Would you write a single application section for both cases or would you place a separate application after each case illustration? Why?

4. Draft one analogy comparing Price's case and the case whose outcome you predict will control.

West because he used language
that may not be understood
and was far away.

5. Draft one distinction between Price's case and the case whose outcome you predict will NOT control.

language isn't obviously clear.

Exercise 8.2.4: Applying Common Law Principles to New Sets of Facts

The law distinguishes between a promise that is enforceable and one that is unenforceable because it was given with a lack of consideration. Under basic contract principles, a contract is a promise or set of promises in which consideration, that is money or some other valuable, is being exchanged.

Sometimes promises can be gratuitous, meaning that something is being given as a gift rather than for a bargained exchange. Here is an example:

Friend 1 says to Friend 2: "I will give you my fur coat because I like you!"

If Friend 1 does not provide the coat, does Friend 2 have grounds to sue for breach of contract?

The promise to give a gift in this example would be unenforceable.

The case of *Kirksey v. Kirksey* concerns what makes a promise gratuitous. Read the landmark case of *Kirksey*, followed by a recent Ohio case, and then respond to the questions that follow.

Kirksey v. Kirksey, 8 Ala. 131 (Ala. 1845)

The question is presented in this Court, upon a case agreed, which shows the following facts:

The plaintiff was the wife of defendant's brother, but had for some time been a widow, and had several children. In 1840, the plaintiff resided on public land, under a contract of lease, she had held over, and was comfortably settled, and would have attempted to secure the land she lived on. The defendant resided in Talladega County, some sixty, or seventy miles off. On the 10th of October 1840, he wrote to her the following letter:

"Dear sister Antillico—Much to my mortification, I heard, that brother Henry was dead, and one of his children. I know that your situation is one of grief, and difficulty. You had a bad chance before, but a great deal worse now. I should like to come and see you, but cannot with convenience at present. * * * I do not know whether you have a preference on the place you live on, or not. If you had, I would advise you to obtain your preference, and sell the land and quit the country, as I understand it is very unhealthy, and I know society is very bad. If you will come down and see me, I will let you have a place to raise your family, and I have more open land than I can tend; and on the account of your situation, and that of your family, I feel like I want you and the children to do well."

Within a month or two after the receipt of this letter, the plaintiff abandoned her possession, without disposing of it, and removed with her family, to the residence of the defendant, who put her in comfortable houses, and gave her land to cultivate for two years, at the end of which time he notified her to remove, and put her in a house, not comfortable, in the woods, which he afterwards required her to leave.

In the lower court, a verdict being found for the plaintiff, for two hundred dollars, the above facts were agreed, and if they will sustain the action, the judgment is to be affirmed, otherwise it is to be reversed.

Judge Ormond wrote for the majority:

Although plaintiff sustained loss in moving to the defendant's, a distance of sixty miles, my brothers, however, think that the promise on the part of the defendant, was a mere gratuity, and that an action will not lie for its breach. The judgment of the Court is for the defendant.

Even today, state cases still regard contracts lacking consideration as unenforceable. Assume your client's facts take place in Ohio and you came across this case in your research:

Orwell Nat. Gas Co. v. Fredon Corp.,
30 N.E.3d 977 (Ohio Ct. App. 2015) (citations omitted)

A contract is not binding unless supported by consideration. Consideration is a bargained for legal benefit and/or detriment. A benefit may consist of some right, interest, or profit accruing to the promisor, while a detriment may consist of some forbearance, loss, or responsibility given, suffered, or undertaken by the promisee. Further, gratuitous promises are not enforceable as contracts, because there is no consideration. *Kirksey v. Kirksey*, 8 Ala. 131 (Ala. 1845). In other words, for there to be consideration, the promisor (the party binding himself to perform) must receive some benefit, and/or the promisee (the party receiving the benefit of the performance) must sustain some detriment.

1. In your own words, based on the holding and reasoning of *Kirksey* and *Orwell Nat. Gas Co.*, what distinguishes a gratuitous promise from one that is enforceable?

A gratuitous promise is one given that the promissor does not expect to benefit from and is of no detriment to the promisee.

2. For the following legal scenarios, decide whether the promises have consideration (making them enforceable) or whether these are gratuitous promises that lack enforceability. Assume your facts take place in Ohio. Explain your answer.

a. Parent says to child: "When you get home after school, I will make you your favorite meal—spaghetti and meatballs." Parent does not make the child's favorite meal, but instead serves a heaping plate of liver and vegetables. Child is furious and contacts you, the family lawyer, asking if she can recover for breach of contract. Your advice is:

_____ *No* . _____

_____

_____

_____

_____

b. Neighbor X says to Neighbor Y: "If you mow my lawn on Tuesdays, I will pay you $15 each time you mow my lawn." Y says she will mow X's lawn on Tuesdays for that price. X says, "great, thanks in advance." Neighbor Y mows the lawn on the following Tuesday, but Neighbor X refuses to pay, saying he changed his mind. Y seeks your advice.

_____ *Yes Promise Unilateral Contract.* _____

_____

_____

_____

_____

c. Student A says to Student B: "I am no longer using my textbook. I will bring it to school and give it to you." Student B says, "thanks!" Student A never gives B the textbook. Does B have a claim against A?

_____ *No* _____

_____

_____

_____

_____

Chapter 9
Tying It All Together: Introducing, Connecting, and Concluding Legal Arguments

By this point, you have learned a lot about reading cases and statutes, extracting and synthesizing rules from different sources of law, organizing your authorities, and crafting sound legal analysis. Now you will practice tying all of these pieces together to create a full discussion section by introducing, connecting, and concluding your legal arguments.

For the discussion to make sense to the reader, you will need to give the reader a clear roadmap of where the analysis is headed and provide road signs to keep the reader oriented throughout the analysis. You will also want to tell the reader your final answer and what next steps should be taken. This chapter will help you craft those connecting components—the introductions, point headings, and conclusions for each legal argument and for the memo as a whole.

I.   Roadmaps and Umbrellas: Introducing Legal Arguments

When writing about the law, lawyers like to start with the ending. Lawyers want to know the bottom-line answer first for a few reasons. For one thing, lawyers want to know where they are headed prior to wading through pages of detailed analysis. When you know the ultimate legal prediction, you can read more critically, testing your assertions and discerning whether the law supports the facts in the way you have set out.

Lawyers introduce arguments primarily in two places: (1) the main introductory section after the "Discussion" heading and (2) in the first paragraph that follows point headings (or sub-headings) for individual legal arguments. The main introductory section can be called many things—the roadmap paragraph, the umbrella paragraph, the landscape paragraph, or the thesis paragraph. Likewise, the shorter introduction sections for sub-topics or individual arguments might also have different names—the mini-roadmap, the mini-umbrella, the mini-landscape, or the mini-thesis paragraph. Use the name that your audience prefers.

Although the name given to these introductory sections or paragraphs can vary, the function should not. The ultimate goal of any introductory section is to remind your reader of the legal issue, set out your bottom-line appraisal of that issue, and signal where the analysis is headed. Thus, an introduction should typically give the reader the following information:

- The ultimate conclusion for the legal questions at issue;
- The governing rule that controls the legal questions;
- The main points of the governing rule (such as elements or factors) that will be discussed and the order in which those points will be presented;
- A statement disposing of any parts of the governing rule not being discussed or that do not warrant a full discussion; and
- A short explanation of the reasons for your ultimate conclusion (when needed or when space allows).

The length of the introductory section will vary according to the number of legal issues being addressed and the complexity of those issues. For a short legal memorandum with one or two issues, you might have a single introductory paragraph. When analyzing multiple issues or several elements or factors of one issue, you might have several paragraphs. Introductory sections for short arguments within the memorandum or sub-issues are usually quite brief, and a single, succinct paragraph will suffice.

To get a sense of the parts of an introductory section, look at Example 9.A, which examines an introductory paragraph for a claim.

Example 9.A: Reviewing an Introductory Roadmap Paragraph

This introductory paragraph begins with the issue being addressed and the writer's ultimate prediction for that issue.

In this case, Paul Hewson will be able to prove that his relationship with Natalie Gutierrez did not meet two elements of common law marriage under Utah law. A marriage that is not solemnized according to Utah law is legal and valid if it arises out of a contract between a man and a woman who "mutually assume marital rights, duties, and obligations" and "who hold themselves out as and have acquired a uniform and general reputation as husband and wife." Utah Code Ann. § 30-1-4.5 (1)(d)–(e) (2018). To establish mutual assumption of marital rights, duties, and obligations, the court will consider financial and domestic factors. *Clark v. Clark*, 27 P.3d 538, 542 (Utah 2001). To establish acquisition of a uniform and general reputation as husband and wife, the court will consider factors such as last name, reputation among friends and family versus the public, and whether the couple introduced each other as

The writer starts with the governing rule for the claim then moves to the standards established by the courts (the rule and the synthesized rule) for each element being examined.

husband and wife. *Hansen v. Hansen*, 958 P.2d 931, 936 (Utah Ct. App. 1998); *Clark,*
27 P.3d at 542. The court will most likely find that Paul and Natalie did not mutually
assume marital rights, duties, and obligations because they did not share financial
accounts or own joint property. Although a close argument, the court will likely
find the couple had a divided reputation because several friends did not believe
them to be married. Thus, Ms. Gutierrez will not be able to claim a common law
marriage under Utah law.

> The factual reasons supporting the prediction are stated then the paragraph ends with the ultimate conclusion for the claim.

A. Start with a Prediction

When crafting a prediction, answer the question that is asked with as much certainty as
your analysis will allow.

First, answer the specific question that was asked, and avoid stating broad conclusions
when the legal issue is narrow. For example, if you are asked to determine whether the
element of "contemporaneous perception" is met in a claim for Negligent Infliction of Emotional Distress, then answer that question about that particular element, rather than the
larger question about the cause of action itself. If, however, you are asked to assess the entire
claim, do so.

Next, be as concrete as possible when describing the likelihood of your prediction. Avoid
waffling or being too vague. Avoid words like "might" or "maybe" because those words, or
any variation of them, could suggest that you have not weighed the authorities or assessed
the issue closely enough. You can have some degree of uncertainty—often we may not
be able to guarantee an outcome—but give your best prediction. If the ultimate outcome
could go either way, you may say that. The table below gives you tips on crafting degrees
of certainty:

Table 9.B: Phrasing Your Degree of Certainty When Introducing an Argument[1]

Degree of Certainty	Words	Ways to Phrase Prediction
When certain about a predicted outcome	Almost certain Will Cannot	"A court **should find** that . . . ." "Our client **cannot establish** . . . ."
When you predict an outcome, but a possibility exists that the court could decide contrary to your conclusion	Very likely or very probable Likely or probable More likely than not Unlikely or improbable Very unlikely or very improbable	"A court **will likely find** that . . . ." "A court **will most likely** find that . . . ." "The court's probable decision will be that . . . ."
When the outcome is too uncertain to predict		"A court's decision on this issue **could go either way** because . . . ." **But avoid:** "A court might find . . . ." "A court may find . . . ."

1. Adapted, in part, from, Joe Fore, *"A Court Would Probably Find . . .": Defining Verbal Probability Expressions*
in Predictive Legal Analysis, 16 Legal Comm. & Rhetoric: JAWLD *35 (forthcoming 2019).

B. Introducing the Governing Rule and Other Rules

After presenting their ultimate prediction in an introduction section, legal writers state the governing rule that controls the entire issue. Once the governing rule is established, any supporting rules are then presented. When establishing the supporting rules, start with the general rules controlling the issue and move to the more specific. When introducing the rules, especially for a more complex legal issue, you might put the synthesized rules in a separate paragraph before then explaining the rules with case illustrations in later paragraphs.

When writing the governing rule, replicate the rule as it is stated in the primary source (and cite that source). When the governing rule comes from a statute, regulation, or constitutional provision, lead your discussion with that precise language. If the rule from a statute, regulation, or other provision has been further interpreted or applied by a court, then provide that material next.

If the rule is not stated clearly, you have a few options. You may put it entirely in your own words or paraphrase some portions and quote only the key phrases. Yet another option is to quote the rule entirely, then restate the rule more clearly for your reader in your own words. Be sure to cite appropriately.

II. Point Headings: Directing the Reader

Point headings act as road signs for your reader, signaling the main point of the section that follows and helping the reader see how that section relates to other sections in the document. As an added benefit, the point heading gives the reader's eye a place to rest, letting the reader digest the analysis that has gone before and prepare for the analysis coming next.

Collectively, for longer discussions or multiple legal topics in a memorandum, the point headings serve as a table of contents, showing the reader the main points, any sub-points, and the order in which those points will be presented. Because of their many functions, point headings should be well-crafted sentences that work hard in your document.

Point headings should be short, but they also should be interesting and descriptive. This section will help you practice crafting effective point headings.

An effective point heading usually has two parts:
- The conclusion about the legal discussion that follows, and
- The main reason for that conclusion.

If, however, the point heading is too long or too complex, omit the reason for the conclusion. Typically, effective point headings are full sentences with punctuation, but short phrases can also be effective. Look at the following examples in Table 9.C.

Chapter 9. Tying It All Together | 173

Table 9.C: Examples of Point Headings

Level of effectiveness	Example
A full sentence is an effective point heading, especially when it states the main conclusion for a section and the reason for that conclusion.	A. Our client was likely acting in a reasonably prudent fashion because the actions that led to a violation of the statutory time limit were not intentional.
A phrase can be an effective point heading when it clearly identifies the topic to follow.	A. Intentional actions required to find a statutory violation
Phrases that do not fully inform the reader of the points to follow are often not effective.	A. Intentional actions

The tension between being concise and complete always exists in legal writing, and you will find that same tension when drafting point headings. With point headings, however, the answer is a little easier: When in doubt, write less. Readers like shorter point headings.

Even so, headings that just announce a topic rather than explaining the main point of the section will likely be less useful to your reader at the predictive writing stage, and far less useful if the document is ever turned into a brief for a judge.

III. Using Transitions to Connect the Dots

The best legal writing guides the reader through the legal analysis and shows how the legal dots are connected. One tool lawyers frequently use is transition words. Transition words not only help the flow of the writing, but they serve other more substantive roles: They tell the reader how ideas are connected, they show the relationship among cases, and they act as road signs to guide the reader through the organization structure.

As a legal writer, you can utilize many different types of transition words. Sometimes, even a single word such as "likewise" creates a far more clear and effective document that your reader can easily understand. Be thoughtful about the kinds of words you use though. Formal, serious transitions can often read like legalese and lessen the overall effectiveness of the transition. Shorter, simple transitions tend to work best in legal writing. Formal transitions are like old Victorian sofas: They may look nice and be serviceable, but they are not as sleek or comfortable as some of the modern sofas available now. Table 9.D shows you a few transition words that can help tie sections of analysis together.

Table 9.D: Transition Words

Type of Transition Word	Examples	
Transition words showing order, steps, parts, or sequence	First, second, third Initially, next, finally	
Words showing consistent connection	Moreover Likewise Similarly	In addition Like
Words showing opposing ideas	However In contrast	But Unlike
Words showing relationship or conclusion	Because Despite But Still Thus	Although And However Yet Therefore
Words signaling location within an organizational scheme	"**Under** the UCC" (signals the writer is in the rule or the explanation) "**Here**, the contract was not breached" (signals the writer is turning to the application sections) "**Therefore**," (signals writer is concluding)	
Formal transitions	Notwithstanding Accordingly Nevertheless	Inasmuch as Subsequently

IV. Drafting Conclusions

Since legal analysis avoids the kind of crescendo or suspenseful build up that other types of writing may employ, legal conclusions are used strategically to keep the reader focused on the point at hand. Legal analysis begins with the conclusion that will be reached, and the analysis ends with a conclusion as well. Earlier in this chapter, you saw, for example, the bottom-line conclusion used up front in the introductory sections.

Let's look at the places in which conclusions are used most frequently to end a legal analysis. Whether concluding one legal argument or drafting the formal Conclusion section for a whole memorandum of law, a conclusion should succinctly and directly sum up the bottom-line outcome for the preceding analysis and, when applicable, describe the next steps the attorney should take.

A. Concluding Individual Legal Arguments within a Memorandum

Conclusions can be helpful to the legal reader at the beginning and end of a document, at the beginning and end of individual arguments within a document, and even at both the beginning and end of a single paragraph. Just as you must introduce individual legal arguments, you will also want to conclude them.

Conclusions to individual legal arguments are short and usually appear at the very last sentence or paragraph of analysis. The conclusion should simply state how that issue or sub-issue will turn out. The conclusion may also state whether any unknown information—facts or law—should be gathered.

B. Drafting a Conclusion Section of a Memorandum

The Conclusion section of a memo is where the loose ends of the memorandum are wrapped up. Just like in the introductory paragraphs, you will want to include a succinct statement of your predicted outcome of the case. But do not stop there. Part of our job as lawyers is not only to predict what outcome is most likely, but we must also use our own judgment to determine what steps the supervising attorney should take next. That "next steps" advice should also be in the Conclusion section.

Just like in the introduction section, be as concrete as possible with your prediction. Avoid waffling and predict the outcome that you think is most likely based on the application of the facts to the law.

V. Exercises

The following exercises will acquaint you with and help you practice the various ways to introduce, connect, and conclude legal arguments. In the exercises you will assess the introductory paragraphs, evaluate the effectiveness of point headings, and think about how transitions between or among sentences can help improve readability. You will also evaluate a conclusion.

Exercise 9.1: Organizing an Introductory (Roadmap) Paragraph

An introductory roadmap paragraph should walk the reader through the upcoming analytical points in an orderly fashion, moving from general rules to specific ones. Signposts help the reader navigate the ideas. The following paragraph is the introduction to a memo[2] examining the legal issue of whether a defendant threatened the use of imminent force during a robbery. Using numbers in the blanks beside each sentence, order the sentences below to form an effective roadmap paragraph.

—   **Further, this requirement is met if the victim merely believes the defendant has the intention, ability, and means, to inflict harm.** *Saffold*, **951 So. 2d at 781.**

—   **The issue is whether Mr. Madison threatened the imminent use of force against Mr. Harrison.**

—   **Under the Alabama Code, a third-degree robbery is committed if in the course of committing a theft a person either (1) uses actual force; or "(2) threatens imminent use of force against the person . . . with intent to compel acquiescence to the taking of or escaping with the property." Ala. Code § 13A-8-43(a) (2016).**

—   **Mr. Madison will likely be charged with robbery in the third degree because waving the weighted lacrosse stick at Mr. Ronit put Mr. Ronit in fear of bodily injury.**

—   **Determining whether a defendant threatened the imminent**

---

2. This exercise is adapted from a problem developed by Professor Lucy Jewel at the University of Tennessee College of Law.

use of force has a low threshold because the victim's fear, the defendant's intention, or the defendant's ability and means alone may be sufficient to establish the standard.

— Courts have found the threat of imminent force is based on the victim's perception, specifically whether, during the course of a theft, the victim is placed in fear. *See Cook v. State*, 582 So. 2d 592, 594 (Ala. Crim. App. 1991); *Saffold v. State*, 951 So. 2d 777, 781 (Ala. 2006).

— Here, Mr. Madison did not touch Mr. Ronit in any way, so no actual force was used.

Exercise 9.2: Identifying Components of an Introductory Paragraph

Review the following introductory paragraph, then answer the questions following.

Robert Scott might be charged with kidnapping because he held Lindsey Hohmann for "ransom or reward or otherwise." 18 U.S.C. § 1201(a) (2018). Section 1201 of the Federal Kidnapping Statute states that "whoever unlawfully seizes, confines, inveigles, decoys, kidnaps, abducts, or carries away and holds for ransom or reward or otherwise any person. . . shall be punished." In this case, Scott held Hohmann for "ransom or reward or otherwise" when he took her from her home in Idaho to the wilderness therapy program in Colorado because he received a benefit.

1. As a reader who is new to this legal topic, what parts of the introductory roadmap do you think are missing?

_____

_____

_____

_____

_____

2. What is the governing rule? What is the precise legal question being addressed here?

_____

_____

_____

_____

_____

_____

3. How would you reword the opening sentence to have clearer degree of certainty if the analysis shows that the defendant meets the element in question, but the other side has a viable, but weak, counter argument?

_____

_____

_____

_____

_____

_____

Exercise 9.3: Understanding the Parts of an Introductory Paragraph

You are a senior level associate at a law firm. A first-year associate sends you a draft of a memo[3] to review for a potential new case. Below is the introductory paragraph to that memo. Read through the introductory paragraph and think about its effectiveness.

Discussion

The memo analyzes whether Mr. Hernandez's claim against our client, OnTime Bus Transport, will satisfy the "contemporaneous perception" element necessary for a bystander to recover under a claim for Negligent Infliction of Emotional Distress ("NIED"). Mr. Hernandez's experience following the bus accident involving his stepdaughter is not sufficient to satisfy the bystander recovery test required under Cascadia state law for a claim of NIED. *See Jones v. Smith*, 111 N.W.2d 222, 224 (Cas. Ct. App. 2018). To recover for NIED, a plaintiff must prove three elements: (1) that the plaintiff was located near the scene of the accident; (2) that the plaintiff suffered shock from a contemporaneous perception of the accident; and (3) that the plaintiff and victim were closely related. *Bullard v. Imperial Lanes*, 333 N.W.2d 444, 446 (Cas. Ct. App. 2015). Here, because the facts indicate that Mr. Hernandez was located near the scene of the accident and that he was closely related to his stepdaughter, only the element of "contemporaneous perception" is at issue. A bystander experiences "contemporaneous perception" of an accident when the bystander either learns about the experience through firsthand knowledge or plays an intimate role in the discovery or immediate aftermath of the incident. *Id.* Here, Mr. Hernandez heard about the bus crash from a fellow driver before rushing to the scene, had some perception of what had happened before he saw the wreckage, and was not intimately involved in some other way. Thus, the court will likely hold that the NIED claim should be dismissed.

After reviewing the introductory paragraph, review each of the following sentences and describe the function it serves.

1. Describe the function of the following sentence: The memo analyzes whether Mr. Hernandez's claim against our client, OnTime Bus Transport, will

---

3. This problem is based on a fictitious jurisdiction.

satisfy the "contemporaneous perception" element necessary for a bystander to recover under a claim for Negligent Infliction of Emotional Distress.

_____

_____

_____

_____

_____

2. Describe the function of the following sentence: To recover for NIED, a plaintiff must prove three elements: (1) that the plaintiff was located near the scene of the accident; (2) that the plaintiff suffered shock from a contemporaneous perception of the accident; and (3) that the plaintiff and victim were closely related. *Bullard v. Imperial Lanes,* 333 N.W.2d 444, 446 (Cas. Ct. App. 2015).

_____

_____

_____

_____

_____

3. Describe the function of the following sentence: Here, because the facts indicate that Mr. Hernandez was located near the scene of the accident and that he was closely related to his stepdaughter, only the element of "contemporaneous perception" is at issue.

_____

_____

_____

_____

_____

_____

4. Describe the function of the following sentence: A bystander experiences "contemporaneous perception" of an accident when the bystander either learns about the experience through firsthand knowledge or plays an intimate role in the discovery or immediate aftermath of the incident. *Id.*

_____

_____

_____

_____

_____

5. Describe the function of the following sentence: Mr. Hernandez heard about the bus crash from a fellow driver before rushing to the scene, had some perception of what had happened before he saw the wreckage, and was not intimately involved in some other way.

_____

_____

_____

_____

_____

6. Discuss the function of the following sentences: Thus, he cannot have experienced a "contemporaneous perception" of the accident. *Id.* at 445. The court will likely hold that the NIED claim should be dismissed.

_____

_____

_____

_____

_____

_____

Exercise 9.4: Identifying Components of a Paragraph Introducing a Single Legal Argument (Mini-roadmap, Mini-umbrella)

Our client signed a contract with a home security company, and he now believes that some terms of the contract were unreasonably harsh. An associate wrote a memo to the supervising attorney and asked you to critique it. Review the following paragraph that introduces a legal argument[4] within the body of a Discussion section, and then answer the questions that follow.

In determining whether a clause meets the procedural element of unconscionability, courts look to a variety of factors including: education, age, business acumen, and experience of the parties; bargaining power; conspicuousness and comprehensibility of contract language; oppressiveness of terms; and presence of meaningful choice. *Mullis v. Speight Seed Farms, Inc.*, 505 S.E.2d 818, 820 (Ga. Ct. App. 1998). Georgia courts have consolidated these considerations into two factors: "oppression" and "surprise." *Id.* The SecureHome contract involves oppression and surprise, and the court will likely find it meets the element of procedural unconscionability.

1. **In analyzing the element of procedural unconscionability, what two factors will be analyzed in this section and in which order?**

_____

_____

_____

_____

_____

_____

2. **What is the writer's conclusion to the legal question being asked?**

_____

_____

_____

_____

_____

_____

---

4. Adapted from a problem used by Professor Hadley Van Vactor, Lewis & Clark Law School and used with permission.

3. As a new reader, does this paragraph give you enough context to understand the two factors? Would adding the following sentence assist the reader, and if so, where would it be placed?

The *Mullis* court observed that oppression arises from inequality of bargaining power and absence of meaningful choice, whereas surprise involves the extent to which terms of bargain are hidden.

_____

_____

_____

_____

_____

_____

Exercise 9.5: Identifying and Drafting Effective Point Headings

For each of the following, assess whether the point heading is effective or ineffective and why. When the point heading is ineffective, revise it.

1. Verbal threats that make a victim assume that the assailant can and will harm the victim are a threat of imminent force and actions that make a victim assume that the assailant will harm the victim are a threat of force.

_____

_____

_____

_____

_____

_____

2. How the victim perceives a threat.

_____

_____

_____

_____

_____

_____

3. Physical action as a threat under *Mullis*, 505 S.E.2d at 820.

_____

_____

_____

_____

_____

_____

4. The Owens case will not likely meet the substantive element of an unconscionable contract.

_____

_____

_____

_____

_____

_____

5. The SecureHome contract will not be deemed substantively unconscionable because the terms do not include an unreasonable allocation of risk or an unreasonably one-sided term.

_____

_____

_____

_____

_____

_____

Exercise 9.6: Understanding How and When to Use Terms of Transition

You are a senior associate who has been asked to review memos from a first-year associate before they are given to the senior partner. For the first memo, indicate in the margins where a transition word would be helpful to the reader and list any transition words or phrases that you think would work. (Hint: Transitions may be helpful in multiple places.)

Memo 1

An experiential perception of an accident can result from the shock of unwittingly coming upon an accident scene moments after the accident occurs. *General Motors Corp. v. Grizzle*, 642 S.W.2d 837 (Tex. Ct. App. 1982); *Freeman v. City of Pasadena*, 744 S.W.2d 923, 924 (Tex. 1988). In *Grizzle*, the plaintiff came upon an accident involving her son and other relatives "moments after the collision." 642 S.W.2d at 844. The court held that unknowingly coming upon a scene moments after an accident creates a sensory perception that causes mental injury sufficient to prove contemporaneous perception. *Id.* In *Freeman*, the plaintiff was at home at the time of the accident and was informed about it by a third party. 744 S.W.2d at 924. He then rushed to the scene, where he saw the wreckage and his injured stepson, covered in blood, lying on a gurney. *Id.* The court held that because the plaintiff neither contemporaneously perceived the accident, nor experienced the shock of unwittingly coming upon it, he could not recover. *Id.* at 924.

For the next memo, underline the transition words you see and notice how they connect the ideas.

Memo 2

The benefit must be personal to qualify as "ransom or reward or otherwise." *Walker*, 137 F.3d at 1220. An action that benefits the transgressor qualifies as "otherwise." For example, in *Walker*, the defendant forced his victim into the victim's car and drove from Utah to Idaho, hoping to keep her in a relationship with him. *Id.* at 1218. The court determined that keeping his victim in the relationship personally benefited the defendant. *Id.* at 1219. Because Walker personally benefitted, he met the "ransom or reward or otherwise" clause of the statute. On the other hand, keeping someone for reasons other than self-interest did not qualify as "ransom or reward or otherwise." *Chatwin*, 326 U.S. at 460. In *Chatwin*, the defendant transported a minor across state lines without the consent of her parents or guardians. *Id.* The two of them lived together, in hiding, as husband and wife. *Id.* The court found that Chatwin did not hold the girl against her will. *Id.* Their cohabitation was mutual. The defendant received no singularly personal benefit, and he did not hold her for "ransom or reward or otherwise." *Id.*

Exercise 9.7: Drafting Effective Conclusions

You are reviewing the final page of a memorandum for a colleague who is analyzing whether a client, Ms. Perkins, could be charged with Robbery in the Third Degree. (You may remember her situation from Chapter 5.) Ms. Perkins took a necklace from a former boyfriend after waving a track cleat with sharp, metal prongs near his face. The colleague was to analyze the issue and then explain to the supervising attorney what options the client has. Review the final paragraph of the document below, and then answer the questions that follow.

Conclusion

Ultimately, Perkins will be charged with Robbery in the Third Degree because she threatened imminent force in an attempt to compel acquiescence. Her yelling at Miller while holding a spiked cleat, waving it toward Miller's face, and making a verbal threat, constitutes threat of imminent force. Miller felt that Perkins was going to and had the ability to harm him, regardless of their differences in physical size.

1. **If you were the supervising attorney, would you consider this Conclusion paragraph effective? Explain your reasons.**

_____

_____

_____

_____

_____

_____

2. **What is missing from the Conclusion?**

_____

_____

_____

_____

_____

_____

3. Will the attorney know what steps should be taken next? How do you think adding recommendations of next steps will help the supervising attorney?

_____

_____

_____

_____

_____

_____

Chapter 10

Drafting the Question Presented and Brief Answer

I. Structuring a Question Presented

II. Refining the Three Parts of a Question Presented

III. Crafting the Brief Answer

IV. Exercises

The Question Presented and the Brief Answer sections of a legal memorandum allow busy readers to comprehend and understand quickly the basic legal issues presented in the analysis. These sections serve multiple purposes. Not only do they allow the reader to see the answers to the pivotal questions being asked, but they also prepare the reader for the more detailed analysis to come. Further, these sections apprise future readers of the information and decisions made at a particular point in your client's case. Finally, these sections can be helpful to other attorneys who may be researching the same or similar issues in the future.

The core skill a Question Presented requires is the ability to formulate issues (simple or complex) thoroughly and succinctly. Formulating an issue is the first step in preparing any legal document—a client who comes to you for advice will come with a set of facts and you will need to discern the legal issues that arise from those facts. That issue will be further refined with the documents you draft, whether an objective memo for another attorney or a persuasive brief for the court.

Similarly, the Brief Answer will require an equally succinct and straightforward response that answers the Question Presented. The Brief Answer will need to establish your bottom-line answer to the question along with the most important reasons supporting your determination. The Brief Answer is not a place to explain your answer in depth, nor should it recap every reason for your decision about the issue. The Brief Answer should, however, give the reader a good sense of the likely outcome for the issue and the facts that support that prediction.

As you begin researching and writing your memorandum, you will likely formulate the issues by asking the following questions:

- What are the facts of your client's case?
- What body of law governs?
- What is the relevant authority?
- What precise part of the relevant authority is at issue?
- What facts are the most important in analyzing that authority?

As you move from research to outline to a fully composed legal argument, you will refine the question that is being asked and the answer to that question. Typically, you will have one Question Presented and corresponding Brief Answer for each distinct legal issue in your memo.

In truth, the Question Presented and Brief Answer should be the most polished part of your memo—these sections are not only what the reader sees first, but they also contain the answers which an attorney will rely on in deciding the next steps of the case. Because of the importance of these sections, take time to craft them well.

I. Structuring a Question Presented

Questions Presented often come with different names and styles depending on the preference in your office. No matter the name, a strong Question Presented will have three parts:

- A description of the specific governing rule that applies (and may include the jurisdiction and type of primary source);
- The precise legal question; and
- The key facts of the case on which the question will turn.

Your goal is to draft a clear and concise question that contains these three parts. The Question Presented can be structured in different ways, but the three parts are always necessary. The most common structures include:

- Under/Does/When
- Statement/Statement/Question
- Whether/Which/When

Common structures for the Question Presented are listed in Table 10.A.

Table 10.A: Common Structures for the Question Presented

Type of Structure		Components
Under	→	the controlling law—state the jurisdiction, the law, and what the law allows or prohibits
Does/Is/Can	→	this legal consequence occur
When	→	these key determinative facts are present
Statement	→	the controlling law—state the jurisdiction, the law, and what the law allows or prohibits
Statement	→	the key determinative facts upon which the issue turns
Question	→	the precise legal question presented for review
Whether	→	the precise legal question and controlling law
Which	→	specific rule
When	→	these key determinative facts are present

Current trends in legal practice are moving to the multi-sentence structure. The statement/statement/question format (sometimes known as the "deep issue" format) is becoming the most preferred standard because it is often easier to construct, particularly when the law or the facts are lengthy or complex.

In addition to these three structures, you might have a more complex question in which a legal issue has multiple parts, thus making formulating a single Question Presented difficult. For example, you might have an overarching governing rule that has multiple parts or you might have a controlling law that could turn on different legal facts. In those situations, you may find it easier to create an "umbrella question," in which you can establish the overarching question then break down the details in separate parts. (See Example 10.E below.)

The structure may be tailored to fit the needs of each case. Review the following examples to see the different structures in action. Notice how each variation presents the same three component pieces of the controlling law, key determinative facts, and the precise legal question being asked.

Example 10.B: Under/does/when

Under Alabama Code Section 13A-8-43 (2016), governing third degree robbery, which requires the threat of imminent force, **is** imminent force established **when** a person waves a track cleat with two protruding metal spikes at another while shouting, "get out of my way or you'll wish you had," while taking items, which do not belong to her?

Example 10.C: Statement/statement/question

Under Alabama Code Section 13A-8-43 (2016), third degree robbery is established when a person commits a theft while using a "threat of imminent force." In this case, our client waved a track cleat with sharp metal spike at her roommate while saying loudly, "get out of my way or you'll wish you had," and leaving with his roommate's property. Is the waving of the cleat, coupled with those words, enough to establish the element of imminent force?

Example 10.D: Whether/which/when

Whether under Alabama Code Section 13A-8-43 (2016), a person can be charged with the offense of third degree robbery, **which** requires the "threat of imminent force," **when** she waves a track cleat with metal prongs at another while saying loudly, "get out of my way or you'll wish you had," and leaving with the roommate's belongings.

Example 10.E: Formulating the Umbrella Question

I. **Under** Title VII of the Civil Rights Act of 1964, governing workplace discrimination based upon sex, a hostile work environment is created when the conduct, imputed to the employer, is severe and persuasive.

    A. **Is** severe and pervasive conduct established **when** a co-worker (1) leaves a drawing of a nude woman in the photocopier with our client's name on it; (2) gives our client the silent treatment for three months; (3) drops a cup of hot coffee on our client's desk, while she is sitting there; and (4) enters our client's office, presumably to ask a business-related question, with his fly unzipped?

B. **Can** the conduct be imputed to the employer **when** (1) a supervisor found a sexually suggestive drawing of our client and declined to comment; (2) the employer conducted sexual harassment training; and (3) took no action when our client complained to her direct supervisor about a co-worker?

Questions:

1. **What differences do you see when comparing the different structures?**

The first is looking to define what severe and pervasive

Can be categorized.

Both looking to see if legal consequence can occur.

The second one incorporates possible alternate explanations/ counterarguments.

2. **Which structure do you prefer? Why?**

First.

When deciding which structure to use for a question presented, gear your legal writing to your audience. If your office has standard structures, use the one your reader will prefer. If your audience is flexible, consider the complexity of the law and facts then choose the structure a reader can most easily absorb.

II. Refining the Three Parts of the Question Presented

The Question Presented can be challenging to craft not only because of the variety of structures you can use to formulate it, but also because you can have many variations as to the order and content of the three component parts.

Your ultimate goal is always to encapsulate the precise legal question being asked in the clearest way possible. Thus, while these three stock structures give you an idea of how to formulate an issue, you may determine in what order to present the controlling law, precise legal question, and key determinative facts. Table 10.F gives you a few tips on constructing the parts.

Table 10.F: Tips for Drafting Component Parts of the Question Presented

Component Part	Tips
Controlling law	• Try to indicate both the controlling law and the relative jurisdiction (state, federal, statutory, or case law). • Always tell what the law prohibits, requires, or allows. • Think about the level of specificity you need for this section—ask yourself what level of detail is best for the reader and whether the reader needs details about the statutory section numbers or case names.
Precise legal question or consequence	• This part is straightforward, but be as specific or precise as possible.
Key determinative facts	• Use only the key facts needed to resolve the issue. • You will not be able to use all of the key facts, so choose the most relevant two or three facts.

In addition, when formulating the QP, you may need to sacrifice completeness for clarity if the QP becomes too long for the reader to absorb.

In constructing the Question Presented, take special care to avoid this mistake: Avoid using legally significant phrases that assume the answer to the question being asked. Instead of falling into that circular reasoning and assuming the conclusion in the question, ask the question by using the key determinative facts.

One other technique to avoid is characterization of the facts. A lawyer's job in the predictive writing stage is to present the facts in a neutral way. Characterizing the facts (typically by using adjectives and adverbs to describe something) may not be helpful to the reader. For example, in Example 10.B above, to describe the action by saying the client "gently waved the track cleat" would characterize the action rather than just stating the facts.

III.   Crafting the Brief Answer

Each Question Presented should have a corresponding Brief Answer that succinctly answers the legal question and provides the most important supporting reasons for that answer. The Brief Answer should be directly responsive to the Question Presented, and the reader should be able to see the connection between the two sections.

The first sentence of the paragraph should actually be short and direct—a brief "yes" or "no" will suffice. If the answer could go more than one way, you may include a qualifier that states your level of uncertainty. "Most likely, yes," for example, would be a way to qualify your answer if you cannot fully predict the outcome.

After the initial conclusion sentence, the remainder of the Brief Answer should get directly to the point. First, establish the rules that govern the legal question. If the legal question is answered by assessment of a combination of rules or sub-rules, winnow down the field, choosing only those rules that best explain the principles a court will likely use to determine the issue. Next, concisely apply the rules to those key facts and determine the outcome of the case. Remember, the Brief Answer is not intended to convey the full analysis; instead, it is a very short statement of the most important rules and facts; the rest of the memorandum will explain your answer in full.

In the following examples, notice how the Brief Answers complement the Question Presented both in structure and content.

Example 10.G: A Brief Answer for an Under/does/when Structure

No. Because the State will not be able to establish that the track cleat was a dangerous instrument, our client cannot be charged with robbery in the first degree. An object is found to be a dangerous instrument based on the manner in which the object was used, including whether it was highly capable of causing serious physical injury in the circumstances surrounding the incident, and the victim's reasonable belief the object was a dangerous instrument. The absence of actual use and injury along with the circumstances of the incident are inadequate to support a reasonable belief the track cleat was a dangerous instrument.

Example 10.H: A Brief Answer for an Umbrella Question Structure

I. A hostile work environment under the Civil Rights Act cannot be established. When the conduct is not severe or pervasive, then no hostile work environment is established, even if the conduct can be imputed to the employer.

    A. No. In terms of severity or pervasiveness, courts will look to (1) the plaintiff's subjective observation of the environment; (2) a factor test to determine whether the conduct was so severe and pervasive as to objectively create a hostile work environment; and (3) whether the conduct was the result of discriminatory animus. Though the plaintiff may have subjectively felt that she was immersed in a hostile work environment, objectively, in looking to all the circumstances, the conduct would not be so severe or pervasive as to render the work environment hostile when only three significant incidences occurred over a long time period.

    B. Yes. If there is culpable conduct, the employee's conduct can be imputed to the employer, meaning that the employer would be liable. In terms of imputing the conduct to the employer, courts will look to whether the employer knew or reasonably should have known of the conduct, and if any corrective action was taken. If the employer had knowledge and did not take any remedial action, then it will be found vicariously liable. The supervisor's knowledge of such actions and lack of action would make the employer liable.

IV. Exercises

The following exercises are designed to help you think about the structure and content of both the Question Presented and Brief Answer. In the exercises, you will critically evaluate several Questions Presented and practice crafting a Question Presented using three different structures. In the final exercise, you will practice working with Brief Answers.

Exercise 10.1: Formulating an Issue from Facts

Before drafting a Question Presented, work on your skills in formulating an issue. Read the following facts and then answer the questions below.

For four years, Joanna Rivera worked for Al's automobile dealership in the city of Cleveland, Ohio. On the first day of her employment, she signed an agreement that restricted her from working for a competitor for one year from the date of her termination and within a geographical radius of 100 miles. Ms. Rivera eventually resigned from her job. Six months later, she began working for a competitor, Buster's, which is 200 miles from Al's. However, she travels to Cleveland to meet with Buster's customers in its satellite locations, many of which are within a 25-mile radius of Al's. Al's brought an action to prevent Ms. Rivera from working for its competitor. On the new job, Ms. Rivera slips and falls and brings a case of negligence against her new employer. Your supervisor has asked you to write an objective memorandum of law about the likelihood of success that Al's may have against Rivera.

1. **What issues are presented from this fact scenario? How would you state the issue(s) in your own words?**

> Under the common law, can non-compete
> agreements that prohibit former employees from
> working for competitors w/in a certain geographical
> region be enforced against employees
> whose new competitor is HQ'd beyond
> the geographic region but on occasion have
> to travel w/in the geo. prohibited area?

2. **What facts are relevant? How do the facts pertaining to the negligence action affect your client's case?**

_____

_____

_____

_____

_____

_____

3. **What body of law governs?**

> Common law

_____

_____

_____

_____

_____

_____

4. What facts are not relevant to the issue being researched?

_____

_____

_____

_____

_____

_____

In moving from your preliminary formulation of the issue to a more concise Question Presented, you might start with the whether/which/when construction. Read this initial draft of a structured QP and answer the next questions.

Whether an employer can enforce anti-competition agreement against a former employee **when** she was restricted from working for a competitor within a 100-mile radius, and she began working for a competitor 200 miles away, but meets with customers within a 25-mile radius.

5. Why do you think proper names are not used in this initial Question Presented?

_____

_____

_____

_____

_____

_____

6. If you were asked to revise this Question Presented, how would you further refine it? Would you change the QP's structure? If so, why?

_____

_____

_____

_____

_____

_____

Exercise 10.2: Parsing the Parts of a Question Presented

Remember the case of *Marietta Title Insurance Company v. Rath*, from Chapter 3.2? (The text of the decision is set out below.) Read the following fact scenario then use the implied rule from *Marietta* to respond to the questions that follow below.

> Mary Jones (defendant) was a Vice President of a real estate company (plaintiff) in Milwaukee, Wisconsin. Jones had signed a covenant not to compete when she was employed with the company. She has since resigned and set up a competing real estate company in violation of the covenant. An associate at your firm has done research and anticipates that the covenant would be deemed reasonable in terms of its geographic scope and time limitations. The issue for you to address pertains to whether Jones had unique services.
>
> Jones, while employed with plaintiff's company, worked in the back office on financial accounting matters. Out of 400 clients, she had limited interaction, if any, with clients on a regular basis. She had no special knowledge of computer programs or any system of the company. She resigned from the company and now the company seeks an injunction for breach of the non-compete covenant.

Marietta Title Insurance Co. v. Rath, State Court of Utopia (2016)

Plaintiff Marietta Title Insurance Co., with offices in Park County, brings this action against Paul Rath asserting breach of noncompete covenant. Plaintiff seeks injunctive relief and asks that this Court permanently enjoin defendant from working in the title insurance business in the state of Utopia for two years. Plaintiff grounds its case upon the assertion that Rath's services were unique and, therefore, he should not be permitted to work for a competitor.

Marietta hired Rath in 2012 as Senior Vice President in charge of several major sales accounts. On the first day of his employment, Rath signed a covenant not to compete, restricting him from working for another title insurance company for two years following his termination of employment services from Marietta. However, in August 2014, Rath abruptly terminated his employment with Marietta and signed on as senior vice president of a competitor, Charles Schwartz Title Co., also based in Park County. At the hearing, evidence was produced indicating that Rath had relationships with specific customers of his assigned accounts and that these customers would engage only Rath for Marietta business. Rath had a special knowledge of a computer program that was helpful for his customers' business. Rath had frequent contact with his customers. Rath's territory was limited to Park County. The accounts he oversaw were limited in the same geographic locales.

In the state of Utopia, assuming a covenant by an employee not to compete is reasonable in time and geographic scope, enforcement will be granted to the extent necessary: (1) to prevent an employee's solicitation or disclosure of trade secrets; (2) to prevent an employee's release of confidential information regarding the employer's customers; or (3) in those cases where the employee's services to the employer are deemed special or unique. In a case where (1) is met, but not (2), Utopia courts have granted injunctions to enforce covenants not to compete based upon the unique services of the defendants. In *Matheson Savings Bank v. Jonas*, the state court found that the former employee's relationships with the clients were special and qualified as unique services. The *Jonas* court deemed these relationships unique because of the highly competitive banking industry and the rare talent that rose to the top of the banking world. In addition, the *Matheson* clients had regular contact with Jonas. Thus, the court granted injunctive relief.

In analyzing whether an employee's services are unique, the focus is less on the uniqueness of the individual person and more on the employee's relationship to the employer's business and the clients.

Here, facts produced at the hearing indicate that Rath's services were, and continue to be, unique. Therefore, this Court grants plaintiff's permanent injunction; however, defendant Rath is restricted from working for title insurance companies having offices within the geographic parameters of Park County only.

Based upon the implied rule from *Marietta Title Insurance Company v. Rath*, how would you draft a Question Presented? Use the following questions to help you.

1. **What is the controlling law and what does it allow, prohibit, or require? What jurisdiction is the law in?**

_____

_____

_____

_____

_____

_____

2. **What is the precise legal issue or legal consequence at issue?**

_____

_____

_____

_____

_____

_____

3. What key facts from the problem will determine the outcome of the issue?

_____

_____

_____

_____

_____

_____

4. Now that you've assessed the three parts of the legal issue, craft a Question Presented using one of the structures mentioned earlier in the chapter.

_____

_____

_____

_____

_____

_____

5. Why did you pick that particular structure?

_____

_____

_____

_____

_____

_____

Exercise 10.3: Identifying Missing Components from a Question Presented

Review the following Questions Presented and then explain what components are missing from the question, what additional information the reader will need to understand the issue, or how the question should be rewritten to avoid assuming the answer to the legal question being asked.

1. Can property be owned through adverse possession when the claimants show actual, open and notorious, exclusive, hostile, and continuous possession of the disputed property for ten years?

_____

_____

_____

_____

_____

_____

2. Under Ohio law, can a person recover for emotional distress when someone else's internet posts cause the person to lose business and seek psychiatric treatment?

_____

_____

_____

_____

_____

_____

3. Under the Ohio law of negligent infliction of emotional distress, can a person recover for emotional distress when his former spouse's sibling, who lives in a different state, posts numerous pieces of information on the internet suggesting that the person was a sexual predator, did not pay child support or taxes, accusing him of attempted bribery, and disclosing his personal contact information including his name and address, so that the person had severe emotional disturbances and had to get psychiatric counseling?

_____

_____

_____

_____

_____

_____

4. Does a father satisfy the contemporaneous perception element of a negligent infliction of emotional distress claim when he perceives the accident at the time it happens? (Hint: Generally, the rule for contemporaneous perception is that a person perceives the accident at the time it happens or is brought so close to the aftermath that he becomes a part of the accident.)

_____

_____

_____

_____

_____

_____

Exercise 10.4: Using Different Structures to Formulate a Question Presented

Review the following law and the client's facts, and think about what components you would need for a Question Presented.

The client, Nicole Burke, was injured on an "extreme" ropes course as a result of incorrect safety instructions given by the course leader (who is employed by the owner of the course). The obstacle course is a recreational activity, but it is located on property owned by the State's Department of Public Parks and leased to the business owner. Before the activity, Burke signed a release of liability, which expressly stated that the course leaders would not be held liable for any negligence. She wants to know if the exculpatory clause will prohibit her from recovering for her extensive injuries. Specifically, she wants to know if such waivers violate public policy. You have looked up the statute and a some background information on these types of releases and found this:

California Civil Code § 1668

"A contract violates public policy if it seeks directly or indirectly to exempt anyone from responsibility for his own fraud, or willful injury to the person or property of another, or violation of law, whether willful or negligent."

Background information from state treatise:

A release (also known as an exculpatory clause) is a contract by which the potential plaintiff purportedly agrees to relieve the potential defendant of tort liability.

A release violates public policy if it concerns an important public function. *Tunkl v. Regents of the University of California*, 60 Cal. 2d 92, 101 (1963). Two factors used in determining if an activity concerns an important public function is whether such activities are suitable for public regulation and are of great public importance. *Id.* at 98–99. Recreational activities are usually not deemed to be important public functions. The maintenance of State Park lands is of great public importance.

1. **How would you phrase the issue using the statement/statement/question format?**

_____

_____

_____

_____

_____

_____

2. **Now rewrite the issue using the under/does/when format.**

_____

_____

_____

_____

_____

_____

3. **Finally, rewrite the issue using the whether/which/when format.**

_____

_____

_____

_____

_____

_____

Exercise 10.5: Constructing a Brief Answer

Assume a client has come to you after being charged with Third Degree Robbery for taking a necklace from a former boyfriend while waving a metal-pronged track cleat at him and scratching his arm. The legal question is whether the element of "threat of imminent force" was met when she waved the cleat. (The scenario was used in Exercises 5.3 and 9.7.) Read the two Brief Answers that follow and answer the questions.

Brief Answer 1

Ms. Perkins violated state law when she attacked her former boyfriend with a spiked track shoe. Given the aggressive manner in which Ms. Perkins approached her friend while holding the spiked shoe, she threatened imminent force.

1. **Assuming that this selection is intended to answer a Question Presented (like those in Examples 10.B–10.D), what information is missing from this Brief Answer? (Hint: More than one thing may be missing.) What information included in the Brief Answer is not relevant to the legal question?**

_____

_____

_____

_____

_____

_____

2. **If another associate drafted the Brief Answer and asked you to give feedback on it, what revisions would you suggest the associate make?**

_____

_____

_____

_____

_____

_____

Review the following Brief Answer and answer the questions that follow.

Brief Answer 2

Yes. Our client most likely threatened the "imminent use of force" to compel Mr. Miller to part with his possessions. The court will rely on the defendant's apparent intention, ability, and means to harm in assessing whether the defendant threatened the imminent use of force. The court will also look at how the victim perceived the threats made by the defendant. A defendant has the intention, ability, and means to inflict harm if the defendant makes a verbal threat while brandishing a weapon and the victim unwillingly parts with belongings because of that threat. Here, Ms. Perkins made a verbal threat while waving a metal-pronged cleat, giving the appearance that she had the means to harm Mr. Miller, and causing Mr. Miller to part with his belongings. Because our client threated Mr. Miller with a "dangerous instrument," she can be charged with first degree robbery.

3. What information does Brief Answer 2 contain that was missing from Brief Answer 1?

_____

_____

_____

_____

_____

_____

4. As a reader, do you have all of the information you need for the issue from this brief answer? If not, how would you recommend this Brief Answer be revised?

_____

_____

_____

_____

_____

_____

Chapter 11
Statement of Facts

I. **Choosing the Relevant Facts and an Organizational Framework**
   A. **Selecting Relevant Facts**
   B. **Selecting an Organizational Framework**
   C. **Other Drafting Considerations**
II. **Exercises**

The Statement of Facts in an interoffice memorandum of law tells the legal story of a client's case. The Statement of Facts should be written **objectively**. What does that term mean? Visualize a client telling you about the facts that brought her to your office, for which she has strong conclusions. How did she sound when she communicated these facts to you, her attorney? Then visualize a different scenario—your supervising attorney asking you to research how the law applies to certain facts in a client's case. How did those facts sound to you as the partner relayed them?

In both scenarios, the conclusion is yet to be determined but the facts may be skewed toward one side. The facts from the client's perspective may be slanted—after all, when a person consults a lawyer, that person may have been wronged or that person may have been accused of wrong doing. The partner may also convey the facts in a somewhat slanted way, especially when considering how to get a good result for the client.

Your job in writing an objective memo, however, is to present the facts from the perspective of a neutral observer, perhaps seeing them as a judge would. Thus, the facts are not slanted. Put differently, the facts are not written as an attempt to persuade the reader of an outcome. Instead, they are explained from the perspective of a neutral observer without the lawyer's clever pen striking a persuasive flair.

The exercises in this chapter will walk you through the many considerations a lawyer faces when writing the Statement of Facts.

I. Choosing the Relevant Facts and an Organizational Framework

The Statement of Facts plays several roles in a legal memorandum. First, the section lays the foundation for the legal questions that have arisen, allowing the reader to see the entire story. The section allows you to synthesize the facts from all different kinds of sources—like documents, interviews, police reports, depositions, and testimony—and present those facts clearly in one section. The section also memorializes the facts as you understand them. By writing a Statement of Facts, you might see holes in the underlying story, or at the very least, let the supervising attorney or client correct errors, see omissions, or understand what facts were known at that date in time.

Most importantly, the Statement of Facts tells the reader how the factual story of the case supports your analysis. Most of the time, the application of the law turns on the facts. Crafting a thorough and accurate statement of relevant facts lets the reader see that your analysis is well supported.

A. Selecting Relevant Facts

Lawyers group facts into three primary categories: legally significant facts, background facts, and emotional facts. Although lawyers do not actually use these designations in the written legal document, these categories help a lawyer mentally sort and triage the kinds of facts at play in the story.

- **Legally significant facts.** The facts from the client's case that a court will need to decide the legal outcome. Also known as "key facts" or "critical facts."
- **Background facts.** Background facts are not needed to decide the legal issue, but they may provide context that will help the reader understand the story.
- **Emotional facts.** Facts that help the reader feel sympathy or understanding for one party or another. Again, the legal issue may not turn on those facts, but strategic use of these facts may help to sway the judge deciding the legal issues.

Selecting relevant facts is often most easily done when you are going through the file. Using a short table like the one below in Exercise 11.1 can help you sort facts efficiently according to the issues you are researching.

When sorting and choosing relevant facts, a few tips can help you.

- Include *all* relevant facts, even ones that do not favor your client's position. The other side will certainly know about most negative facts, and it will be better for the supervising attorney to hear those facts and frame them in the least damaging way for your client.
- Note any unknown facts that are relevant to the legal issues being decided.
- Include one to two sentences indicating the procedural posture of the case at the time the memo is being written (either at the beginning or the end of the facts statement).

B. Selecting an Organizational Framework

Once you have sorted the facts and determined the most relevant and legally significant facts of the case, you must now organize the facts. Facts can be written using one (or even a combination of) three organizational frameworks:

- **Chronologically**, describing events along a time line;
- **Topically**, grouping facts by issue or category; or
- **Perceptually**, presenting facts from the various participants' vantage points.

Most often, you will use a straight chronological framework unless the facts will be more easily understood if organized differently. For example, if you are working on a memorandum that includes conflicting testimonies from multiple witnesses, you might choose the perceptual framework.

You might even use a combination of these frameworks. Say, for example, that you are working on a breach of contract case involving an airplane manufacturer who is suing two suppliers for faulty wing flaps. The manufacturer's headquarters is in Tacoma, Washington, but the planes are constructed in Bend, Oregon. The supplier of the computer equipment controlling the flaps is in Redding, California, and the supplier of the metal flaps is in Columbus, Georgia. With a complicated facts scenario involving multiple parties, a straight chronological organization might be confusing; instead, you might organize the facts section topically by describing with whom and where each contract was executed. Within that topical construct, you might then organize the facts chronologically.

C. Other Drafting Considerations

When writing the Statement of Facts, you will want to adhere to the same formal conventions that you will use in the other parts of the legal memorandum. Here are a few specific ways to improve your Statement of Facts.

- Use **vivid verbs** and **good word choice** to tell a story.
- **Avoid characterizing facts**. Vivid verbs create a good story; adjectives and adverbs can sometimes slant the story too much for an objective legal analysis. ("The defendant waved the spiked cleat" uses an action verb. "The defendant viciously waved the cleat" is a characterization.)
- **Use good paragraph structure** to make the section more readable and to chunk related facts together.
- **Use headings** within the Statement of Facts, particularly when using a topical or perceptual organizational framework, or whenever a heading will aid the reader.
- Unless the name of a person is particularly important, **use the person's role in the story** rather than their name. For example, "the investigating officer" may be less confusing or distracting than "Officer Brooks Whitney."
- **Keep the past in the past**. Describe past facts in past tense.
- **Cite your sources**. When reviewing a real file or record for a client, you may have dozens, if not hundreds, of documents including interviews, letters, and records, from which to draw your facts. Be kind to yourself, your supervising attorney, and anyone else who works on the case by clearly and accurately citing the source of the fact.

With these ground rules in place, you are ready to develop your skills in writing a Statement of Facts.

II. Exercises

The following exercises will help you identify and sort relevant facts and help you discern the most important facts to use in a memorandum. You will get practice deciding how to utilize various types of facts and how to distinguish legally significant facts from background and emotional facts.

Exercise 11.1: Sorting and Categorizing Facts

A potential client, Tom Balt, comes to your law firm for legal advice. He wants to know if he can sue another person, Mr. Walsh, who posted derogatory pictures and information about him on social media. The supervising attorney asks you to get started on the Statement of Facts for a memo, but first you are advised to read for context the Restatement of Torts and an accompanying case. Your ultimate goal is to provide reasoned analysis as to whether Balt would be successful in a lawsuit against Walsh grounded upon the tort of intentional infliction of emotional distress. For now, you are asked to focus on just one element of the tort: whether Walsh engaged in extreme and outrageous conduct. First, review the elements of the tort claim.[1]

Restatement (Second) of Torts § 46
§ 46 Outrageous Conduct Causing Severe Emotional Distress

(1) One who by extreme and outrageous conduct intentionally or recklessly causes severe emotional distress to another is subject to liability for such emotional distress, and if bodily harm to the other results from it, for such bodily harm.

(2) Where such conduct is directed at a third person, the actor is subject to liability if he intentionally or recklessly causes severe emotional distress

(a) to a member of such person's immediate family who is present at the time, whether or not such distress results in bodily harm, or

(b) to any other person who is present at the time, if such distress results in bodily harm.

After researching New York law, you identify the governing rule from a leading case.

Chanko v. Amer. Broad. Co., 49 N.E. 3d 1171 (N.Y. 2016)
(citations omitted)

New York courts have identified four elements of the tort of intentional infliction of emotional distress: "(i) extreme and outrageous conduct; (ii) intent to cause, or disregard of a substantial probability of causing, severe emotional distress; (iii) a causal connection between the conduct and injury; and (iv) severe emotional distress." Liability can be found only where the conduct has been "so outrageous in character, and so extreme in degree, as to go beyond all possible bounds of decency, and to be regarded as atrocious, and utterly intolerable in a civilized community."

---

1. This fact pattern was inspired by a true story reported in a radio interview conducted over National Public Radio on August 4, 2017. Names and some events were changed.

You are told by your supervisor to assume that Balt can establish the other three elements of the tort (intention, causation, and that Balt actually suffered severe emotional distress). Next, you are instructed to review the client's version of the facts and work through the directions that follow.

Your Client's Facts:

Tom Balt worked in the fishing industry on Long Island until his back and arms (which had been injured many times) were too weak to lift the heavy nets. At age 55, after working in the business for 35 years, Balt left his job and filed for permanent disability. Balt resides in a house that he owns in Franklin Square, New York. On a monthly basis, Balt receives a check in the amount of $700 per month for his disability. However, he has two other people in his house to feed. His son, John, is nineteen years old and unemployed. John attempted to go to community college, but he stopped attending classes. Balt's wife, Angela, has always worked as a stay-at-home mom, and occasionally takes on sewing or clothing alterations projects.

On April 15, Balt opened the refrigerator and saw that there was so little food that his family would not make it to the end of the month. Balt decided to take matters into his own hands, and he drove to Uniondale, a town five miles away. He parked his car in an intersection where a steady stream of cars passed. Balt got out of the car and held up a sign for the passing drivers to see that said, "I'm disabled and need money to feed my family." Some people slowed down and yelled slurs at him, calling him "white trash," and taunted him with comments like "get a job!" Others showed compassion and gave him money. Balt went home that night with $50 and was able to buy groceries for the week.

The next week, on April 22, Balt went back to the same town and tried again. He felt uncomfortable begging for money. A town resident, Joe Walsh, saw Balt and approached him. Walsh said, "I can do you one better. I can offer you a job. How about working at Burger Heaven? I'm a manager and I'm hiring." Balt replied, "No thanks. I'd rather not." Balt did not give Walsh any further explanation.

Walsh was furious at Balt's response. Walsh had seen many people in town on public assistance that had not applied for jobs. Walsh returned to where Balt was standing, this time with his own sign. Walsh's sign said, "I offered this jerk a job and he turned it down. You gonna give him your hard-earned money?" Balt stood there, frozen for about 10 minutes, and then he packed up and left. Before Balt left, Walsh took a picture of Balt.

The next day, Balt got a phone call from someone he knew who said that they had seen a photograph of him on Facebook. Walsh had posted this comment on his Facebook page: "Look at this jerk—he turns down a job and now wants your money." Next to that statement was Balt's picture taken the previous day, holding a sign, with Balt's face blurred. Balt's name was not mentioned on Facebook. Walsh removed the posting after six weeks. Since then, Balt has felt emotionally weak and has sought counseling.

1. **Using the facts listed above, sort and select the facts you would put into a Statement of Facts based upon what you know now. You can use the table below or your own scratch paper.**

IIED Case Fact Chart			
Elements of Claim	**Legally Significant Facts**	**Background Facts**	**Emotional Facts**
Extreme and outrageous conduct			

Exercise 11.2: Critique a Statement of Facts

This exercise asks you to evaluate and critique two separate Statements of Facts. Review each and provide feedback to the author (in the margin) as you would if you were the supervising attorney. Then answer the questions that follow.

Statement of Facts Sample 1

On April 22, Tom Balt traveled to a busy intersection, five miles from his residence, to beg for money. Balt held up a sign that read, "I'm disabled and need money to feed my family." He had done this same thing a week before, and some passing drivers shouted comments like "get a job!"

Joe Walsh then approached Balt and offered him a job, which Balt turned down. Walsh then held up his own sign that said, "I offered this jerk a job and he turned it down." Before Balt left, Walsh took a photograph of Balt holding his sign. The next day, Balt learned from an acquaintance that Walsh had posted the picture on Facebook with a comment that said, "Look at this jerk—he turns down a job and now wants your money." Balt's face was blurred in the picture and his name was omitted from the post. Balt felt bad and sought counseling following the incident.

Statement of Facts Sample 2

Mr. Balt was forced to file for permanent disability at age 55 because of an injury caused by the cumulative effect of working in the fishing industry for 35 years. Each month, Balt receives a check for $700; however, due to his family needs, the amount is not nearly enough to cover the family's monthly living expenses. On April 19, when the family was nearly out of food, Balt decided to take action. He drove to a neighboring town to beg at a busy intersection. He held a sign that read: "I'm disabled and need money to feed my family." He was bothered and embarrassed when some drivers would yell, "Get a job!" Balt collected $50 that day and was able to buy enough groceries to feed the family until the next week.

On April 22, Balt returned to the same location in hopes of getting grocery money. As Balt held the sign, Joe Walsh, the manager of the local Burger Heaven, approached Balt and offered him a job. Without explanation, Balt denied the offer. Upset by the rejection, Walsh returned to where Balt was standing holding his own sign describing how he had offered "this jerk" a job and he refused. The sign was meant to interfere with Balt's ability to solicit donations. Embarrassed, Balt tried to leave, but not before Walsh took his photograph. The next day, Balt was notified by an acquaintance of a Facebook post. The posting, by Walsh, contained a blurred photo of Balt with the comment: "Look at this jerk—he turned down a job and now wants your money." The post was removed after six weeks. Balt has felt emotionally weak and has sought counseling since the event.

1. **Which Statement of Facts do you think is the best version for a memorandum of law? Why?**

_____

_____

_____

_____

_____

_____

2. **What should the writer of the weaker version do to strengthen and improve the Statement of Facts?**

_____

_____

_____

_____

_____

3. If the one that you selected as the better version needs improvement, what changes would you make?

_____

_____

_____

_____

_____

_____

Exercise 11.3: Selecting and Categorizing Facts using Sections 50/51 of the New York Civil Rights Law

The following are your supervising attorney's interview notes with a celebrity client. The attorney has asked you to review the notes as you prepare to research the claim. As with most interviews, the conversation jumped around a bit.

Lorna Sheena is a celebrity and has appeared in numerous full-length movies and television shows. She appears on Saturday Night Live approximately twice each year. She also has had a few roles in Broadway shows. Lately, she has been working on producing a film based upon the women's movement. Her mother, Toma, is a well-known feminist who was an outspoken activist in the #metoo movement.[2]

She comes to your firm and complains that a video game, created by Show-Me Games, Inc., used an avatar of her without her permission. The avatar is a character who looks like her and has the same sounding voice.

The video game is called "Grand Diamond Heist" ("Heist"). Heist was released to the public on July 1, for use on the current PlayStation and Xbox video game consoles. Heist video game takes place in the fictional city "Los Jamaica," which itself is in a fictional American state of "San Utopia." Heist was described by a consumer magazine as "an 'open world' video game, allowing each player to freely explore its virtual environment and choose to experience (or not) missions, random events, and activities. Heist depicts a stinging parody of California culture through its fictional locations, characters, and consumer products."

Players control one of several main characters at various points in the game, engaging in approximately 80 main story missions as well as many optional random events. The player steps into the shoes of one of the three main characters to complete various "missions" and "random events" and reach a goal of "100% completion." To reach 100% completion, the player must complete 14 out of 56

---

2. Facts of this exercise were inspired by the brief filings and court decisions of this case: _Gravano v. Take-Two Interactive Software, Inc._, 142 A.D.3d 776, 37 N.Y.S.3d 20 (1st Dep't 2016), _aff'd_, 31 N.Y.3d 988, 73 N.Y.S.3d 780 (2018).

"random events." Each random event is an individual story that focuses on a specific character or event.

Heist tells the story of three complicated men—Monty, Fredo, and Trey—all getting rich by stealing jewelry. The main storyline runs about 50 hours and consists of approximately 80 missions. More than 100 hours of additional gameplay is available, including over 60 random events and dozens of activities. At various times, players can choose to control Monty, Fredo, or Trey. These three characters have unique, well-defined abilities and personalities: Monty is an ex-convict; Fredo is a college student who strikes up an unlikely friendship with Trey, who remains a dangerous criminal.

Ms. Sheena claims that during certain optional random events, called "Escape the Cops," the player encounters a character hiding in an alleyway, called Andreas Fault, who is a depiction of her. Sheena tells you that Fault, depicted in 3-D animation, looks like her face and body. It also uses a similar voice, which is uncanny to Ms. Sheena. (Your supervisor played the video game and agrees that there is a resemblance in the voice, although the avatar's face is different.)

Specifically, Sheena says that the Fault character uses the same phrases she uses when being interviewed by the media. For instance, Sheena often says, "get like real," and Fault says the same thing on two occasions in the game.

There are four different versions of the random event, depending on whether the player is controlling Monty, Fredo, or Trey, but the content of the random event is essentially the same in all four. Should the player encounter the optional random event and choose to participate, the character must evade the chasing police cars and drive Fault home. Fault states in the game that the cops are chasing her because she is a "really famous" actress but she just shoplifted a bracelet from a jewelry store, and the character expresses surprise that the player does not recognize her. Fault enters the player's automobile. She tells the driver that she must evade the "cops, like they are following me like mad." During the drive, the player's character may recognize Fault as the star of romantic comedies and a cheerleader dance-off movie. The Fault character is programmed to make a variety of random statements to the player's character during the drive to her home. Among them are that she is an "actress slash singer" and the "voice of a generation." The Escape the Cops random event takes about five minutes to complete.

Sheena tells you that Heist uses her portrait and voice for its character, although her actual voice is not used, she is not depicted by use of a true picture, nor is she mentioned by name. Both Sheena and Fault are young blonde women. (When your supervisor played the game, he did not think that there was a striking physical resemblance.) Toma, Sheena's mom, is also interested in the case, because she believes there is too much violence against women in video games.

Sheena was caught shoplifting in real life, but she was attempting to steal a necklace, not a bracelet. The newspapers ran headlines about her shoplifting for weeks. Sheena also had starred in a few romantic comedies in real-life, and one character she played was a cheerleader.

Sheena complains that Heist uses identical events to her life, referring to the portrayal of a Hollywood figure being chased by cops. She also claims that Heist features a hotel similar to the Hollywood West Hotel, where she once resided. Heist is a parody of Los Angeles, and Hollywood West Hotel is well known. The Fault character, however, states that she lives in a home on Canyon Drive in the "Hills," not in a hotel. Sheena feels that the avatar is closer to reality than fiction and said, "It's me, it's totally me." Sheena has sought the help of a publicist to improve her public image as well as a counselor to help her with depression that Heist has triggered.

You are asked to write a memorandum of law to your supervising attorney predicting whether Sheena could be successful on a claim that an avatar (that is, a graphical representation of a person, in a video game or like media) may constitute a "portrait" within the meaning of Civil Rights Law §§ 50 and 51 and, if so, whether the images in question in the video game central to this matter are recognizable as Sheena.

Review the statutes and case excerpts below then answer the questions to help you assess, sort, and organize the facts relevant to this case.

New York Statute §§ 50 & 51
(called "The Civil Rights Law")

The statutory purpose of Sections 50 and 51 of the Civil Rights Law is to protect persons against the nonconsensual use of their "name, portrait, or picture" in commercial circumstances ("trade or advertising"). Section 50 makes it a misdemeanor if this law is violated. (Note: there is scant history of any defendant actually receiving criminal sanctions.)

> Section 50 states: "A person, firm, or corporation that uses for advertising purposes, or for the purposes of trade, the name, portrait or picture of any living person without having first obtained the written consent of such person, or if a minor of his or her parent or guardian, is guilty of a misdemeanor."

> Section 51 creates a civil remedy. Section 51 states: "Any person whose name, portrait, picture or voice is used within this state for advertising purposes or for the purpose of trade without consent first obtained [as provided in section 50] may maintain an equitable action . . . to prevent and restrain the use thereof, and may also sue and recover damages for any injuries sustained by reason of such use."

Case 1

Costanza v. Seinfeld
Intermediate Court for State of New York

An individual, Michael Costanza, brought an action against the creators of a television show based upon state statute §§ 50 & 51 in the lower court. The trial court granted defendant's motion to dismiss and Costanza brings this appeal.

According to the facts, plaintiff claimed that defendants used his name and persona to create a character, George Costanza, for the hit "Seinfeld" television program. This court affirms the lower court's decision. Defendants did not use the plaintiff's actual name within the meaning of the statute. The first names differed. Also, the court found that the defendants did not use his photograph or persona. Plaintiff did have a brief appearance in one episode, however, this was not sufficient to be actionable. Held for defendant.

Case 2

Hampton v. Guare
Intermediate Court for the State of New York

This civil case is on appeal from the trial court, which granted defendant Guare's motion to dismiss. Plaintiff, Hampton, is an aspiring actor, but with a criminal background. Previously, plaintiff had been convicted of attempted burglary and for criminal impersonation, and other related offenses. In this present civil action, plaintiff seeks compensatory and punitive damages against the author and producer of the award-winning Broadway play, "Six Degrees of Separation." The play was inspired in part by a widely reported criminal scam in which the plaintiff had convinced several affluent New Yorkers to allow him into their homes and to give him money and other things of value by pretending that he knew their children from college and that he was the son of the actor Sidney Poitier.

We agree with the lower court, that plaintiff has failed to state a cognizable claim for commercial misappropriation under sections 50 and 51 of the Civil Rights Law of this state. Plaintiff's name, portrait or picture was not used in the play, and works of fiction and satire do not fall within the narrow scope of the statutory phrases "advertising" and "trade." Affirmed.

Using the Lorna Sheena fact scenario, answer the following questions, adhering to any directions.

1. **Based on the law provided in the statutes and case excerpts, what are the elements or factors that Sheena will need to prove for a successful claim?**

_____

_____

_____

_____

_____

_____

2. **Using a colored highlighter pen, highlight the facts relevant to proving the claim. Briefly describe the key determinative facts upon which the court's decision will turn in this case.**

_____

_____

_____

_____

3. List the background facts that would be important to include in your memo. Beside each fact, describe why you would include that fact.

_____

_____

_____

_____

_____

_____

4. List any emotional facts not really relevant to the legal issue but important to the case.

_____

_____

_____

_____

_____

_____

Chapter 12
Statutory Interpretation

I. **Statutory Analysis: Understanding the Statute**

II. **Interpreting the Statute**

   A. **Understanding a Court's Methodology**

   B. **Sources of Evidence and How They Are Used**

III. **Exercises**

Laws are increasingly being codified in statutes and regulations, so you may often find yourself doing statutory analysis. As you practice law, you will likely analyze statutes in two main ways. First, you might analyze a statute to see if the facts of your case fit within the boundaries of that statute. Second, when words or phrases in the statute are ambiguous, you might need to interpret what the legislature intended the statute to mean. Since ambiguous words in a statute can be interpreted in more than one way, your client's case may turn on which interpretation is used.

This chapter will allow you to revisit the skills for the deep reading of a statute that you learned in Chapter 3.1, *Reading Statutes,* and help you practice the skills for proficiently analyzing an ambiguous statute.

I. Statutory Analysis: Understanding the Statute

Whenever a statute, regulation, or any other codified law is part of your analysis, your first task is to read the statute carefully and parse every word. You went through the three-step process of deep reading and parsing in Chapter 3.1. Apply those steps to the reading of statutes in this chapter:

1. Get context (see how the statute is organized and where the statute fits in the broader statutory scheme);
2. Skim the pertinent statutory sections (look for big concepts and how the parts fit together); and
3. Read the statute carefully and question it.

In employing those steps for statutory analysis, you are moving from broad ideas (looking to understand how the statute generally works and its component parts) to more narrow ideas (what the words of the statute actually mean and how they apply). After completing the three steps, you will start to answer the questions relating to how the statute works:

- To whom does this statute apply?
- Is this statute intended to prohibit or punish conduct?
- Or is it intended to encourage or regulate action?
- Is the statute civil or criminal?
- Where does this statute fit in the overall statutory scheme?

Further, you will better see how the component parts fit together. In reviewing the component parts, note what the subsections say and the relationship among the different parts of the statute. Pay special attention to the major components:

- The **elements or factors** that make up the statute, and
- The **red flag words** (the operative words that restrict, expand, or order the elements or factors within the statute)

Once you've assessed the statute and have a good understanding of the statute's component parts and how it generally works, you are ready either to apply the statute, as you did in Chapter 3.1, *Reading Statutes,* to your case or interpret any ambiguous terms.

II.   Interpreting the Statute

Although you may frequently need only to apply a statute to your facts, the second way in which you might work with a statute is to analyze an ambiguous term or phrase within the statute itself before applying it to your client's case. This kind of analysis is often called **statutory interpretation** or **statutory construction**.

When interpreting an ambiguous statute, you will need to know two things: First, you must know the methodology, or steps of analysis, courts in your jurisdiction will use to interpret the statute. Second, you must know what kinds of evidence the court will rely on during each step of analysis. Understanding these pieces and how they intersect will allow you to fully answer your client's question in the same way that a court would.

A. Understanding a Court's Methodology

Courts from different jurisdictions may be more or less rigid in the methodology they use. When analyzing your client's problem, you must first determine the number of analytical levels courts in your jurisdiction prefer. In addition to understanding the levels, you will also need to know the types of evidence courts will consider on each level.

When divining the legislature's intent, courts generally start with the statute and work outward. Courts rely on three types of evidence to ascertain the legislature's intent—intrinsic evidence, extrinsic evidence, and policy as explained in Table 12.A.

Table 12.A: Examples of Intrinsic and Extrinsic Evidence

Type of Evidence	What It Is	Examples
Intrinsic Evidence	Cues from the within the statute itself.	• Words, phrasing, syntax, grammar, and punctuation of the statutory text • Judicial canons of construction evaluating the words themselves
Extrinsic Evidence	Any source outside the statute that provides evidence of how the statute should be interpreted.	• Legislative history • Regulations • Cases dealing with the general subject at issue or that can be analogized to the statutory phrase in question • Canons of construction pertaining to general maxims • Scholarly commentary
Policy	Policy-based sources (also a form of extrinsic sources) explain the reasons behind the law and help courts interpret what the legislature intended.	• Canons of construction that are not neutral on policy: these might espouse social values (like that of reasonableness or fairness), due process, or preference for one branch of government over another.

As explained above, in conjunction with the three types of evidence, a jurisdiction's methodology determines what kinds of evidence can come in at each level of analysis. Some courts do not explicitly espouse a methodology, but start with the words of the statute and then fluidly move on to other kinds of evidence. Other courts, however, do use a defined methodology. For example, consider Oregon's methodology. Based upon a statute and a seminal case,[1] the Oregon Supreme Court set out a methodology following a three-tiered structured as illustrated in Table 12.B below. Under that methodology, the court could move beyond the text and context of the statute only in instances in which an ambiguity remained.

---

1. *P.G.E. v. Bureau of Labor and Indus.*, 859 P.2d 1143, 1145–47 (Or. 1993).

Table 12.B: Example of a Three-Tiered Methodology (Under Previous Oregon Law)

Level	What evidence is examined	Kind of evidence
Level I	Text and Context "if, but only if" an ambiguity existed in the words and context of the statute could the court go on to the next level.	Intrinsic
Level II	Legislative History	Extrinsic and Policy
Level III	Everything else	Extrinsic and Policy

After that case was decided, the Oregon legislature amended the statute to be less restrictive on the use of legislative history. In response, the Oregon Supreme Court adhered to the statute and altered its methodology[2] to follow a two-tiered structure, illustrated in Table 12.C, that allows legislative history to be presented even when analysis of the text and context resolve any ambiguity.

Table 12.C: Example of a Two-Tiered Methodology

Level	What evidence is examined	Kind of evidence
Level I	Text and Context Legislative history (only if proffered by the parties to support an argument)	Intrinsic Extrinsic and Policy
Level II	Everything else	Extrinsic and Policy

Because jurisdictions may allow various kinds of evidence to come in on different levels, a jurisdiction's methodology should be at the forefront of your mind when interpreting a statute. A failure to grasp the methodology could lead to faulty legal analysis. You could not, for example, analyze an ambiguous statute by presenting legislative history first. Instead, you would need to start with the words themselves then examine the context of the ambiguous words and phrases in that statutory section.

Since courts in different jurisdictions vary on the number of levels and what kinds of evidence can come in on each level, be sure to give your objective analysis firm footing by understanding what your jurisdiction requires. The next section will provide a little more information as to the different sources of evidence.

B. Sources of Evidence and How They Are Used

The evidence used to support statutory construction can come from many different sources of primary law. As explained above, courts divine the intent of the legislature by first starting with intrinsic sources arising from the words of the statute or the cues surrounding the statute. Courts then move outward to the context of the statute. If a word or term is still ambiguous, courts will continue moving outward to other sources of law like regulations, legislative history, and other extrinsic sources.

---

2. *See State v. Gaines*, 206 P.2d 1042 (Or. 2009).

Table 12.D: Types of Authority Used in Statutory Construction

Kind of evidence	What it is	Types of evidence	Examples
Intrinsic	Evidence from within the text of the statute itself	Text of the statute	The plain meaning—what the words say on their face. Words (ordinary words given their ordinary meaning and technical words given their technical meaning), syntax, grammar, and punctuation of text.
		Context	The ambiguous words in context with the rest of the statute or with other related statutes. May also include: • the overall statutory scheme, • prior cases interpreting the language at issue, and • textual canons of construction.
		Cases that apply the ambiguous term	
Extrinsic	Evidence coming from sources outside the statute	Legislative History Cases	Cases that apply the statutory language or deal with issues relating to the statute at issue (but not those cases interpreting the ambiguous terms).
		Agency interpretations or regulations	
		Non-textual canons of construction	
		Law review articles	

When interpreting a statute, courts frequently use judicial **canons of construction**. These canons are judicial maxims that courts rely on to support their analyses. Canons of construction come in two main varieties, intrinsic canons and extrinsic canons. Intrinsic canons are maxims that look at internal cues from the statute itself—its words, grammar, linguistics, syntax, or the context in which the ambiguous words or phrases are placed. Extrinsic canons are those maxims that guide the interpreter by using judicial norms coming from outside of the statute. Extrinsic canons are further broken down into two main kinds: Non-textual (substantive) canons of construction and substantive policy canons. Table 12.E sets out examples of the different canons.

Table 12.E: Canons of Construction

Type of Evidence	Type of Canon	Examples

Intrinsic	Textual Canons[3]	**Canon regarding the plain meaning rule**
		• "If language is plain and unambiguous it must be given effect."
		
		Canons regarding specific words:
		• "'May' means permissive; 'shall' means mandatory."
		• "'And' means conjunctive; 'or' means disjunctive."
		   Example: "fruits, seeds, nuts, vegetables, honey, sheep, cattle, pigs, *and* poultry." A person must produce all of these things to come under the statute. Change "and" to "or," and a person would have to produce only one of them.
		
		Canons regarding lists of things
		• **Noscitur a sociis:** Interpret an ambiguous word in a list by the company it keeps, that is, in light of the surrounding words.
		   "including pigs, cattle, sheep, and poultry." "Poultry" would not include exotic birds. Could llamas be included?
		• **Ejusdem generis:** General, catch-all phrases at the end of a list are construed to mean the same kind or type as the rest of the list.
		   If "motor vehicle" is defined as a "car, truck, motorcycle, moped, or any other self-propelled vehicle with a seat not designed for running on rails," does it include a lawnmower? A motorized (standing) scooter?
		• **Expressio unius, exlusio alterius:** Enumeration of specific things implies the exclusion of all others. If the word is not in, then it is meant to be out.
		   "rain, sleet, and hail" excludes snow.
		
		Canon explaining that a statute cannot go beyond its text.
		
		Canon saying that language does not have to be given effect if a literal interpretation would lead to an absurd result or thwart the purpose of the statute.
		
		In pari materia: Statutes with the same subject or purpose should be read together to effectuate that purpose.
		   For example, a statute setting out the punishment for kidnapping should be read in conjunction with a statute setting out sentencing guidelines for felonies.

---

3. Table adapted from Christine Nero Coughlin, Joan Rocklin, and Sandy Patrick, *A Lawyer Writes* 201–02 (3d ed. 2018). These examples of canons have been frequently used over the years, and the original source of the examples is unknown.

Type of Evidence	Type of Canon	Examples
Extrinsic	Non-textual (or Substantive) Canons[4]	**Here are a few non-textual canons:** 1. Statutes in derogation of the common law will be narrowly construed. 2. Statutes are to be read in the light of the common law, and a statute affirming a common law rule is to be construed in accordance with the common law. 3. Remedial statutes will be construed broadly. 4. Penal statutes will be construed narrowly. 5. A statutory provision requiring liberal construction does not mean disregard of unequivocal requirements of the statute.
	Substantive Policy[5] Canons	Separation of Powers Canons **Canon to reinforce the separation of powers** **Canon to avoid interpretations that would make a statute unconstitutional** **Canon of severability that favors severing an unconstitutional provision** Due Process Canons **Canon against interpreting statutes to deny a person the right to a jury trial** **Canon presuming that judgments will not be binding upon persons not party to a proceeding**

---

4. *See* Kent Greenawait, *Legislation, Statutory Interpretation: 20 Questions* 206–09 (1999); Linda D. Jellum & David Charles Hricik, *Modern Statutory Interpretation: Problems, Theories, and Lawyering Strategies* 429 (2006). Both sources rely on excerpts from Karl N. Llewellyn, *Remarks on the Theory of Appellate Decision and the Rules or Canons About How Statutes Are to be Construed*, 3 Vand. L. Rev. 395, 401–06 (1949).

5. Adapted from Jacob Scott, *Codified Canons and the Common Law of Interpretation*, 98 Geo. L.J. 341, 382–88 (2010).

III. Exercises

The exercises below will help you to identify and work with the nuts and bolts of a statute. They will ensure that you can grasp commonly used terms when engaging in statutory interpretation and analyze ambiguous terms precisely.

Exercise 12.1: Understanding Key Terms of Statutory Interpretation

Match each term to its correct definition by writing the letter of the definition in the blank.

_____ plain meaning rule

_____ intrinsic evidence

_____ extrinsic evidence

_____ red flag words

_____ ambiguous word

_____ text

_____ a court's methodology

_____ context

_____ legislative history

_____ canons of construction

_____ textual canons of construction

_____ substantive canons of construction

A. Sources outside of the statute that provide evidence of the legislature's intent

B. The operative terms in a statute

C. The analytical steps courts of a jurisdiction will use to interpret a statute and the specific evidence a court will allow at each step

D. The exact words of the statute

E. Reading the words as written and interpreting them on their face

F. Legal maxims that judges rely on to interpret the law

G. The historical record of a bill as it makes its way through bicameral or unicameral government

H. Canons that look to the text of the statute—words, grammar, and syntax—to discern what the legislature intended

I. A word that is susceptible to more than one meaning

J. General legal maxims that do not address the text of the statute, but that consider general legal norms

K. Cues from within the text or context of the statute that illuminate the legislature's intent

L. The words, phrases, or related statutes that surround the ambiguous words or phrase

Exercise 12.2: Working with a Case That Is Interpreting a Statute

Review the case of *Chatwin v. U.S.* (adapted and summarized below), and respond to the questions that follow:

United States Supreme Court
Chatwin v. United States
326 U.S. 455 (1946)

Mr. Justice MURPHY delivered the opinion of the Court.

The Federal Kidnapping Act punishes with imprisonment for a term of 25 years to life anyone who "seizes, confines, inveigles, decoys, abducts or carries away and holds for ransom or reward or otherwise any person, except a minor by a parent." The sole issue confronting us in this case is whether the stipulated facts support the conviction of Appellant under this Act. The parties have stipulated that the defendant inveigled, carried away and held a minor child for a stated period. We are not called upon to determine or characterize the morality of the actions. Nor are we concerned here with liability under any other state or federal statute.

In August 1940, appellant Chatwin, who was then a 68-year-old widower, employed Dorothy Wyler as a live-in housekeeper in his home. The girl was almost 15 years old at the time, but she had a mental age of 7. Wyler's parents approved their daughter's employment by Chatwin. While residing at Chatwin's home in her employed capacity, the girl was continually told by Chatwin that plural marriage was essential to her salvation and in conformity with the true principles of their religion. As a result of these teachings, the girl was converted and entered into a marriage ceremony with Chatwin on December 19, 1940. Thereafter she became pregnant, which was discovered by her parents on July 24, 1941. The parents then informed the State juvenile authorities of the situation, and they took the girl into custody as a delinquent on August 4, 1941, making her a ward of the juvenile court.

On August 10, 1941, the girl accompanied a juvenile probation officer to a motion picture show in a nearby town. While the officer was out, the girl left the picture show and met Chatwin's two married daughters who gave her sufficient money to go back to Chatwin's home. Chatwin and two friends convinced her that she should abide "by the law of God rather than the law of man" and that she was perfectly justified in running away from the juvenile court to live with Chatwin. They further convinced her that she should go with them to Mexico to be married legally to Chatwin and then remain in hiding until she had reached her majority under Utah law. Chatwin and his friends transported the girl to Mexico, where she went through a civil marriage ceremony with Chatwin on October 14. She was then brought back to the U.S. where she lived in hiding with Chatwin under assumed names until discovered by federal authorities two years later, on December 9, 1943.

Having waived jury trial, Chatwin was found guilty as charged and sentenced to 25 years to life. The court below affirmed the conviction. We granted certiorari, because of our doubts as to the correctness of the judgment that the Appellant was guilty under the State Kidnapping Act on the basis of the foregoing facts.

Great stress is placed by the Government, however, upon the admitted fact that the girl possessed a mental age of 7 in 1940, one year before the alleged inveiglement and holding. A stipulated mental age of 7 cannot be said necessarily to preclude one from understanding and judging the principles of celestial marriage and from acting in accordance with one's beliefs in the matter. The serious crime of kidnapping should turn on something more substantial than such an unexplained mathematical approximation of the victim's mental age. There must be competent proof beyond a reasonable doubt of a victim's mental incapacity in relation to the very acts in question before criminal liability can be sanctioned in a case of this nature.

The stipulated facts of this case reveal a situation quite different from the general problem to which the framers of the Federal Kidnapping Act addressed themselves. This statute was drawn in 1932 against a background of organized violence. Kidnapping by that time had become an epidemic in the United States. Ruthless criminal bands utilized every known legal and scientific means to achieve their aims and to protect themselves. Victims were selected from among the wealthy with great care and study. Details of the seizures and detentions were fully and meticulously worked out in advance. Ransom was the usual motive.

It was to assist the states in stamping out this growing and sinister menace of kidnaping that the Federal Kidnapping Act was designed. Its proponents recognized that where victims were transported across state lines, only the federal government had the power to disregard such barriers in pursuing the captors. H. Rep. No. 1493 (72d Cong., 1st Sess.); S. Rep. No. 765 (72d Cong., 1st Sess.). Given added impetus by the emotion that gripped the nation after the famous Lindbergh kidnapping case, the federal statute was speedily adopted. Comprehensive language was used to cover every possible variety of kidnapping followed by interstate transportation. Armed with this legislative mandate, federal officials have achieved a high and effective control of this type of crime.

However, the broadness of the statutory language does not permit this court to tear the words out of their original context to apply them to every unattractive, immoral or unlawful situation. There is nothing in the language of the statute or in the legislative history to suggest the Act was to be used to assist the state in such matters, however unlawful or obnoxious the character of these activities might otherwise be. In short, the purpose of the act was to outlaw true kidnappings. The broad language of the statute is certainly not broad enough to encompass every transgression of law or morality that involves some deception and travel.

Were we to sanction a careless concept of the crime of kidnapping or were we to disregard the background and setting of the Act, the boundaries of potential liability would be lost in infinity. A loose construction of the statutory language conceivably could lead to the punishment of anyone who induced another to leave his surroundings and do some innocent or illegal act of benefit to the former, state lines subsequently being traversed. The absurdity of such a result, with its attendant likelihood of unfair punishment and blackmail, is sufficient by itself to foreclose that construction.

The judgment of the court below affirming the convictions of the petitioners must therefore be reversed.

Now that you've read the case, answer the following questions.

1. **Is this a civil or criminal case?**

   _____

   _____

2. **Who is the appellant? Who is the appellee?**

   _____

   _____

   _____

3. **What is the definition of kidnapping under the Federal Kidnapping Act?**

   _____

   _____

   _____

   _____

   _____

   _____

4. **What part of the Act does the court analyze?**

   _____

   _____

   _____

   _____

   _____

   _____

5. **What is the legislative history underlying the Act?**

   _____

   _____

   _____

_____

_____

_____

6. Why does the court reject a broad interpretation of the Act?

_____

_____

_____

_____

_____

7. Explain why the court was concerned about the effect of a broad interpretation of "ransom or reward or otherwise."

_____

_____

_____

_____

_____

8. What is the court's holding?

_____

_____

_____

_____

_____

9. Why do you think the court held as it did? Do you agree with the holding in this case? Why or why not?

_____

_____

_____

_____

_____

_____

Exercise 12.3: Interpreting an Ambiguous Statute

A new client has recently been charged with violating the National Motor Vehicle Theft Act after she stole a glider from a former business partner. Vanessa Arund is one of the only female certified glider pilots in the western states. She worked as a flight instructor at the Aero Aces Flight School, teaching lessons in flying various small planes and gliders. Vanessa had a falling out with her former business partner, Mark Grimble, and left the business. As part of her severance package, Mark was to pay her a sum equivalent to the cost of a glider. He did not, and months of a contentious relationship ensued along with a legal battle.

One night, in a fit of rage, Vanessa decided she would take matters into her own hands. She made her way into the school located at a small airport outside of Portland, Oregon, and convinced Cyd Maurer, a new instructor (who did not know about Vanessa's history with Grimble), to pilot the towplane that would take her up in Grimble's glider. Maurer agreed, and they set off with the towplane in front and the glider behind. Up in the air, however, once the glider was released from the towplane, Vanessa did not take the route on her flight plan. Instead, she glided into a small airport outside of Camas, Washington, where she landed and promptly sold the plane.

Vanessa was arrested a few days later for violating the National Motor Vehicle Theft Act, 18 U.S.C. § 408.

Language of the Statute, _"The National Motor Vehicle Theft Act,"_ 18 U.S.C. § 408
(from United States Code, Title 18: Crimes and Criminal Procedure)

The Act punishes "whoever transports, or causes to be transported, in interstate or foreign commerce a motor vehicle knowing it to have been stolen."

Definition of "Motor Vehicle"
(from the "Definitions" section of statute, 18 U.S.C. § 10)

"The term 'motor vehicle' when used in this section shall include an automobile, automobile truck, automobile wagon, motor cycle, or any other self-propelled vehicle not designed for running on rails."

Legislative History

The act was passed in 1920 to protect owners as automobiles and motorcycles became commonplace on America's roads and highways. Congress has had several opportunities to change the language in the definitions section, but has not. Airplanes were in existence in 1920.

Judicial Commentary:

"Although it is not likely that a criminal will carefully consider the text of the law before he murders or steals, it is reasonable that a fair warning should be given to the world, in language that the common world will understand, of what the law intends to do if a certain line is passed."

You want to argue that a glider is not a motor vehicle because it has no engine. The prosecution will argue that a glider is a motor vehicle.

Having read the excerpts above, answer the following questions.

1. **Get context for the statute.**

   a. Is the statute criminal or civil? _____

   b. When was the statute was enacted? _____

   c. Where is the statute in the overall statutory scheme, that is, in what part of the code is it placed? [Hint: Look at the name of Title 18.]

   _____

   _____

2. **Skim the most pertinent sections.**

   a. What exact language needs interpretation?

   _____

   _____

   _____

   _____

   _____

   b. Does the statute prohibit, require, or simply permit behavior?

   _____

   _____

_____

_____

_____

_____

c. What is the statute's limiting language?

_____

_____

_____

_____

_____

_____

d. Do any definitions from other sections affect or control words in our statute? List them here.

_____

_____

_____

_____

_____

3. **Read the text closely and question it.**

a. What exact words concern your client? Highlight or underline them. What are the red flag words in the relevant section? Circle them.

In plain words, what does the operative portion of the statute say?

_____

_____

_____

_____

_____

_____

b. What does "ambiguity" mean?

_____

_____

_____

_____

_____

_____

c. What exact words need interpretation because of ambiguity?

_____

_____

_____

_____

_____

_____

d. What are the dictionary definitions of the word or words at issue?

_____

_____

_____

_____

_____

_____

Now, get into pairs or groups of 4 with other colleagues. Half of you should evaluate the statute from one interpretation, and the other half should evaluate the opposing interpretation. Each side should answer the following questions.

1. **What is clear and what is confusing about the statute as a whole?**

    _____

    _____

    _____

    _____

    _____

    _____

2. **What does context add to your interpretation?**

    _____

    _____

    _____

    _____

    _____

    _____

3. **What intrinsic tools can your side use to support your argument?**

    _____

    _____

    _____

    _____

    _____

    _____

4. What extrinsic tools support your side?

_____

_____

_____

_____

_____

5. What legal points would you use to say the plain meaning of the disputed word or phrase supports your side?

_____

_____

_____

_____

_____

6. What would you use to argue that context supports your side?

_____

_____

_____

_____

_____

7. What would you use to argue that extrinsic tools support your side?

_____

_____

_____

_____

_____

Now, get together with someone from the opposing side and discuss the strengths and weaknesses of each side's interpretation.

Chapter 13
Revising, Editing, and Polishing

I.   Editing the Memorandum
    A. Editing the Content and Organization of Legal Arguments
    B. Editing the Context and Flow of the Discussion Section
II. Polishing Your Legal Document
III. Exercises

In legal writing, the "magic" happens during the editing and polishing stages—through these stages the document transforms from just a draft (whether a solid draft or a problematic one) to a powerful piece of legal analysis that can influence others' thinking. Whether you are drafting a predictive argument for a supervising attorney or a persuasive document for a judge, engaging in the separate steps of editing and polishing must be a vital part of your process.

As you may have already noticed, the whole process of creating a strong analytical document is recursive. You may have been able to write a single draft in your past educational or professional experiences, but legal analysis requires more. Legal analysis requires layers of thinking and a process that allows you to synthesize, draft, think, maybe research more, think, synthesize, and redraft. Really, you will likely spend only about forty percent of your time on researching and writing the first draft. The next forty percent of your time should be spent revising. The remaining time will be spent on the fun parts—polishing—in which you get to be an artisan "wordsmith" for every paragraph, sentence, and word in the document. The number of legal arguments and the more nuanced those legal arguments are, the more drafts you may need to create.

Editing and polishing will require looking at parts of your legal analysis independently, and then looking at the document as a comprehensive whole. This chapter will help you identify problems with the structure, content, organization, and flow of your legal document. By using these exercises, your legal document will not only be a credible and professional piece of writing, but it will also be an effective analysis of the law.

I. Editing the Memorandum

Through the editing process, your job is like that of a structural engineer.[1] Structural engineers are tasked with designing and constructing new buildings or overseeing modifications or additions of existing buildings. Whether creating or remodeling, structural engineers must ensure the structural integrity of the edifice so that it will not collapse. Structural engineers must also ensure that the structures can withstand the various elements a structure will face. Likewise, you must ensure that the structural integrity of your document is sound and that it can withstand the critical scrutiny of skeptical legal readers. To be a good structural engineer of your document, you are going to make sure that the organizational structure of each individual argument is sound; that each individual argument is accurate, thorough, and succinct; and that the document as a whole is cohesive, with each individual argument logically connecting to other arguments presented. When editing arguments on a hard copy, use the Editor's Marks shown in Example 13.A below.

A. Editing the Content and Organization of Legal Arguments

Begin the editing process by reviewing your paper using each of the steps in Example 13.A below.

Example 13.A: Checklist for Reviewing the Content and Organization of Each Legal Argument

1. Label the parts of each individual legal argument according to your preferred paradigm (CREAC, TREAC, IREAC, IRAC, CRPAC, CREXAC, etc.). *This exercise will use the CREAC structure (Conclusion, Rules, Explanation, Application (and Counter-Analysis), and Conclusion.*

2. Review all rules
   - Have the rules for the legal issue been stated (moving from general rules to specific rules)?
   - Have you included any synthesized rules required for the legal issue?
   - Does each paragraph of the E start with a hook (or a rule) that clearly states the legal point that paragraph will prove or that the precedent will illustrate?
   - Is the rule stated in present tense?
   - Is the rule cited (preferably in a citation sentence following the rule rather than embedded in a textual sentence)?
   - Have you deleted any references to your client's case in these paragraphs?

3. Explanation: Case Illustrations
   - Did you illustrate the rule?
   - How many cases did you use? Can you show a parameter of the rule with cases on opposite ends of the legal spectrum?
   - What tense did you use? (past cases, past facts = past tense)
   - Did you include all parts of the illustration?
     - Hook
     - Trigger facts
     - Holding
     - Reasoning

---

1. Loosely based on Bryan Garner's description of four steps of writing expression by Dr. Betty Flowers: madman, architect, carpenter, judge. Bryan A. Garner, *The Winning Brief* 12–13 (3d ed. 2014).

- Can a new reader understand the precedent with the information given on the page?
- Can the reader see how the rule worked when applied to facts in the previous case? Do you need less information? More information?
- Which illustration comes first? Why? Did you make a deliberate choice?

4. Application

- Does each paragraph start with the point you will prove?
- Have you addressed the points in the same order presented in any case illustrations?
- Did you use rule-based reasoning or analogical reasoning or both?
- Have you connected your ideas to the precedent cited in the R/E by either directly applying a rule or using an analogy?
- Does each analogy have the following?
  - Have you stated the point?
  - Have you used relevant fact-to-fact comparisons?
  - Have you explained why the comparison matters? (Is the "so, what" answered?)
- What tense is used? (past facts = past tense)

5. Counter-Analysis

- Have you set out the weaker side's argument?
- Have you connected the ideas to the law stated in the case explanation?
- Have you used analogies (if appropriate) or rule-based reasoning (if appropriate)?
- Have you explained why, despite any viable arguments, the weaker argument will not likely be successful?

6. General Considerations

- Verify that all ideas explained are applied—is all of the law explained in the R/E used in the A or the C/A below?
- Have any legal explanations of law or applications of law been omitted?
- Do the legal arguments make sense?
- Will the argument stand—do any holes in the analysis require more research or drafting?

7. Conclusion

- Have you stated your final conclusion for the legal question asked in our case?
- Have you crafted a succinct conclusion that does not rehash all details, but simply ties up the legal issue?

Use the preceding checklist to assess the strength of each legal argument. Once those arguments are solid, move to the next step.

B. Editing the Context and Flow of the Discussion Section

Editing the context and flow of legal arguments is the final part of the editing process. **Context** helps the reader understand the legal argument's place in the document and within the factual story, and **flow** helps the reader transition within a single legal argument and among the various legal arguments in the document.

As you remember from Chapter 9, *Tying It All Together*, legal writers use one or more introductory paragraphs (often called **roadmap** or **thesis** paragraphs) to acquaint their readers with the legal issue, its governing rule, the legal arguments that will be addressed (as well as those that will not be addressed), and the ultimate prediction for how the legal question will be resolved.

These introductory sections can be one paragraph or more, depending upon the number or the complexity of the issues being discussed. In a longer introductory section, the first paragraph may be a general statement of the rule, with more detailed statements of the rule following in later paragraphs. Small sub-sections of the argument may also be introduced with paragraphs often called mini-roadmap or mini-thesis paragraphs. No matter what your supervising attorney calls these introductory paragraphs, your reader will need these paragraphs for context. In Example 13.B below, work on editing and polishing skills for these kinds of paragraphs.

Example 13.B: Checklist for Reviewing the Roadmap and Mini-roadmap Paragraphs for a Single Legal Argument

1. Look at the introductory paragraphs (the roadmap, umbrella, or thesis paragraphs):
   - Have you included an ultimate prediction, that is, a bottom-line conclusion, about the legal question you were asked?
   - Have you included the governing rule(s)?
   - Have you started with the broadest rule and moved to the more specific rules?
   - If applicable, do you have a synthesized rule?
   - After reading this part, is the reader clear on the legal question that is being asked and any questions that are not being asked?

2. Review the introductory paragraphs following each point heading if document has multiple issues or sub-issues (the mini-roadmap, mini-umbrella, or mini-thesis):
   - For any issue or sub-issue that has multiple rules, have you included a mini-roadmap paragraph?
   - Has a bottom-line conclusion been stated up front about the outcome for this issue?
   - Have you started with the broadest rule and moved to the more specific rules?
   - Do you have a synthesized rule?

II. Polishing Your Legal Document

The last step of the writing process is polishing. When polishing, you critique every word, sentence, punctuation mark, and citation to make sure that the document is precise and clear. The following exercises will help you achieve that precision and clarity.

Proofreading is the final step before submitting a legal document. You have probably been proofreading with every draft of your document, but you will always need to proofread a final time once the document is finished. Your own credibility and reputation as a competent, professional lawyer will rest, in large part, on your ability to turn in a clean document that is free from errors.

Proofreading is tricky—your eyes can see what is not actually on the page. The more time you have spent revising the document, the less likely you will be able to see errors, particularly when reading on a screen. The following exercises will help you implement strategies for catching those errors and submitting a clean and professional document that will enhance your credibility.

In addition, when proofreading, pay attention to citations. People may not notice when your citations are good, but they will always notice when your citations are incorrect. Not only will readers notice the error, but they will also start making assumptions about the credibility and accuracy of the work's substance. Although this workbook does not teach citation, these exercises might help you think about errors in your own work.

III. Exercises

The following exercises will help you develop your skills in revising, editing, and polishing. You will practice polishing techniques, including skills used in polishing citations, proofreading, and critiquing another's work.

Exercise 13.1: Drafting Clearer Introductory Paragraphs

Our client, James Doe, was charged with burglary in the second degree after he entered a neighbor's tree house and then stole a flashlight, a radio, and a board game.[2] The neighbor's children used the tree house as an afternoon play space, and the children frequently had sleepovers in the tree house during the summer. It contained a mattress, blankets, pillows, and some folding chairs. It also contained some miscellaneous items such as flashlights and a radio, along with other items like art supplies, snacks, and bottled water. Although the tree house did not have running water, it had electricity with two wall lights and one electrical plug.

Doe has been charged with the crime of burglary in the second degree, which requires that the structure entered be a dwelling. The New York Penal Code defines a "dwelling" as a building that is "usually occupied by a person lodging therein at night." N.Y. Penal Law § 140.00(3) (Westlaw 2019). Courts have explained that when considering whether a structure is a dwelling, courts should consider: (1) the nature of the structure; (2) the intent of the owner to return; and (3) whether on the date of the burglary, a person could have occupied the structure overnight. *People v. Sheirod*, 124 A.D.2d 14, 510 N.Y.S.2d 945 (4th Dep't 1987) (holding a home that was vacant for a year was a structure suitable for "overnight accommodations," and thus was a dwelling). However, if the building does not have the "customary indicia of a residence and its character or attributes," then it is not a dwelling. *People v. Quattlebaum*, 698 N.E.2d 421 (N.Y. 1998) (holding a school with two offices that contained a chair and a bed in each was not a dwelling).

Evaluate the parts of the following introductory paragraphs and choose the correct answer for each.

1. **Which sentence better articulates the issue for the Roadmap paragraph?**
   a. The issue is whether a burglary occurred.
   b. The issue is whether a tree house constitutes a dwelling as an element of the crime of burglary in the second degree.

2. **Which sentence better articulates the conclusion for the Roadmap paragraph?**
   a. A court may find that a burglary occurred, but there is a strong counterargument.

---

2. The facts of this exercise were inspired by shared materials from the faculty at St. John's University School of Law; these materials may be derived from various authors in the greater legal writing community, but original authors are unknown.

b. A court will probably find that a tree house is not a "dwelling," and thus this element of the burglary statute is not met.

3. **Which statement best expresses the core legal analysis?**

a. The tree house is similar to the vacant house in the case of *People v. Sheirod*.

b. Because the tree house was frequently used for overnight lodging complete with bedding, food, and electricity, and because at the time of the theft, one could have occupied the structure overnight, a court will likely find the tree house to be a "dwelling."

Exercise 13.2: Identifying Effective Hooks and Thesis Sentences

Follow the directions for each part of the exercise below.

1. **Out of the choices below, circle the letter of sentences that serve as useful hooks to introduce case illustration paragraphs. The writer is using the hook to explain whether the object used by the defendant was a dangerous instrument. Revise any sentences in which the hook is not useful to the reader. (Assume that citations would be included where appropriate.)**

a. A body part cannot be considered a dangerous instrument.

b. Circumstantial evidence beyond a reasonable doubt is needed to ascertain that the defendant was in possession of a dangerous instrument.

c. Courts in New York have held that a jury can rely on circumstantial evidence to determine whether defendants have committed assault in the second degree with a dangerous instrument. In *People v. Wilson*, ...

d. In the case of *People v. Wilson*, the court held that the evidence was sufficient to support a charge of assault in the second degree where a deadly instrument was not recovered.

e. The court in *People v. Owusu* stated, "that 'any instrument, article or substance,' no matter how innocuous it may appear to be when used for its legitimate purpose, becomes a dangerous instrument when it is used in a manner which renders it readily capable of causing serious physical injury."

f. Courts examine the facts of the case before rendering a decision.

g. In *People v. Pena*, the two defendants, Turrell and Pena, stole a coat and $10 from the victim, Irons.

2. **Circle the letter of any sentences useful to a reader when introducing application paragraphs addressing the issue of a dangerous instrument. Revise any sentences that do not effectively introduce the application paragraph.**

a. Similarly, in this case, no instrument of any kind was found on the defendant John Spinner after he was arrested.

b. Similar to the facts in *Wilson*, in our case, the defendant was also found to not be in possession of an "instrument" at the time he was apprehended.

c. In the case at hand, there was no object found, similar to *Pena* and *Wilson*.

d. Mr. Cain followed Mr. Spinner in pursuance of his wife's pocketbook.

e. It is important to note that Mr. Spinner sustained said knife wound.

Exercise 13.3: Using Editor's Marks

When proofreading, having a common set of "editor's marks" is necessary so that both the reader and the writer understand what changes should be made. In the remaining exercises, practice using the editor's marks listed in the table below to indicate what changes need to be made.

Editor's Marks Table

Mark	Means	Example
(insert mark)	Insert	The bike does qualify (not)
(delete mark)	Delete	The bike does not not qualify
(move mark)	Move	The rule (only) allows the court
(transpose mark)	Transpose	To boldly go
(insert space mark)	Insert Space (not a hashtag)	Under the statutory section
(close space mark)	Close space	The legisla ture
stet	Keep original as it is ("let it stand")	the car, which was stet
/	Use lowercase	The County Agency
≡	Capitalize	The sixth circuit Court of Appeals
(comma mark)	Insert punctuation: Comma	In addition
(colon mark)	Colon	table that follows
(semi-colon mark)	Semi-colon	is a motor vehicle however
(apostrophe mark)	Apostrophe	The burglars tool
(end punctuation mark)	End punctuation	Does the statute apply
(quotation mark)	Quotation mark	The bike is a motor vehicle as defined in the statute
△	Insert hyphen	Well written brief
┬ M	Insert em-dash (a dash as wide as a capital M, used to set off phrases or clauses)	A full case illustration should have four parts the rule, the holding, the court's reasoning, and the key facts that triggered the court's decision.
┬ N	Insert en-dash (a dash as wide as a capital N, used for a span of numbers)	The details are on pages 419 21.
_____	Italicize	In Modern Legal Scholarship,
< >	Set in regular type	To threaten imminent force
(indent mark)	Indent	The citation issued to Ms. Day should be dismissed because
⌐	Flush left	The legislature
¶	New paragraph	The case applies. The context also

Exercise 13.4: Polishing with Correct Punctuation, Spelling, and Grammar

Many of the following sentences contain grammar, spelling, and punctuation errors. Correct the errors you see using the editor's marks from Exercise 13.3. For sentences without errors, mark in the margin as "Correct."

1. Warnings to be effective under the holding of *Miranda* must precede the defendant's questioning.

2. After each round of questioning the detective stated that he then typed up a confession and had the defendant read it.

3. The credibility of that defendant was for the lower courts to assess, we did not review their conclusions.

4. Moreover, this Court should refuse to adopt any rule that would have the affect of automatically invalidating a confession.

5. Inside the holding cell the prisoner sat handcuffed.

6. The court began the daily calendar call by asking the attorney's to take a seat, informing them briefly of protocol, and reminding them to turn off their cell phones.

7. The judges took their recess at the end of a long morning calendar, which consisted mostly of civil motions.

8. The attorneys who represent the plaintiff wish to file a motion for summary judgment before trail.

9. Litigators need briefcases that are sturdy.

10. The police report contained in the top box". . . Information filled in by the . . . arresting officer."

11. "It is up to the prosecution" the Court observed in *Melendez* "to decide what steps in the chain of custody are so crucial as to require evidence."

12. The defendant was convicted in the District Court. Of aggravated driving while under the influence of intoxicating liquor.

13. Although the shareholders retained full possession of the company's stock. The stock market reflected low prices for the shares.

14. The obligation to propel retesting when the original analyst is unavailable is the State's not the defendants.

15. The *Crawford* and *Melendez* cases therefore weigh heavily in the defendants' favor.

Exercise 13.5: Polishing with Correct Citations

1. Which of the citations below are correct? [Put a "check" mark if correct, and an "X" mark if incorrect.] In the margin, note what is wrong with the citation and the citation rule that governs.

_____ *Swift v. Redding Transp. Co.*, 178 A.2d 235 (Pa.).

___✓___ *Swift v. Redding Transp. Co.*, 178 A.2d 235 (Pa. 1985).

___✓___ *Swift v. Redding Transp. Co.*, 178 A.2d 235, 236 (Pa. 1985).

___✓___ *Swift*, 178 at 237.

___✓___ *Id*, at 238.

_____ *Id.* (quoting *Devitt v. Heimbach*, 456 N.W. 747).

_____ *Id.* (quoting *Devitt v. Heimbach*, 456 N.E. 747, 747 (N.Y. 1990)).

_____ *Ladany v. William Morrow & Co.*, 465 F. Supp. 2d 870, 882 (S.D.N.Y. 1978).

_____ *Ladany v. William Morrow & Co.*, 465 U.S. 870, 882 (S.D.N.Y. 1978)).

_____ *Ladany v. William Morrow & Co.*, 465 F.Supp.2d 870, 882 (S.D.N.Y. 1978).

_____ *Ladany v. William Morrow & Co.*, 465 F.2d 870, 882 (S.D.N.Y. 1978).

Polishing with String Citations

General Rule: Try to limit yourself to no more than three citations in a string cite.

When to Use String Citations:

- To demonstrate that the principal case establishing a rule is still applied today.
- To demonstrate that a rule is applied across a variety of jurisdictions (these may include persuasive, not just controlling jurisdictions).
- To demonstrate that a rule is applied across a variety of factual scenarios (using explanatory parentheticals).
- To distinguish a group of cases. One option is to introduce with signals that indicate contradiction—such as "*Contra*," "*Compare*," or "*But see*." When using signals, remember to include an explanatory parenthetical to help the reader understand why the case is being used.

When to Avoid String Citations:

- In the place of providing analysis for a relevant case (if you want the supervising attorney or the court to know the case, or if you are using it in your analysis or counter-analysis, then put it in the body of the document).
- To give the court an excessive amount of examples from the same jurisdiction.
- To add volume to your brief.

[handwritten margin note: Counter arg for real relationship — not a 4th abuser]

Suppose the next two examples are excerpts from a case before the United States Court of Appeals for the Ninth Circuit. After reviewing the rules below, correct all citations in the examples, including the signals. Indicate whether each citation within the string cite is necessary, and consider re-organizing the order of the citations. In the margin, list the citation rules that apply.

1. Assume the rule is the same in all of these sources and the goal is to show a string cite. How would you organize these authorities if your court is the Ninth Circuit Court of Appeals?

Obviously, there was some suggestion inherent in defendant's custodial status, but it was a routine safety precaution that defendant was handcuffed in the car, and that factor alone did not transform this viewing into an unduly suggestive one. *See, e.g., People v. Johnson*, 102 F. Supp. 2d 616, 627 (E.D.N.Y. 1984); *People v. Huggler*, 50 U.S. 317 (1976); see also *People v. Thomas*, 105 F.2d 35 (9th Cir. 1984); see also *People v. Rodriguez*, 108 F.2d 58 (9th Cir. 1986).

2. Assuming all of these authorities state the same proposition quoted below, rank the cases in the order of how you would list them in a string cite (number 1 would be first and 4, last). Then correct any errors you see in the citations.

"Thus, the courts have accepted that such 'show up identifications' are appropriate, desirable, and far more accurate than suggestive."

[handwritten margin note: 51]

___ *People v. Logan*, 106 F. 2d 184 (6ᵗʰ Circuit 1985), cert. denied, 396 U.S. 1020 (1987)

___ *See also, Frank v. Blackburn*, 95 F.2d 910 (9ᵗʰ Cir. 1979), *vacated en banc on other grounds*, 97 F. 2d 873 (5ᵗʰ Cir. 1980), *cert. denied*, 454 U.S. 830 (1981)

___ *Singletary v. United States*, 383 A.2d 1064, 1068 (D.C. Cir. 1978)

___ *Cummings v. Zelker*, 455 F.2d 714, 716 (2d Circuit 1972)

Exercise 13.6: Proofreading Strategies

For any legal document you are writing now, choose a strategy from Category A (below) and a second strategy from Category B to proofread your document. Use the editor's marks from Exercise 13.3 to denote changes. Compare the two strategies and evaluate which was most helpful.

[handwritten margin note: Quote appropriate statutory language in this.]

Category A:

1. Enlarge your viewing screen to 200% or higher and review your document on your computer screen. Highlight in yellow all of the errors you see.

2. Print a copy of your document. With a yellow highlighter pen, read your document, marking any errors.

Category B:

1. Print a copy of your document, place a brightly colored piece of paper under each line of text as you read it. Circle any errors.

2. Print a copy of your document. Stand up. Read the document aloud, highlighting any errors or unclear sentence phrasing as you read.

Exercise 13.7: Checklist for Peer Editing

One of the best ways to edit and polish your paper is to let someone else read it. Using the checklist that follows (along with the memo problem that you are currently working on), peer review a colleague's work and provide feedback on how to make the document more effective. (This document can also be used for self editing.)

A Checklist for Peer Editing (or Self Editing)

Student _____

Peer Review Partner _____

When reviewing the entire document, mark the document as instructed below:

- Put a * by any place in the memo that is especially effective.
- Put [ ] brackets around any part that is incomplete or unclear.

Effectively Executed	Discussion	Suggestions For Making More Effective
	Governing Rule (GR): The writer has explained the governing rule, setting out relevant definitions, rules, or tests. The writer has included a sentence or paragraph establishing a context including: • The overarching rule (GR) • Which elements/factors the analysis will examine and which are not at issue • The conclusion to the precise legal question of whether each element/factor is met (thus, whether the underlying claim will be successful).	
	Each Point Heading (PH) is a complete sentence or phrase that gives the reader a clear understanding of the topic that follows. Each PH is of readable length, coherent, logical, & favorable to the client.	
	Synthesized Rule(s) (SR): The writer has accurately and objectively set out the general rule for EACH element with a citation, synthesizing multiple cases when appropriate. R: The writer has set out the correct rules or sub-rules for the element, and has set out general rules before specific rules. **The first sentence of each paragraph (hook) tells the legal point that the paragraph will prove.**	
	E: The writer has included *accurate and adequate* descriptions of analogous cases, setting out trigger facts, holding, and rationale. The writer has clearly explained **how** the case illustrates the rule, giving enough detail about the precedent cases. The writer does not bring up client's facts in this section. Only the rule is stated in present tense; the facts, holding, and rationale are stated in past tense.	

Effectively Executed	Discussion	Suggestions For Making More Effective
	A: The writer has explained the application of the rules to the facts, **point by point**, in the same order the points were explained in the E. **The first sentence of each paragraph tells what the paragraph will prove.** The writer has properly used rule-based reasoning or analogical reasoning. In using analogical reasoning, the writer has **compared the facts of one case to the facts of another case.** The writer has compared fact to fact, not fact to a case name.	
	A: The analysis is not **conclusory** because the writer has explained **the significance of the comparison.** Thus, the writer has explained **why** the factual similarities between the analogous cases and the client's case are legally significant, or **why** it would be consistent with the policies underlying the rule to decide the case in a particular way. Put differently, the "so, what" has been explained.	
	C/A: Counter-analysis has a good thesis sentence. The writer explains analysis with analogies or direct application of rule to fact, and ends with a rebuttal of why the argument is not as strong as the argument in the A.	
	C: The writer has included a conclusion for each sub-issue (element or factor) predicting how the question will be decided.	
	Overall organization of discussion: The writer has clearly and logically organized the discussion section.	
	Citation	
	All non-original ideas (rules, reasoning, and holdings) have been attributed to their sources. Since the A is the writer's own reasoning, the writer has omitted case citations except when including a direct quote.	
	While citation may not be perfect at this stage, the citation form conforms to lessons and rules in the *Bluebook*.	

Effectively Executed	Discussion	Suggestions For Making More Effective
	Polishing: Grammar, Punctuation, Legal Writing Style	
	The attorney can understand the discussion section after reading it once.	
	The paragraph divisions are logical, and the paragraphs are neither too long nor too short.	
	Signposts, thesis sentences, and transitions make clear the connections between ideas.	
	The writing has strong writing mechanics: the document is grammatically correct and correctly punctuated (e.g., commas and periods go within quote marks, punctuation marks are correct).	
	The writer has used appropriate legal style, and has no weak phrasing such as "it is/there are," "in order to," "the fact that," and so on. The writer has referred to our case as "this case" and precedent cases as "that case."	
	Professionalism: The paper has been proofread and has no errors.	
	Professionalism: The paper is properly formatted according to office guidelines as to type size, typeface, line spacing, margins, and page numbering.	

Arrington case

Public Interest exception

    - What counts as
    Public Interest?